Aratus Astronomical Poem

AL
7060

4° A. gr. a.
118

Aratus

Hbh
~~X~~
257
KL 7060

ROYAL SOCIETY OF

ARATUS' ASTRONOMICAL POEM,

(With Ten lines not heretofore known,)

WITH CICERO'S LATIN TRANSLATION;

EDITED FROM

A MS. IN THE BRITISH MUSEUM OF THE
2ND OR 3RD CENTURY;

WITH A DISSERTATION,

IN PROOF OF THE

Use of Minuscule Writing by the Ancient Romans.

BY W. Y. OTTLEY.

Twenty-one very Fine and Curious Plates,

FACSIMILES

OF ANCIENT WRITINGS, &c.

ANTIQUARIES, LONDON.

III. *A Letter to* JOHN GAGE, *Esq. F.R.S. Director, by* WILLIAM YOUNG OTTLEY, *Esq. F.S.A., &c., on a Manuscript in the British Museum, believed by him to be of the Second or Third Century, and containing the translation of Aratus's astronomical Poem by Cicero, accompanied by Drawings of the Constellations: with a preliminary Dissertation in proof of the use of Minuscule Writing by the ancient Romans; and a corrected edition of the Poem itself, including ten lines not heretofore known.*

Read 13th February, 1834.

DEAR SIR,

YOU are aware that I have, at intervals, employed myself a good deal in the manuscript room of the British Museum, during the last four years, in researches among the Illuminated MSS. of the fifteenth century, on the subject of *Costume*; for the purpose of helping me to form a right judgment of the ages and country of certain books of wood-engravings, which are known by bibliographers under the name of *Block-Books*; and are commonly supposed to have given rise to the invention of Typography: for the controversy concerning this subject has long occupied my attention; and, although so many books have been written upon it during the last two centuries, I have become more and more persuaded, that the evidence on both sides must be subjected to a nicer examination, and sifting, than it has yet had, before we can hope to come to a right decision concerning it.

Until very lately, few painters have attempted historical accuracy in matters of Costume; and even at this day, perhaps, no one has perfectly attained it. If we begin from the close of the fifteenth century, and go upwards, we shall find that from that period to the most ancient times, nothing of the kind was so much as thought of; and an artist, when called upon to delineate a Paris, an Alexander, or a Cæsar, would represent him, without scruple, dressed in the fashion of his own time. It therefore follows, that by such studies, aided by a competent knowledge of the different styles of design, composition, and colouring, which have prevailed in different parts at different periods, much may now be done towards ascertaining the date of an early work of art, and the country where it was executed.

One day, when I was thus employed, a gentleman of the establishment, knowing that, though the object I was pursuing limited my researches to manuscripts of the fifteenth century, I was no-wise averse to have my attention directed occasionally to such as were more ancient, placed before me the Harleian MS. No. 647, which is the principal subject of the present communication: I say the principal subject, because two other manuscripts were afterwards found, anciently copied from this, which I shall have occasion to speak of in connection with it.

This MS. contains Cicero's well-known translation of the astronomical poem of Aratus, with figures of the constellations, of somewhat a large size, done in colours; and it is remarkable that, within the outlines of the figures, the prose accounts of these constellations, as given by Hyginus, are written in small capitals; like the small poems of Simmias Rhodius, which we see inscribed in the shape of an egg, a pair of wings, a battle-axe, an altar, &c. in the "Poetæ Minores Græci." The volume also contains some small prose tracts, which I shall enumerate hereafter. Upon turning over the leaves, I presently lost all remembrance of the Costerian controversy, and the fifteenth century; and, from the style and character of the drawings, soon became persuaded that they are genuine remains of ancient Roman art; and that the manuscript they decorate, or rather, I ought to say, the most ancient portion of it, may vie in antiquity with the far-famed Virgils and the Terence of the Vatican.

But though I felt confident in this opinion, I could not get those gentlemen of my acquaintance, who were the most conversant with early manuscripts, to join with me in embracing it. For the verses of Cicero are written in bold and well-formed *minuscule* characters, or round hand; and they considered this circumstance as fatal to its claim to any very high antiquity. This sort of writing, they told me, they were not accustomed to meet with in manuscripts anterior to the tenth or eleventh centuries, when it was much used. Afterwards, indeed, I succeeded in finding one so written, containing some prefatory verses proving it to be of the first half of the ninth century; (namely, the four Gospels in Latin, Harl. Coll. 2790); and perhaps, could I have been satisfied with dating the manuscript in question a hundred years earlier than that, they might have been brought to agree with me. But between the eighth and the second or third century, to which I was disposed to ascribe it, there was an immense distance; and I saw that the only chance that remained to me of making converts to my belief, was by producing, if possible, good evidence, that the notion prevalent with the best informed persons in this country, and I believe taken from Casley, that *the ancients were unacquainted with minuscule writing*; or that, if they did use minuscule writing, *it must have been very different from that practised in later times*, is ill founded.

It is true that, without doing this, I should still, as I think, have had the balance of proof in my favour: for the argument opposed to me was merely negative; and, when fairly examined, amounted only to this—that my friends were unacquainted with MSS. written in minuscules, or in minuscules of a similar character to those of the Aratus, earlier than the tenth century: and in fact they told me, that beyond the tenth century they had nothing to guide them. Whereas the evidence in favour of my opinion was of a twofold character; positive and negative: for at the same time that the *costume*, and the *style of art*, in the figures in question, perfectly accord with the ancient period to which I ascribe them, they will not, as far as I know, accord with a later.

Of the small dependance that ought to be placed on negative evidence alone, especially in inquiries touching the date of the introduction of this or that usage, new proofs are furnished every day. In the second volume of that fine work " Le Pitture Antiche d'Ercolano," printed in 1760, there is, among others, a figure of the muse Erato, with her name and title thus: ΕΡΑΤω·+ΑΛΤΡΙΑΝ· (See Plate IV. No. 1.) The writers (p. 34, note 2), in speaking of it, inform us that Montfaucon observes in his " Palæographia," that the *psi*, in the form of a cross, as it is here, is found in manuscripts of the eighth and ninth centuries,—so long, in early times, did the same usage continue. They take this occasion, also, to notice the following inscription, which was found in the excavations at Resina, March 6, 1743, upon a wall that formed the angle of a street leading to the theatre, and was written in black and red, in minuscule characters, with accents, in the manner exactly represented in Plate IV. No. 2.

"ὡς ἐν σοφὸν βόλευμα τὰς πολλὰς χεῖρας νικᾷ."

"*A single piece of sage council overcomes many hands :*"
which, they observe, is a verse of Euripides cited by Polybius, I. 35.

"It was customary," say they, "to write similar sentences on the walls of places of public resort; and it is related of the Emperor Alexander Severus, that he was so delighted with the golden maxim : ' quod tibi fieri non vis, alteri ne feceris,' that, besides that it was ever in his mouth, he ordered it to be written on the walls of his palace and in other public places." They add, that "the above inscription, of which the antiquity is beyond all doubt, may put to rest the question as to the age of the Greek accents, which a few critics have suspected may have been used as early as the time of Cicero; but which the great majority of writers have supposed to have been first introduced towards the seventh century;[a] and also that of the forms of the Greek minuscules."

On the other hand, much may be urged of the value of the evidence which the drawings, in the manuscript under consideration, furnish of its antiquity. Trombelli, in his work upon "The Art of discovering the ages of Manuscripts," (from which two years ago I had the pleasure of furnishing you with an extract, for your valuable paper on St. Æthelwold's Benedictional), prefaces what

---

[a] The writers here cited do not intend to say, that the antiquity of the *invention* of the Greek accents has ever been doubted; for in a note, at page 328 of the same volume, they inform us, that "they are believed to have been first introduced about 200 years before Christ, by Aristophanes of Byzantium, who adapted musical notes to the characters, in order to facilitate the learning of the Greek language, and the reading of it with a proper pronunciation; and that their use is attested by Athenæus, xi. 10, p. 484, and 13, p. 496, and by Plutarch (Quæstion. Platon.); besides that the Grammarians give the rules concerning them. "But from all this," say they, "it has been supposed, that they were only adopted by the grammarians, and used in the schools; and that they were not generally admitted by the ancients in writing." The Greek manuscripts published in fac-simile, in the two volumes of the "Herculanensium Voluminum quae supersunt," do not appear to have them. But all these manuscripts are written in capitals. Perhaps in ancient times, as at present, they may have been considered unbecoming the dignity of this kind of writing, and applicable only to writing in minuscules.

he says of the Illuminations, with which so many of them are decorated, by observing that they constitute a surer means of judging of the age of a manuscript than any other: and though I would not too implicitly rely upon his authority in this matter, as his knowledge of art was, probably, not very extensive, still I believe this opinion to be in the main true; since the style and character of the writing used throughout the Western Empire, from the beginning of the Christian era to the twelfth and thirteenth centuries, when the black-letter began to be introduced, appear to have undergone but few changes, in comparison with those by which works of art, executed at different periods of that long interval, are to be distinguished from each other; or rather, I ought to say, by which they would readily be distinguishable, were we thoroughly acquainted with the variations of *style* in art, and the alterations in *costume*, which, during so many centuries, were continually taking place every where. This complete knowledge, indeed, especially as respects some of the middle centuries, no one probably now possesses. But we know enough of Classical times, to enable us to discriminate between works of art executed in those times, and such as were done in later centuries. It is well known, that the arts of Painting and Sculpture, which had flourished under the first Emperors, notably declined before the time of Constantine; that after that period they fell away rapidly,[b] though still for a time some remains of the ancient Roman manner continued to obtain; and that after pictures and images began to be introduced into the Christian churches, as objects of devotion, a new and barbarous style found its way every where from the capital of the Greek Empire. And I think, therefore, that as the drawings in the manuscript under consideration exhibit not only the *costume,* but also *the style of art which prevailed in the good times of the Roman Empire,* we are not justified in ascribing the manuscript to a later period.

I learn from the " Nouveau Traité de Diplomatique," (vol. iii. p. 57) that among the papers of Emanuele a Schelestrate, librarian of the Vatican, was found the following interesting memorandum of an examination of the famous manu-

[b] Let any one, who may be disposed to think that I overstate this fact, or am desirous to make too much of it, look at Gori's interesting work upon ancient Diptychs; in which, if I forget not, he will find several, of soon after the time of Constantine, in as rude a style of art as need be.

script fragments of Virgil, made one day by himself and two other eminent antiquaries. One of them, indeed, Mabillon, was probably better qualified to form a right judgment of the ages of old manuscripts in general, than any person has been since his time; and the other, Gio. Pietro Bellori, it may be sufficient to say, was the editor and illustrator of all those numerous collections of ancient Roman paintings and sculptures, which were engraved by Pietro Santi Bartoli; and, consequently, could hardly fail to be as thoroughly acquainted with every thing relating to the ancient Roman customs and dresses, and to ancient Roman art, as any man that ever lived.

"Sept[r]. 16th, 1686, in the Vatican Library, present the Rev[d] Father Jo. Mabillon, of the order of St. Benedict, Gio. Pietro Bellori, and I the undersigned; the MS. No. 3225, preserved in the said library, was examined. It is a quarto of a square form, written in majuscule characters, without any separation of the words, except marks of punctuation; whereof those points which are placed at the tops of the lines, represent our period; and those in the middle or at bottom, our comma. The letter A is without any transverse stroke, thus Λ; the upper part of the letter P is but half closed; the V is always rounded at bottom; the T has the cross stroke at top very short; the stroke distinguishing the G from the C, is like a comma; and in the letters E and F, the horizontal strokes are little more than points. It contains numerous coloured drawings, which it is evident are earlier than the age of Constantine, and are perhaps of the time of Septimius Severus; as in them we do not only observe ancient temples, victims, edifices, gallies with two rows of oars, Phrygian caps, and dresses appertaining to the sacrifices of the Trojans and the Romans; but also a degree of perfection in the drawing of the figures, which indicates a superior and a better age. It is possible, indeed, that the artist who did these drawings, may have followed the inventions of some more noble and ancient painter; as nothing is to be seen in them unworthy the majesty of the first age of the Roman Empire.

EMANUELE A SCHELESTRATE."

And Mabillon, in his Travels in Italy ("Museum Ital." Par. i. p. 63) agrees in this opinion: "Ex latinis," says he, "Virgilius quantivis pretii cum figuris, antiqua sacrificia et alia id genus reconditæ Gentilium eruditionis tam peritè et eleganter exprimentibus, ut Constantini Magni tempus superare videantur."

The above testimonies of Schelestrate and Mabillon shew the paramount importance which these two learned men attached to *the kind of evidence* I am now dwelling upon; although it is probable that neither of them was so well qualified to judge either of the style of art, or of the details of costume, in the figures of this MS. Virgil, as was Bellori, who had assisted at their examination of it: and I think that the chief reason why Schelestrate, upon this occasion, spoke so particularly of the forms of certain letters in this manuscript, was because *he considered the antiquity of the manuscript to be well proved by the drawings*: and therefore looked upon it as *a good authority*, the peculiarities in the characters of which might help him and others, hereafter, in judging of the probable dates of other very early manuscripts. (See specimens of the writing in this MS. Plate VI. Nos. 2, 3.)

Should it be doubted whether the figures in our manuscript of Aratus really carry with them the same decisive evidence of their antiquity, I answer, that, although, from the nature of my studies during more than forty years, I may fairly lay claim to some knowledge in these matters, I do not call upon any one to rely merely upon my judgment. I have consulted some of our best artists; among others, the eminent sculptor, Mr. Westmacott; Mr. Eastlake, who has lately spent ten years at Rome; and Mr. Francis Howard, who has very much applied himself to the study of ancient Art; and they are all decidedly of opinion—nay, have no doubt—that these drawings were executed in ancient Roman times, that is, before the age of Constantine.

But, it has been urged by some of my opponents, that these drawings may bear *the appearance of being ancient*, because *they were copied in the eighth or ninth century from ancient originals*. In like manner, the writers of the Nouveau Traité de Diplomatique, having previously persuaded themselves that no manuscripts more ancient than the fourth, or, at the highest, than the third century, are preserved to our days[c], were pleased to argue against the

---

[c] The general argument of the writers of the "Nouveau Traité," against any manuscript, having pretensions to be deemed earlier than the third or fourth century, would seem to stand thus: "All manuscripts written before the third or fourth century have perished. But this manuscript has not perished: therefore it is not anterior to the third or fourth century!" See, in their third vol. (p. 58,) what they say, in speaking of the most ancient manuscript of Terence in the Vatican.

antiquity of the above-mentioned Vatican fragments of Virgil; availing themselves of the *conjecture* with which Schelestrate closes his notice of that manuscript, that " the artist who did the drawings which it contains, *may* have followed the inventions of some more noble and ancient painter," &c. For they say (vol. iii. p. 57) that " *if* we suppose these drawings to have been *copied* from better originals, then can they no longer be considered to denote a period so ancient as that of Septimius Severus, or even as that of Constantine." But, besides that this is founding an argument upon a conjecture, in preference to founding it upon the evidence that presents itself, these writers appear to take the words of Schelestrate in a sense which he did not intend. From the most ancient times, it was common for the painters and sculptors (except perhaps those of the very highest class) to repeat, with small variations, the most admired inventions of the great artists who had preceded them; and Schelestrate, I think, meant only to say, that the artist who did these drawings might perhaps have taken the general invention and composition of them from older originals; and not that, in the strict sense of the term, he copied them. But whichever meaning we give to the conjecture hinted by Schelestrate, the argument which the above writers attempt to draw from it, is untenable; and so, in my opinion, is that now urged against the antiquity of our manuscript of Aratus.

The artists of ancient times,—and the same holds good of those of the middle ages,—when employed to copy drawings, paintings, or other works of art done in a previous age, never appear to have thought of imitating exactly, or of making a *fac-simile* of the thing before them, so as that the copy might be taken for the original. They contented themselves with giving the general design, attitude, and employment, of the figure or figures; adding, of course, where such were introduced in the original work, the particular symbols by which each personage was to be characterized; and in all the rest, they followed the style of art and the costume of their own time. Among the reverses of the copper coins of the Roman Emperors, of the first two centuries and the beginning of the third, one of the most common is a figure of Fortune, seated on a chair, supporting a cornucopia with her left hand, and resting the right upon the rudder of a ship. Upon comparing several of these together, we find the general attitude of the figure the same in all of them; and each has the cornucopia and the rudder: but, beyond this, there is little attempt at similitude between them: the draperies are changed; the chair varies in its shape; as do, also, even the cornucopia and the rudder. Some of them, (one of those of Lucius Verus, for example,) are of excellent workmanship; while others are rude performances.

When we get to the low ages, we find a very different style of art, as well as of costume, prevailing every where, from what obtained in the first three centuries; and were we even to admit the ability of an artist of those barbarous times, to copy accurately the performance of an ancient artist, so as now to deceive persons well versed in the works of the ancients,—which, to say the least, may be doubted,—still it is difficult to believe that either he or his employer would not have given the preference to the style and fashion of his own time: for there can be little doubt that most of those peculiarities in the mode of drawing certain parts of the human figure, in the foldings and ornaments of the draperies, and in numerous other details, which distinguish the paintings and sculptures of those times, and which we now term *gothicisms*, were then thought *beauties*; and although, after the time of Constantine, the detestation of Pagan idolatry among the Christians, was a chief cause of their destroying so unsparingly whatever productions of ancient art came within their reach; still very much of what was done by them in this way, in ruder centuries, may fairly be placed to the account of their utter blindness to their excellence.

What I have here advanced is indeed confirmed, in a very remarkable manner, by the drawings in one of the two early manuscripts, which, as has been said, contain copies of our ancient manuscript. This manuscript (Tib. B. 5, of the Cottonian collection) is of the latter part of the tenth century, as appears from a calendar, at the beginning; and contains numerous tracts on various subjects, in addition to the entire contents of the ancient manuscript. The proofs, that this part of it *was copied direct from the ancient manuscript*, before it had been mutilated, are such as to admit of no doubt, as will be fully shewn hereafter. The attitudes of all the figures are the same as in that MS.; as are, likewise, the general forms of those constellations which are represented by inanimate objects: but all the details are different; and the Saxon artist, who I doubt not thought his copies better than the originals, has every where given us the barbarous style, and, where he could, the costume, of his own day. Thus *Perseus* has his legs bound round with garterings reaching more than half-way up.them, according to the fashion commonly observable in our Saxon illuminations; as in the Benedictional of St. Æthelwold; and so has *Orion*, instead of the classical sandals given to him in the ancient manuscript. The heads of the *Pleiades* are surrounded by fanciful borders of different colours; and, instead of endeavouring to imitate the simple grandeur which we admire in the originals, the artist has taken pains to vary their head dresses; and, as if conscious of his inability to make the ladies handsome, has sought to make amends, by tinting their hair with black, red, orange, and blue. The *Lyre*, so truly classical in its shape, in the ancient manuscript, appears here something between a lyre and a dulcimer; the simple poop of the ship *Argo*, is sadly transformed into the neck and head of a monster; and a strange-looking building of two stories high, rises from the middle of the deck. It is needless to carry the comparison further; and if any one should still be disposed to contend, that an artist of the eighth century would have been likely to copy these ancient drawings better than we find them in the Cottonian MS. Tib. B. v.—nay, so well, as that competent judges, like those I have mentioned, should take them for genuine performances of classic times,—I have only to say that, from all I have seen, I am led to form a different conclusion; and to invite him to produce some evidence in support of his opinion.

I think that, without going further, I have made out my case; and that the drawings, in what I term the Ancient Manuscript, furnish, of themselves, good and sufficient proof of the antiquity of that manuscript. The translation of Aratus's poem by Cicero, is written in that manuscript in *minuscule characters*, under the figures; there is no doubt that the writing and the figures are of the same age; and it therefore follows, that the common belief, that *the ancients were unacquainted with minuscule writing*, or that, if they did use minuscule writing, *it must have been very different from that practised in after times*, is ill-founded.

But, in the beginning of this Paper, I expressed my intention of examining into the grounds of this common belief. With this view, I have spent a considerable time in looking into the best writers of the continent who have treated of such matters. In doing this, as the subject was in a great measure new to me, I made copious notes and extracts; not only concerning the particular point at issue, but also of whatever else I met with, which seemed to me of more than common interest, touching the various modes of writing believed to have been practised by the ancients; and the peculiarities which are said to characterize the earliest manuscripts now known. Much of what I have found is doubtless already known to many Members of our Society. But it may be in part new to others; and, on the whole, I do not think I can better preface what I have to say of the particular manuscript under consideration, than by throwing together such passages from my common-place book as appear to me the most interesting.

The following passage of Pliny (Lib. xiii. cap. xxi. Harduin's edition in fol. 1741) concerning the different materials used in ancient times for writing upon, is commented on at great length by Trombelli: ("Arte di conoscere l'Età de' Codici," 4to 1778.)

"Prius tamen quam digrediamur ab Ægypto, et *papyri* natura dicetur, cum *chartæ* usu maxime humanitas vitæ constet, et memoria. Et hanc Alexandri Magni victoria repertam, auctor est Marcus Varro, condita in Ægypto Alexandria. Antea non fuisse chartarum usum: in *palmarum foliis*" [some have read "*malvarum*"] "primo scriptitatum: deinde quarumdam *arborum libris.* Postea publica monumenta *plumbeis voluminibus;* mox et privata *linteis* confici cœpta, aut *ceris:* [some, says Trombelli, read: "aut *schedis:*" and Harduin seems to think this may be the right reading:] *Pugillarium* enim usum fuisse etiam ante Trojana tempora invenimus apud Homerum." A somewhat obscure passage follows, touching the changes which Egypt had undergone, since very ancient times, in consequence of the soil deposited by the river Nile; after which he says: "Mox æmulatione circa bibliothecas regum Ptolemæi, et Eumenis, supprimente chartas Ptolemæo, idem Varro *membranas* Pergami tradidit repertas: postea promiscue patuit usus rei, qua constat immortalitas hominum."

Pliny, (or Varro) I suspect, in the words: "Antea non fuisse chartarum usum," in the beginning of this passage, did not mean to assert, strictly speaking, that *papyrus* had not been used for writing upon before the time of Alexander the Great; but only that the use of it then first became known to the

Greeks, who, as every one knows, were the only people, except themselves, that the Romans did not consider as barbarians.

"*Palmarum foliis* primo scriptitatum:" We have observed above, that some read *malvarum* foliis, instead of palmarum. According to Isidorus, both kinds were used for writing on; and Trombelli is of opinion that the leaves of various other trees were after some time applied to the same purpose; as is, he thinks, indicated by Virgil; Æneid. Lib. iii. 443.

> "Insanam vatem aspicies, quæ rupe sub ima
> Fata canit, *foliisque* notas, et nomina mandat.
> Quæcumque in *foliis* descripsit carmina virgo,
> Digerit in numerum, atque antro seclusa relinquit.
> Illa manent immota locis, neque ab ordine cedunt."

And again, Æneid. vi. 74.

> ......"*foliis* ne tantum carmina manda,
> Ne turbata volent rapidis ludibria ventis."

Isidorus says: "that the leaves of books were so called, either from their similitude to the leaves of trees, or because they were made *ex follibus*," from skins of leather.

"Deinde quarundam *arborum libris:*" (the word "scriptitatum" understood). For leaves, were substituted the barks of trees, called *libri;* or rather, perhaps, we ought to say, the inward bark or rind of trees, which is the first meaning of the word given by Ainsworth, and agrees with the following passages from Isidorus, (Lib. vi. cap. 13) "*Liber* est interior tunica corticis, quæ ligno cohærit, in qua antiqui scribebant; de qua Virgilius ait: 'Sic alta *liber* aret in ulmo.' Unde et liber dicitur, in quo scribimus, quia ante usum chartæ, vel membranarum, de libris arborum volumina fiebant: id est, compaginabantur. Unde et scriptores a libris arborum librarios vocaverunt."

And (Lib. xvii. cap. 6) "Liber est corticis pars interior dictus a liberato cortice, id est ablato: est enim medium quiddam inter lignum et corticem."

Martianus Capella (Lib. ii. pag. 44, edit. Lugdunen. 1539) thus speaks of books of various kinds: "Cernere erat, qui libri, quantaque volumina, quot linguarum opera ex ore virginis defluebant. Alia ex *papyro*, quæ cedro perlita fuerant, videbantur. Alii *carbasinis* voluminibus complicati libri, ex ovillis multi quoque tergoribus. Rari vero in *philyræ cortice* subnoti."

The *volumina carbasina*, here spoken of, were perhaps not very dissimilar from the *libri lintei* of Pliny, of which I shall say a few words presently. The *philyra* is another name for the *thyina* or *tilia ;* called in Italian tiglia, and in English the linden or teil tree. That paper was made from the *tilia*, appears from the name *Philyra* being often used to signify paper: "In *philyra* scribere:" "In *philyra* scripsit," &c.; for, according to Hyginus, Philyra the daughter of Oceanus was transformed into the tree bearing that name, and more commonly called *tilia :* "In arborem *philyram*, hoc est *tiliam* commutata est." (Hygin. fab. 138.)

Trombelli is of opinion that before the papyrus was furnished to Italy in large quantities, in her commerce with Egypt, paper made from the inner bark of the *tilia*, and perhaps also of other trees, was much used there. Those books, he observes, were certainly not made of papyrus of which Pliny speaks (Lib. xiii. cap. 27,) as having been found in the tomb of Numa; and which he says were of paper.[b]

Many, he says, are of opinion that the term *philyra* was used in the course of time as a generic term, denoting any kind of bark of trees on which people wrote; and the same is said of the term *tilia*.

The authors of the "Nouveau Traité de Diplomatique," (vol. i. p. 512,) after speaking generally of the ancient papers made of the barks of trees, especially the *tilia*, thus describe an unique manuscript in France, which they suppose written on this kind of material:

"If," say they, "there now exists in the world any monument of the ancient paper made of the barks of trees, it is assuredly a manuscript, No. 655, at the Abbey of S. Germain des Prés. We have observed in it very sensible differences from the manuscripts and diplomas (papyri) in the Bibliotheque du Roi, and the Archives of S. Denis; such as are not to be accounted for by the diversities which are to be found in the Egyptian papyri, some of which were made

[b] "Ingentia exempla contra Varronis sententiam de chartis reperiuntur." (Varro has said, as we have seen above, that *paper* was not known prior to the time of Alexander the Great): "Namque Cassius Hemina, vetustissimus auctor Annalium, quarto eorum libro prodidit, Cn. Terentium scribam agrum suum in Ianiculo repastinantem, offendisse arcam, in qua Numa, qui Romæ regnavit, situs fuisset. In eadem *libros* ejus repertos P. Cornelio, L. F. Cethego, M. Bæbio, Q. F. Pamphilo Coss. ad quos a regno Numæ colliguntur anni DXXXV. et hos fuisse e *charta*."

thicker than others, or by the supposition that by accident two or more leaves of this manuscript had got stuck or pasted together." After observing that papyrus was always made of two laminæ or sheets of the plant pasted together, and of no more, &c. they say that the leaves of this manuscript, which are only five in number, are composed of numerous pellicules or layers, pasted one over the other, and that the leaves altogether are thicker and of a coarser appearance (plus grossiers) than the papyrus; and they then give in a note (p. 513) a very minute description of this curious monument, the contents of which appear to be but very imperfectly legible.

"Of the five leaves," say they, "of which it is composed, two have, until now, been pasted to the parchment cover, and the three others let into a border of the same material; so that eight pages only are exposed to view: the binding does not appear to be very ancient. There are never less than four layers of the material used in each leaf, unless where a bit has been removed by accident, or designedly; and in some we discover a greater number.

"Scarcely any vestiges of writing are to be seen on some leaves; and the letters are with difficulty to be distinguished, unless when wetted. It is a most singular circumstance, that upon detaching the upper pellicule, we sometimes discover other writing underneath, different from that above ..... Some of it appears *Roman cursive*; some is *Roman writing, in letters of the size of demi-uncials, but minuscules in their form, and approaching a little to cursive.* In some pages we find lines disposed in opposite directions. The ages of the different sorts of writing appear sometimes more than a century distant from each other. One would say that, over the pages anciently written upon, a coat of white had been applied, in order to make them serve for new writing. Now, if that which is the most recent is of the sixth or seventh century, at the latest (as is evident from the characters); of what antiquity must be the older?

"All the manuscript is Latin; and we doubt not that it contained Public Acts. It is, perhaps, a portion of the municipal registers of some city. We think we have often discovered in it dates of Calends, Nones, Ides, and Consuls. We read very distinctly, at the bottom of the fifth page; *xiiii. Kalendas Maias*. It is true the word Kalendas is abridged, as is the word Consulibus in other places: but they are the ordinary abbreviations of these terms. We

supposed to be of the 2d or 3d century.

have in no place been able to read the names of the Consuls; if we except that of *Theodosius:* and this *seems to have been written by a later hand than the greater part of the writings, although to all appearance it is of the time of that Emperor, and of the fifth century* ...... Judging of this manuscript by the writing of most common occurrence on the outer coats of the leaves, it cannot be later than the sixth century. The little Latin we are able to decypher in it, would seem to indicate a higher antiquity. There is no departure from purity of style, or good orthography; if we except here and there particular letters, in which the writers of all ages have varied," &c.

After observing that, on some leaves, the more ancient writing appears to have had a new coating of the material pasted over it, in order to make them serve for new writing, &c. they tell us they were induced to detach from the covers the two leaves which, as has been said, were pasted within them; and on one of the two pages, which then presented themselves, " We found," say they, "twenty-two lines of Merovingian writing, and consequently different from that of the rest of the MS. This writing is at least as early as the seventh century. But it may be more ancient, as, in fact, our Merovingian characters are the same as those used in the cursive writing of the Romans. We began by making out some of the words in this last page; and soon succeeded in reading several verses of the 22d and 23d chapters of Exodus, and of the 6th and 18th of Leviticus." The remaining part of this long note relates chiefly to the difficulties the authors had encountered in their attempts to read the writing of this curious manuscript, whereof they give some small specimens in their third volume (pp. 302-3, and 423). See our Plate VI. No 6.

It is unnecessary to say any thing of the *leaden books* or *volumes*, of which Pliny speaks; unless that it seems probable, notwithstanding his calling them by the last name, that they were not rolled; but were either square books with leaves of this material, or, if of one piece, were hung upon the walls of buildings destined for the reception of the public archives.

" Mox et privata (monumenta) *linteis* confici cœpta," says Pliny, in the above passage: and Martianus Capella: " Alii *carbasinis* voluminibus complicati libri:" and Vopiscus (In Aurelianum): "Et si his contentus non fueris, lectites Græcos, *libros etiam linteos* requiras, quos Ulpia tibi bibliotheca, cum volueris ministrabit:" indicating at once, as Trombelli observes, the antiquity of these kind of books, and that they had then fallen into disuse. They are indeed spoken of as ancient, two hundred years before, by Livy: (lib. iv. cap. xiii.); "Nihil enim constat," says he, "nisi in *libros linteos* utroque anno relatum inter Magistratus Præfecti nomen." And in cap. xxiii: "In tam discrepanti editione, et Tubero, et Macer *libros linteos* auctores profitentur: Neuter, tribunos militum eo anno fuisse, traditum a scriptoribus antiquis dissimulat. Licinio *libros* haud dubie sequi *linteos* placet." Trombelli seems at a loss to determine what sort of books, or rolls, these were. Harduin, in his note on this passage of Pliny, appears to consider them as mere books of linen cloth.[c]

" Mox et privata (monumenta) linteis confici cœpta, aut *ceris* : *Pugillarium* enim usum fuisse ante Troiana tempora invenimus apud Homerum."

I am not without my suspicion that Pliny meant to say that *waxed tablets*, for writing on, were used even at this very ancient period. *Ceris* seems to be the most common reading: Trombelli, however, following the opinion of Harduin, has a long article upon this passage, in favour of reading " aut *schedis*," instead of " aut *ceris* ;" and maintains, that the *pugillares*, or tablets, which were carried about for the convenience of writing on, were not prepared with wax until much later times. At how early a period we are to date the first use of wax for painting on, by the Greeks and other nations, I pretend not to determine; but I think it cannot reasonably be doubted that it was used as early for writing on; and if so, the use of *waxed pugillares* in very ancient times may be considered as fairly established.

Ovid, speaking of Biblis (Metam. lib. ix.) has these beautiful lines:

" Et meditata manu componit verba trementi :
Dextra tenet ferrum, vacuam tenet altera *ceram.*
Incipit, et dubitat : scribit, damnatque tabellas :
Et notat, et delet ....
Scripta soror fuerat : visum est delere sororem ;
Verbaque correctis incidere talia ceris."

But, because Ovid was a writer of fables, Trombelli will not admit his authority, in proof of the antiquity of the custom ; which seems to me very strange ;

[c] " Linteorum librorum," says he, " frequens apud Livium mentio ...... At non hæc charta nostra vulgaris fuit, quæ fit ex linteis contritis et maceratis : quod multo posteriore aevo repertum. Lintei dicebantur libri, quod in telam linteam descripti, quemadmodum hac ætate pingere in iisdem pictores solent."

especially as he states his belief, that it was practised in very remote times by the Greeks, and by the Etruscans, from which nations the Romans, he thinks, probably learnt it. It would be easy to produce numerous other passages, in proof of its universal use in classical Roman times. The following from Plautus (Bacch. iv. 4. 76.) well describes a quick amanuensis:

"*Chre.* Cape *stylum* propere, et *tabellas* tu has mihi.
M. N. Quid postea? *Chre.* Quod jubebo, scribito istic.
M. N. Ne interturba; jam imperatum in *cera* est."

These tablets were in general use in schools. Prudentius, in his account of the martyrdom of St. Cassianus, who was put to death by the boys whom he had taught, has these lines:

"Innumeri circum pueri, miserabile visu,
Confossa parvis membra figebant *stylis;*
Unde, *pugillares* soliti percurrere *ceras,*
Scholare murmur adnotantes scripserant."

The custom of writing in this manner was very generally adopted; because, says Quintilian, " it is so easy to write on wax, and to cancel that which has been written, and then to write on it again:" (Instit. Orat. lib. x. cap. 3.) " Scribi optime in *ceris,* in quibus facillima est ratio delendi." And also because the writer had not the trouble of dipping his pen every minute in ink, and therefore could be more expeditious: " Quæ (membranæ) ut juvant aciem, ita crebra relatione, quoad intinguntur calami, morantur manum, et cogitationis impetum frangunt."

Sometimes, according to the same author, wax tablets were made of considerable dimensions; and it is probable they were used by students as we now use slates.

Trombelli says, it is commonly believed that the use of these waxed pugillares was discontinued in Italy, soon after the inundation of the barbarous nations. But it continued in Germany in the eighth century. Wililbaldus, the companion of S. Boniface, is said to have written the life of that eminent bishop and martyr, first on waxed tablets (on account of the facility they afforded of erasing and altering) and afterwards to have copied it out fair on parchment (Actor. S. S. cap. iii. num. 14. Vita S. Bonifac. die 5 Junii, pag. 476, tom. i.): and that the practice prevailed elsewhere, several centuries later, we learn from the authors of the "Nouveau Traité de Diplomatique," (vol. i. p. 458.) who describe books of waxed tablets still existing, and containing accounts of the travelling expenses, &c. of Philip le Bel, in the years 1301-7, written at the time. The waxed pages of these books are said to be of a dark colour; and so do those appear, which we see represented, with projecting margins all round, in some of the decorative paintings found at Pompeii and Herculaneum, &c. (See " Le Pitture d'Ercolano.")

The Pugillares appear to have been of various kinds, and not always prepared with wax: some were made in the form of diptychs, or books; and had thin laminæ of wood or ivory, or perhaps leaves of parchment, fixed within the covers: others had the leaves kept together by a wire or ribbon which passed through a hole common to all of them, so that they opened like a fan.

Martial has several Epigrams upon Pugillares of different sorts, in the beginning of his xivth book: among them the two following:

"Pugillares eburnei." (Epigr. v.)

"Languida ne tristes obscurent lumina ceræ,
Nigra tibi niveum litera pingat ebur."

It requires good eyes, he means to say, to peruse what is written with the *style* upon dark-coloured waxed tablets; but letters, written with black upon white ivory, are read with the greatest facility.

"Pugillares membranei." (Epigr. vii.)

"Esse putes ceras, licet hæc membrana vocetur:
Delebis, quoties scripta novare voles."

These appear to have been like our books of ass's-skin: as on waxed tablets, the owner might rub out what he had previously written upon them, and write again as often as he pleased.

Trombelli says, some are of opinion that the term *pugillares* acquired in the course of time a more ample signification than it had originally. In Gruterus (p. 174, Amsterd. 1707) is an inscription in which are mentioned, " *Pugillares membranacii operculis eboreis,*" which were left to his fellow citizens of Reggio, by a certain T. Ebervenius Sabinus; and it is supposed that these were not such as are commonly called Pugillares; but MSS. (codices) with numerous leaves, enriched by handsome covers of ivory. See, says he, what is said by the Canon Mazzocchi, when speaking of the "Dittico Quiriniano."

"Mox æmulatione circa bibliothecas regum Ptolomæi et Eumenis, supprimente chartas Ptolomæo," (that is, Ptolomy having prohibited the extraction of papyrus from Egypt,) "idem Varro *membranas* Pergami tradidit repertas." —Pliny, in the before cited passage.

But Herodotus, Lib. v. num. 58, (Londini, 1679, fol.) who is believed to have lived 480 years before Christ, besides that he speaks of the very ancient use of papyrus (or biblus) says, also, that the skins of goats and sheep had long been used for writing on by the Ionians. The practice of writing, both on papyrus, and on the skins of animals, must therefore be dated several centuries before the times mentioned by Pliny: though in the time of Eumenes, who lived 180 years before Christ, an improved mode of preparing skins may have been discovered at Pergamus; which occasioned fine parchment to be afterwards called by that name in Italy, and to be from thenceforth much more generally used for writing on, than it had been before.

Besides the substances, mentioned in the above passage of Pliny, there is reason to believe that, from very ancient times, various others were used for writing on; and among them the intestines of elephants and other large animals, and the skins of serpents. In the great fire at Constantinople, in the time of the Emperor Basiliscus, a manuscript roll, 120 feet long, is said to have been destroyed, made of the skin of a dragon or serpent; whereon the Iliad and Odyssey of Homer, and the history of the exploits of ancient heroes, perhaps those of the Argonauts, were written in letters of gold. The above supposed length of this serpent, has been thought to throw an air of fable over this notice; but may not the reptile have been in reality but one-third of the above length; and may not his skin have been cut into three breadths, sufficiently wide for the purpose, and joined together at the ends? I learn from the authors of the "Nou. Traité de Diplomatique," (vol. i. p. 477) that Petrarch wore a simple dress of smooth leather, on which he was accustomed at once to write down such thoughts as occurred to his fancy, and as he deemed worth preserving; and that this dress, covered with his writing, was preserved, so long afterwards as 1527, as a precious literary monument.

I cannot help suspecting, that, besides what we should now call *papyrus*, other sorts of paper were manufactured, and used for writing on, in ancient times, as well as for inferior purposes; some of them, perhaps, not so very unlike our ordinary papers as is commonly supposed: though I am aware that Pliny does not seem to countenance such an opinion; but, on the contrary, speaks of the ancient Roman papers, of various sizes and qualities, the *hieratica* or *sacra*, the *Augusta*, the *Liviana*, the *amphitheatrica*, the *Fanniana*, the *Saitica*, the *regia*, the *macrocolum*, and the *amphoretica*, or common waste paper, &c. as having been all made of the papyrus.

I lately mentioned the above conjecture to a friend, whom I knew to be well read in the classics. It immediately struck him that there might be something in it; and he soon afterwards sent me the following lines from Horace: Epist. i. lib. ii. 269-70:

" ' Deferar in vicum vendentem thus et odores
Et piper, et quicquid *chartis* amicitur *ineptis*.'

" He says, that ' he does not wish to be celebrated in bad poetry, nor exposed in an open box with the author, and conveyed into the street that sells frankincense, and spices, and pepper, and whatever is wrapped up in impertinent writings.' This is equivalent to being sent to the trunk-makers.

" But," he adds, " a case, more in point, I have found in Martial's Ep. ii. lib. iii. addressed ' to his book.'

' Festina tibi vindicem parare,
Ne nigram cito raptus in culinam
Cordyllas madida tegas papyro,
Vel thuris piperisque sis *cucullus*.' [d]

" ' Make haste to secure a patron, lest you should be hurried into the smoky kitchen, and your paper be used to wrap up little fish, or be converted into a twisted wrapper to hold frankincense and pepper.' "

" In the Variorum edition which I am using," continues my friend, " there is a Latin note upon the second line—' Ne damneris in culinam pro charta inepta—waste paper.' But the word *cucullus* is very explanatory: it is a hood

[d] It is evident that the poet addresses these lines to his autograph manuscript, written, we may conclude, not on the finest kind of paper: after which he congratulates it upon having been well received by Faustinus: " Now," he says, " you are safe; and copies of you will be made by the caligraphists, perfumed with cedar, and enriched with purple and other becoming ornaments."

or cowl; and here means the twisted paper wrapper into which we put sugar-plums. Now, could the papyrus be converted to such an use?"

In answer to this question I should say, no. The brittle nature of papyrus, if we can at all judge of what it originally was, from what it is now, would have rendered it unfit for wrappers of this kind.

There is another circumstance which seems much to favour my conjecture, that other papers, beside *papyrus*, were used at this time by the Romans for writing on. In the second volume of the " Herculanensium Voluminum quæ supersunt," (Naples 1809), we have certain fragments of a Latin poem; the only manuscript of the collection in that language that has yet been published. In their preface, the editors inform us, that inconceivable difficulties have attended all their endeavours to unroll the Latin papyri; such as they can only account for by supposing the papyrus, on which they were written, to have been manufactured in a different manner from that used for the Greek MSS. And Sir William Gell, writing upon the authority of a treatise by the Canonico Iorio, published in 1825, confirms this. Speaking of the Herculaneum MSS. generally, he says : " Many were found to be illegible from having originally been written with pale ink. Some appeared to have been below the others, and to have been formed by the humidity into a hard and almost petrified substance. These were considered as quite hopeless, having become a well-united mass, scarcely to be penetrated by a needle. Others had a degree of durability equal to plumbago, and might have been used as chalks. The papyri are only written on one side, except in a single instance, where the roll was not sufficiently long. Some were absolutely powder, and when the dust was blown away, the writing disappeared; so that the Canonico Iorio calls them the ghosts of papyri. It appears that *the Latin manuscripts are more difficult to unroll than the Greek, so that, of 2366 columns and fragments already opened, only 40 are Latin.*"

Now, from all this there appears strong reason to suspect that the Latin manuscripts of the collection, generally, were not written on the same material as the Greek manuscripts; although the world has all along been accustomed to call the whole *papyri*.

Something, without doubt, ought to be allowed for the hammering, and other processes, which Pliny states to have been used by the preparers of papyrus, or the paper-makers, of Rome; which may have had the effect of breaking the texture of the thin layers of papyrus of which, pasted together, the paper was made; whereas the papyrus on which the Greek manuscripts were written, may have been imported from Egypt, where the ancient and more simple way of preparing it, we may suppose, continued to prevail. But, this, I think, will not account for the very great difference, above noticed, between the Greek and the Latin manuscripts of the Herculaneum collection generally, and the extreme difficulty which the persons employed at Naples have encountered in all their attempts to unroll the Latin manuscripts.

It appears to me very possible that the ancient paper, or papyrus-makers, of Italy, and among them Fannius himself, who had so large a manufactory of paper at Rome, might, in times of great scarcity of the plant papyrus, have been accustomed to attempt the use of other materials; especially for papers of the inferior kinds; sometimes, perhaps, mixing the less valuable parts of the plant with them; and of course doing it secretly, in order to avoid the accusation, perhaps the penalty, of making their papers, or papyri, as they were called, of adulterated materials. I can conceive this to have happened, without even the inquisitive Pliny's knowing any thing about it; and that thus, even in ancient times, without any historian having been enabled to tell us how or when, the art of making papers of various kinds, some of them much resembling such as we now have, may have been by degrees discovered and practised. But I submit my conjectures on this head, with all due deference, to the future consideration of the learned.

I must, however, notice a well-known passage, in the "Tractatus contra Judæos," (cap. 5) of Petrus Cluniacensis, a writer of the first half of the twelfth century; wherein, enumerating the various substances books are composed of, he speaks of *paper* [for though he uses not the word, it is necessarily implied,] made of *the scrapings of old cloths*, and *other vile materials* : " Legit, inquit, (Judæus)," says he, " Deus in Cœlis, librum Talmuth. Sed cujusmodi librum ? Si talem, quales quotidie in uso legendi habemus, utique ex pellibus arietum, hircorum, vel vitulorum, sive ex biblis vel juncis Orientalium paludum, aut *ex rasuris veterum pannorum, seu ex qualibet alia forte viliore materia* compactos, et pennis avium vel calamis palustrium locorum, qualibet tinctura infectis, descriptos." Trombelli observes, that if paper similar to what we now use, is not here intended to be described, he cannot divine what is. Maffei thought these old cloths must have been of cotton, and so, it is probable some of them were. But there seems no reason to suppose they were all so: and what can be meant by the "seu ex qualibet alia viliore materia;" unless, that all sorts of inferior substances capable of being so applied, among them, perhaps, hemp, and the remains of old cordage, were used at this period in the manufacture of paper. One thing is evident, that, whatever the materials of which this paper was made, it is not here spoken of as a new invention. Nay, it may not unreasonably be conjectured that, even in the twelfth century, it was considered as an old invention; as immediately before his mention of this paper, the writer speaks of the papyrus; the use of which is universally believed to have been discontinued in Europe, some centuries before.

I am strongly inclined to the opinion that, from a very early period, paper was manufactured of mixed materials; though for a long time, perhaps, the use of wire sieves, to let off the superfluous water from the pulp, may not have been thought of; and, till then, paper may have been made by a process very similar to that employed by our hatters in making felt: which supposition may in some degree account for the great strength and thickness which I have commonly observed in the oldest papers I have seen. But I give this as a conjecture, and do not pretend to say when the use of the sieve was first introduced.

It was the common opinion when Maffei wrote, and has since continued, that no other paper, except that made of cotton, was known in Europe till the fourteenth century. In his "Istoria Diplomatica," (p. 77) he says: "Father Harduin asserts the having seen documents upon paper such as ours, of earlier date than 1200; but *it is easy to mistake cotton paper for the other*. In Italy, certainly, where that made from *linen rags* was invented, I do not remember to have seen any writing upon such paper before 1300; and if we speak of instruments, no one has passed through my hands more ancient than a certain investment of tithes; which I mention as being among my family papers, and which was given, in 1367, by Pietro della Scala, Bishop of Verona, to Gregorio Maffei, son of Rolandino."

Now I must observe on this passage of Maffei, that the notion here expressed by him, of dividing all old papers into two distinct kinds; viz. that made from *linen rags*, and that made from *cotton*, has given rise to numerous errors; which have, I think, greatly impeded the endeavours of learned men to trace the history of the invention of paper-making. Meerman had the same idea; [See " Gerardi Meerman, et doctorum virorum ad eum epistolæ atque observationes *de chartæ vulgaris seu lineæ origine.* Edidit, et præfat. instruxit Jacobus Van Vaasen, Hagæ-Comitum, apud Nicolaum Van Dalen. MDCCLXVII.] and, in consequence, when any one of his correspondents sent him a specimen of paper, in which he thought he detected anything not linen, he refused to acknowledge it as our ordinary paper, and immediately called it cotton paper. *If,* as Maffei says, *it be easy to mistake cotton paper for our common paper,* it surely follows that *the latter may sometimes have been mistaken for cotton paper:* and indeed, from what I have seen, I am convinced, that paper made from mixed materials, has been often wrongly termed cotton paper. I may add, that the distinction between pure cotton paper, and the other kinds, is strikingly exemplified in certain letters, which, through the kindness of my friend Mr. Petrie, I have had an opportunity of examining in the Tower of London: the oldest of these, (one of which is addressed to our King Henry III. by Raymond, the son of Raymond Count of Toulouse, and must therefore have been written in the lifetime of his father, who died in 1222) being upon very strong paper, made, certainly as I should say, of mixed materials; whilst in several of the time of Edward I. written upon genuine cotton paper of no great thickness, the fibres of the cotton present themselves every where at the backs of the letters so distinctly, that they seem as if they might, even now, be spun into thread.

With respect to the use of linen rags in paper, I am satisfied that they were so employed very early; and, of course, most in those parts where linen most abounded: but oftener than not I suspect they were mixed with other materials, even in papers of the finer kinds. I shall only add, that I formerly possessed an undoubted original drawing by Giotto, for his celebrated mosaic of the Bark of St. Peter, at Rome, executed by him, I think, before 1290; which drawing is now in the collection of the late Sir Thomas Lawrence. It was formerly engraved in a work of Metz, and more recently in one of my own. It is boldly done with a pen, upon paper somewhat thin, made evidently upon a sieve, and of very inferior materials; and, indeed, as well from its texture as colour, I should say that but little linen had entered into the composition of the pulp, and that hemp was one of its chief ingredients.

The following passage in Maffei, ("Istoria Diplomatica," pp. 78, 79) could we depend on the truth of the opinion expressed in it, would furnish us with a monument of cotton paper, earlier, by several centuries, than any other hitherto known. Speaking of the famous manuscript of St. Mark's Gospel, preserved in the Ducal treasury at Venice, he says:

" The author of the ' Diario Italico,' (Montfaucon,) judged this MS. to be written on papyrus. A letter therein produced of the year 1564, assures us that it was even then in so deplorable a state, that not only it could not be read, but even the number of the gatherings could not be ascertained, (Diar. c. iv et viii. Pal. l. i. c. 2.): so long ago, therefore, the whole was spoiled and stuck together, in consequence of the damp; which could not have happened to papyrus . . . . . But I," he continues, "have now to say, that this manuscript of the Evangelist was neither written on *papyrus*, nor on *parchment*, but on *cotton paper*. Of this fact I have convinced myself by several times examining and handling it. The damp, during so many centuries, has reduced the perished gatherings into a conglutinated mass of a white colour, like the primitive paste of cotton and water of which the paper was originally made . . . . . It is not however, on this account, to be supposed that this celebrated MS. is not of very high antiquity; as it is well known that cotton paper was made at a very early period in the Levant; and as the square form of the MS. is of itself indicative of its venerable age."[e]

[e] The vulgar tradition that this manuscript was written by the hand of the Evangelist himself, has long been discredited among the learned: but there seems good reason to consider it of a date not later than the commencement of the sixth century. Montfaucon assures us that it is, or was, written in Latin, [I express myself thus, as not even a word of it has been legible for some centuries,] and not in the Greek language, as was formerly thought to be the case: in proof of which he notices the frequent occurrence of letters which have no place in the Greek alphabet; the D, for example, and the R. He, as has been said, thought the material it was written on, *papyrus*.

There is a very learned and interesting dissertation upon the subject of this manuscript by Laur. a Turre, p. DXLVII. et seq. in the " Evangeliarum Quadruplex " of Blanchinius: in which it seems to be proved, that it originally made part of a celebrated Latin manuscript of the Gospels, written on thin parchment, and well known under the title of the manuscript of Forli. It appears that, many centuries ago, the Gospel of St. Mark was taken out of this manuscript; that it was afterwards said to have been written by the Evangelist himself; that this Gospel was comprised in seven gatherings; that the two last gatherings were given in 1355 to the Emperor

The manuscripts which have been found in the excavations of Pompeii and Herculaneum, are, as far as I can learn, all of them rolls. This circumstance (notwithstanding that we have the representations of Pugillares with leaves, in several of the paintings) is of a nature to occasion some doubt as to the use of *square books (codices)*, such as we now have, in ancient times; and I am therefore induced here to produce a few passages from writers of those times which relate, or are supposed to refer to them; though as we possess a few square manuscripts in the library of the Vatican and elsewhere, which the best judges have recognized as being of an age nearly, if not quite, as remote as that at which I am disposed to date the particular manuscript under consideration, it may seem scarcely necessary.

Rolled manuscripts, as has been just shewn of those of Herculaneum, were commonly written only on one side; and I therefore conclude that the hundred and sixty books of collections, which came into the possession of the younger Pliny upon the death of his uncle, and which he says (Lib. iii. epist. 5) were written in a very small hand on both sides the paper or parchment, were *square manuscripts*. It is true that in the course of this letter he often uses the term *volumen*; but that word and *liber* appear to have been indifferently used by him and other writers of the time in speaking of every kind of book. The inconvenience of a rolled manuscript written on both sides is manifest.

I have already said that the "*Pugillares membranacii operculis eboriis*," which were left to the town of Reggio by T. Ebervenius Sabinus, are believed to have been square books with numerous leaves; but I am not prepared with the date at which this person lived; though we know that it was in pagan times, as his *pugillares* were deposited in the temple of Apollo. Seneca, however, (De Brevit. Vitæ, cap. xiii.) says: "Plurium tabularum contextus *caudex* apud antiquos dicitur; unde publicæ tabulæ *codices* dicuntur."

Christ. Gottl. Schawrzius, in his work "De Ornamentis Librorum" (4to

---

Charles IV. and deposited in a church at Prague; and that the remaining five gatherings were transported in 1420 to Venice. It is stated in this Dissertation, that in 1720 the father of Blanchinius was permitted by the Venetian government to examine the manuscript in the Ducal treasury minutely; and that, then, not even a letter of the writing could be discerned; but that all those who assisted at the examination, were decidedly of opinion that the material on which it had been written was *parchment*.

Lipsiæ 1756) is decidedly of opinion that Martial, in his Epigrams (Lib. xiv.) headed, "*Ovidius in membranis*," "*Homerus in membranis*," "*Cicero et Livius in membranis*," &c. is to be considered as speaking of *square manuscripts* of those authors, written on parchment, and not of *rolls*. The leaves of square manuscripts, whatever the substances they were made of, were called *tabulæ*, or *tabellæ*, or *folia*, indifferently. Thus in the Epigram 192, lib. xiv.

"Ovidii Metamorphosis in membranis."
"Hæc tibi, multiplici quae structa est massa *tabella*,
Carmina Nasonis quinque decemque gerit."

"This book (massa) which is made of numerous (or many-folded) leaves (tabella), contains the fifteen books of Naso."

And in like manner, in Epigr. 186.

"Virgilius in membrana."
"Quam brevis immensum cepit *membrana* Maronem!
Ipsius vultus *prima tabella* gerit."

"What small-sized parchment contains the great Maro! The *first leaf* bears his own portrait."

He also uses "multiplicem pellem," for "codicem," Epigr. 184.

"Homerus in membranis."
"Ilias et Priami regnis inimicus Ulysses
Multiplici pariter condita *pelle* latent."

"The Iliad, and (the story of) Ulysses, the enemy of the kingdom of Priam, lie compressed, in like manner, in many-folded skins."

Besides that rolled manuscripts, as has been said, were written only on one side, their shape, and the looseness with which they were rolled, necessarily caused them to occupy much more space, in proportion to the matter contained in them, than was the case with square manuscripts; the leaves of which, besides being written on both sides, were also compressed into the smallest possible compass by the bookbinder. To this advantage on the side of square manuscripts (or *codices*) Schawrzius supposes Martial to refer in Epigr. 190.

"Livius in membranis."
"Pellibus exiguis arctatur Livius ingens,
Quem mea vix totum bibliotheca capit."

"Within small skins is compressed the enormous (work of) Livy, which (written on rolls) my bookcase can scarcely contain."

By the term 'bibliotheca,' in this place, I conceive to be meant one of those round or oval boxes, in which the ancients were accustomed to keep their rolled volumes, and of which so many representations may be seen in the paintings of Herculaneum, and in other monuments of antiquity. These boxes were flat at bottom, and had commonly a flat lid with a hinge and fastening. They were of moderate dimensions, so as to be easily portable; each containing from eight to ten or a dozen manuscripts, which stood in them upright. A library, therefore, consisted of a larger or smaller number of these boxes. Catullus, excusing himself to Manlius, for not having sent him certain verses which he had asked for, states, among other reasons, that he had only brought one of his cases of books with him:

" Huc una ex multis *capsula* me sequitur."

They were also called *scrinia*. Thus Ovid, (Trist. lib. i. El. i. v. 105-6), addressing his book:

" Quum tamen in nostrum fueris penetrale receptus,
Contigerisque tuam, *scrinia curva*, domum;" &c.

It seems not improbable that square manuscripts, which before Martial lived, perhaps, had been but rarely used, except for books of accounts and registers, began in his time to come much into vogue; and that he, perceiving the advantage of them over rolled manuscripts, therefore wrote as above.

I may add on this subject, that, in a volume of Italian drawings of antique bassi-relievi at Rome, formerly belonging to the late Charles Towneley, Esq. and now preserved in the British Museum, I find one, which Mr. Towneley observes to have been taken from an urn, with a Greek inscription, then in the Villa Albani, in which, among other figures, are the remains of a sitting figure with a square book, open, in the left hand;—that, upon one of the fragments of ancient drinking-glasses, which are so eruditely illustrated by Buonarruoti, in the work which I shall now have occasion to speak of, Christ is represented preaching, holding in his hand a square book;—and, moreover, that Eusebius, in his life of Constantine (Book iv. chap. 37)—I quote the Latin of Schawrzius—mentions his having transmitted to that Emperor " terniones et quaterniones," (that is, " gatherings containing sometimes three and sometimes four sheets,") " in codicibus magnifice exornata."

I now come to the more important question, as to *the use of minuscule writing by the ancient Romans*. In my endeavours to collect evidence upon this point, the first book I chanced to take up was the very interesting volume of Buonarruoti, intituled, " Osservazioni sopra alcuni frammenti di Vasi antichi di vetro," &c. fol. Firenze, 1716; and it is remarkable that this eminent antiquary happens to have been the first who wrote at any length in support of the belief which I seek to establish; though he did it only incidentally, in the course of his argument in proof of the antiquity of these fragments.

The fragments treated of in this work are the bottoms of broken drinking glasses, which, with other remnants of trifling ornaments of various kinds, have been found at different times in the catacombs at Rome, stuck in the mortar covering the different urns or niches in which the early Christians were buried. They are ornamented with figures, accompanied generally by inscriptions; the whole, in those of most common occurrence, being scratched or drawn upon the glass with a point, upon a gold ground. The subjects of some of them are pagan; but the greater part represent stories from Holy Writ, or the figures of the Apostles Peter and Paul, that of Christ himself, or devout representations of some of the first martyrs. Buonarruoti believes these things to have been placed, as above-mentioned, by the early Christians, as memoranda, which should enable them readily to find the places where their deceased friends were buried, when, upon anniversaries, or other solemn occasions, they desired to visit their tombs. As memorials of the primitive Christian Church, and of the simplicity of her worship, they possess the highest interest: Buonarruoti argues that some of them may be as early as the second century, and that they are all anterior to the Dioclesian persecution.

" The places," says he, " in which these fragments of drinking-glasses have been found, furnish a strong ground in favour of their antiquity. In my time, when for amusement I have visited the catacombs, the diggers, in order to discover a part not hitherto examined, always went seeking for new corridors or galleries; . . . . . . and so, excavating and searching, they discovered such as had not been before explored; either entirely filled up with earth, or at least half so, or as high as three or four rows of sepulchres; and in these places have been discovered these fragments, &c. . . . . . Now, at what time can these corridors have been filled up? Not after the Church enjoyed peace; as we know that the Christians and the supreme Pontiffs took the greatest care of them, and held them in the highest veneration; so that it cannot be believed that they were filled up then. It is therefore exceedingly probable that this was done during the severe persecution of Dioclesian; and that the Christians, in order that the Pagans, without, should see no signs of the excavation of new corridors, necessary for the burial of the numerous martyrs which every day required sepulture, were obliged, with the earth excavated upon those occasions, to fill up the old corridors that were near them. . . . . We may fairly conclude, therefore, that these fragments of drinking-glasses, which have been found in the corridors that had been filled up, are older than the persecution of Dioclesian, and indeed that, being fragments of vases previously broken, they are considerably older: and, in my opinion, they are of a time in which the Church enjoyed a long peace, which was under the Emperor Gordian, and after the reign of Valerian; and, in fact, the head-dresses of certain portraits of women, in some of these fragments, accord very well with that period, as will be shewn hereafter; besides, that, in those times of peace and security, the Christians could have had no fears of being known for such, by the sacred images on their vases."

Buonarruoti then speaks of the well-known monogram ☧, denoting by two Greek letters the name of Christ; and which is found on several of these glass fragments. He is aware of the common belief, that this monogram was first invented by Constantine, and that, consequently, the antiquaries are accustomed to ascribe all monuments, upon which it is found, to the time of that Emperor, or later. This opinion, however, he thinks decidedly erroneous. "It is not credible," he observes, "that the vast number of inscriptions in the catacombs, bearing this monogram, should be all so late as the time of Constantine. Bosio, Severano, and Arringhi, noticed it in several much more ancient than that Emperor; as in that of Marius, under Adrian; of Alexander, under Antoninus Pius; and of Caius, Pope, under Dioclesian, &c. &c. It has been also found on numerous sepulchres having a vase of blood, the sign of the person having suffered martyrdom; and even upon such vases themselves:" and he adds, that "he himself had observed it on a glass of blood taken from the cemetery of S. Calisto, engraved in the midst of other letters, in this manner: ASIN☧PRE;" and which an erudite Italian gentleman of my acquaintance, Count Mortara, suggests may be read: "Asinius, Presbyter." (Plate V. No. 8.)

"It cannot be believed," continues Buonarruoti, "that all these persons suffered martyrdom after the time of Constantine, in the persecution of Julian the Apostate, the only one after Constantine that was felt in these parts; as he persecuted the Church in a covert manner, and as few of the Christians were actually put to death by him. Indeed, these same glass fragments, the greater antiquity of which appears from other evidence, are sufficient to shew that this sacred monogram was used by the Christians long before Constantine. Its being composed of Greek letters, seems to render it probable that the use of it began with the primitive Church, before it left the East. . . . . Perhaps it was first adopted about the time when the faithful were first called Christians; . . . . and is the same to which St. John alludes in the viith chapter of the Revelations, when, speaking of the sign of the elect, he terms it the sign of the living God; and in the xivth chapter, where he expressly calls it the name of the Lamb. . . . . . Indeed Primatius, Bishop of Adrumentinum, speaking of the Apocalypse (L. iv. ch. 13) is of opinion that the Apostle alluded to our monogram.

"But," continues Buonarruoti, "all difficulty upon the subject is removed by a careful consideration of what is said by Eusebius, whose authority is preferable to that of every one else; as he himself heard from the mouth of Constantine the account of the vision which he had before his battle with Maxentius. For Eusebius, who attests the having several times seen the celebrated standard, does not say (in the 31st chapter of the first book of his life of Constantine, where he particularly describes it), that that Emperor *invented* the monogram of Christ, but that he caused that sign to be affixed to the top of his standard; which standard, with its cross-bar, resembled the Cross, seen by him in the sky after mid-day, in conformity to which he had been afterwards commanded in a dream to cause his standard to be made. . . . . It should also be observed that Eusebius speaks of the monogram, in general terms, as a thing well-known among the Christians; from whom it is probable Constantine learned it; as immediately after the vision, and long before the new ensign was prepared, he was instructed in the Christian religion. Moreover, as he was of Illyric origin, and resided almost always in the West, it is not probable, supposing him the inventor, that he would have formed it of Greek characters: and, even should the assertion of Lactantius, in the fourth chapter of his book on the death of persecutors, be insisted on, that Constantine was commanded, in a dream, to cause the above sacred monogram to be inscribed on his shields; still it may be answered, that it is very probable that God revealed to him that sign, in the form in which it was already used among Christians."

I have been unwilling to omit Buonarruoti's argument in proof of the remote origin of this well-known monogram: for though, strictly speaking, it has little to do with my present inquiry respecting ancient minuscules; still, as this monogram is of frequent occurrence in manuscripts, as well as in other early Christian monuments, I thought it well thus to make more generally known what is to be said in support of its antiquity; in order to shew that a monument on which it appears, ought not, on that account alone, to be unhesitatingly placed as low as the fourth or fifth cenrury.

This argument concerning the monogram of Christ, is followed in Buonarruoti's work by another, respecting St. Agnes; whose figure is represented, standing in the act of prayer, on three or four of these glass fragments. He endeavours to shew, and I think successfully, that she suffered martyrdom under Valerian and Gallienus, and not, as Baronius and the compilers of the "Acta Sanctorum" have supposed, in the last great persecution of Dioclesian. It seems that, in the account of her acts, it is said that she appeared after her death to her parents; and that they related the circumstance to Constantius the son of Constantine; and hence the opinion which he combats. But it is also said in that account that she was put to death under Valerian and Gallienus, and mention is made of Aspasius Paternus; who, as we learn in the acts of St. Cyprian, was Proconsul in Africa under the above Emperors, in the year 264 of the Christian era, and in the two following years was prefect of Rome. It is said expressly in the acts of St. Agnes: "Tunc Vicarius Aspasius nomine Paternus, Proconsul, Præfectus, ex Dominis et Principibus suis Valeriano et Gallieno, jussit:" and Buonarruoti, very fairly, insists, that it is much more probable that the acts, or history, of the Saint should have been interpolated, in that part which states the apparition of her to her parents to have been by them related to Constantius, than that the names of Aspasius, and of the Emperors Valerian and Gallienus, should have been added.

But Buonarruoti now comes to what more immediately interests us. "It now remains for me," says he, "in order to remove every doubt of the antiquity of these glass fragments from the mind of the reader, that might arise

supposed to be of the 2d or 3d century. 79

from the forms of particular letters, on some of them, being different from those of the common Latin alphabet of classic times, to shew by examples that those letters, similarly formed, were also used by the ancients."

This variety, he observes, may have arisen from various causes: sometimes from the sculptor of an inscription having carelessly imitated imperfectly formed letters; sometimes from his having made them conformable to a *certain sort of cursive,* which had before been adopted by the scribes, for the sake of convenience, and in order to write with the greater rapidity upon common occasions; and sometimes, from the artist happening to be a native of the provinces of Greece, or Syria, or of other parts, and not perfectly conversant in the Roman letters; in consequence of which, when endeavouring to imitate them, he unconsciously gave them something of the form of the Greek letters which were used in his own country.

I do not think it necessary to follow Buonarruoti in the particular remarks with which he accompanies the numerous ancient inscriptions produced by him for the above purpose; but shall chiefly confine my observations to the inscriptions themselves; the most important of which, or such parts of them as may best help to establish the point I am contending for, are carefully imitated in the accompanying Plate V. I shall take them in the order in which I find them in my common-place book.

ZINNVM LOCI. QVINTINI. ET MARTVRIAE,

for " Signum loci Quintini," &c. (Plate V. No. 1.); that is the mark of the place where they are buried. This inscription was found in the cemetery of Pretestato. The person who wrote or sculptured it appears, inadvertently, to have omitted the first N in Quintini; and to have afterwards rectified the error, by inserting, between the I and the T, a small minuscule n, exactly formed as we make it now.

ANIME INNOCENTI GAVDENTIAE QUE VIXIT
AN. V. M. VII. D. XXI. IN PACE.

So far this inscription is in large capitals; but the line under it that follows, and which was probably scratched upon the wet mortar used in closing the tomb, or written in black or red, by the father of the child himself, is all in minuscule or cursive characters: (Plate V. No. 4.)

" mercurius pater filiae d (deposuit) v. idus novemb. urso et polemio coss."

This inscription of Gaudentia, Buonarruoti informs us, was transmitted to him, exactly traced from the original, by Monsignor Bianchini. I conclude that his copy of it is reduced in size, but in all other respects like the original. Its date, he observes, is the year 338 of the Christian era, as is proved by the names of Ursus and Polemius, the Consuls.

It will be observed that the *r*, in this inscription, is as it appears in the celebrated manuscript of the Pandects of Justinian, of the beginning of the sixth century, at Florence, with the shaft of the letter descending below the line; and much the same as we frequently find it in early Saxon writings. It is the same in the inscription of the sculptor Atticianes, which will be noticed presently; and I mention the circumstance, merely to shew that the same letter was written in different ways in very early times: for more commonly we find it written, in early Latin manuscripts, in conformity to our manuscript of Aratus; as in the St. Hilarius of the Vatican, which was collated in the year 510 at Kasulis in Africa; and the Severus Sulpicius at Verona, the writing of which was completed in 517.

The *n*, in this inscription, and in that of Quintinus, is exactly as we make it now; (satisfactorily proving that the idea which some have entertained, that this particular minuscule was not introduced till after all the others,—See "Nouv. Trait. de Dipl." vol. ii. p. 491, note—has no foundation;) and the same may be said of the *b*, the *d*, the *p*, and almost all the others. The *e* is made, by a *c*, and a light stroke proceeding from the middle of it; which is, however, in two instances omitted; viz. in the words *et*, and *polemio*, where the top stroke of the *t*, and the first rising stroke of the *m*, are made to do instead; and it is remarkable that we have a similar instance in our manuscript, and another in an English document of the seventh century in the British Museum, (See Plate VI. No. 8.), as I shall again have occasion to observe. After all, this inscription is as much cursive as minuscule writing; and is not to be considered as the performance of a professed scribe. That the true minuscule *e*, as we now make it in writing, was used in Italy three centuries before the death of Gaudentia, will be shewn hereafter.

The following inscription, from the cemetery of Ciriaca, though chiefly in capitals, presents an F, such as we often find in early manuscripts; and examples of the minuscules f (s) and *m*, both of them well formed. (Plate V. No. 2.)

"DIOGENIA fILIAE BONAE QVAE VIXIT ANNOS
fexf mx DIOGENES PATER INfELIX."

In the next (Pl. V. No. 14.) "RINCENTIVS KARO FILIO KARIffIMO BENE-MERENTI POSVIT TABVLA QVI BIXIT ANNOS III ET DIES XXII." we have again the minuscule f (s) twice repeated in 'karissimo ;' and this inscription, moreover, gives examples of the *b* substituted for *v*, and the *k* for *c*.

The following is from a cemetery near S. Lorenzo, outside the walls of Rome. (Pl. V. No. 11.) The first part is in capitals; but most of the letters of the remainder may be considered as minuscules: the *t* in the last word is decidedly so. "DOMITI IN PACE LEA FECIT."

A statue of a Muse, in the gallery at Florence, bears the name of the sculptor who did it. I have no remembrance of the statue itself; but, judging of its merits from the print done from it, (and besides, it was one of those which the French afterwards thought worth taking to Paris), I should think it could not have been sculptured later than the close of the second century, or the beginning of the third; and it may be of the first century. The inscription, which is cut in the marble, is thus: (Plate V. No. 3.)

'opuſ atticianiſ afrodifieniſ,'

and, the letters, except the N, may be all considered as minuscules. The *s* in 'opus,' it will be observed, is extended both above and below the line, so as to resemble the long *s* which we make now in writing; and so it is in three or four instances in the inscription of Gaudentia before noticed.

I notice the following inscription, which was taken by Buonarruoti from the work of Monsignor Fabretti, because the letter *b*, which occurs in it four times, is in every instance a minuscule: (Plate V. No. 7.)

"D. M.

" Q. TERENTI . PRISCIANI . VIXIT . ANNIS . IIII . MENSIbVS . VII. FRVMENTVM PVbLICVM . ACCEPIT . MENSIbVS. VIIII. TERENTIA . SAbINA ALVMNO . FECIT."

The following was copied from the before mentioned cemetery near S. Lorenzo, outside the walls of Rome: (Plate V. No. 5.)

"uERO DULCISSIMO FILIO PARENTES SUI BENE MERENTI IN SECULO UIXIT ANN u MENS IIII ET DIES XIIII EX HOC DEFUNCT EST XVIII KAL. MAI."

Here we have the v rounded at bottom, thus u, as it is frequently found in very ancient manuscripts; the L, also, is higher than the other letters, as is commonly the case in them; and the capital H, in 'hoc,' is of a very remarkable shape, such as it appears sometimes in an ancient manuscript of Terence, and another of Prudentius in the Vatican. We have here also an example of the T, following N, being made by simply adding an horizontal line over the last stroke of the N, as we occasionally find it in manuscripts, from the earliest period to the twelfth century and later.

The first three inscriptions that follow, were found in the cemetery of S. Lorenzo, called Ciriaca; and the fourth in that of Priscilla.

" SARIψA VIXIT ANμOS XVIIII Mϵρ SES VI DS XIII SERNA FECIT SEbiBO." (Plate V. No. 10.)

" EVAGRENI . FILIAE . CARISSIME . BENEMERENTI. QVE VIXIT. AN. XVIIII. M. VII. D. XXIII. MAXINVS. ET TALAME. PARENTES fECERVNT DECES. IIII. NON. OCTO." (Plate V. No. 13.)

" POSVIT . TABVLA MAgISTER DISCENTI
PANPINO BENEMERENTI." (Plate V. No. 6.)

" INNOCENTIA CONIVNX ISSIgVARIS QVAE CVM EVM VIXIT BENE ANNIS X dIES DVODECIM QVAE DE SAECVLO EXIBIT IDIBVS AVg gALLICANO CONS." (Plate V. No. 12.) I learn from Marini, (" Atti e monumenti de' Fratelli Arvali," vol. i. p. xlvii.) that Gallicanus was Consul, A. D. 150.

We see, in the first of these four inscriptions, the *n* three times repeated, similar in form to that used by the Greeks, μ, in their manuscripts; and differing essentially from the real Latin minuscule *n*, as we have it in the inscriptions of Quintinus and Gaudentia: in the second, we have the minuscule f, well formed; and in the third and fourth, a round *d*, and a very decided approximation to our minuscule *g*.

On the whole (if we admit the above *g*), these inscriptions of Buonarruoti give us examples of *all the minuscule letters of the Roman alphabet*, except the *h*, which letter occurs only once in the whole of them, and the *q*. This last minuscule I have since found, accompanied by other minuscule characters, in the following inscription in Fabretti, (" Inscriptionum antiquarum quæ in Ædibus Paternis asservantur explicatio ;" &c. Rom. 1699, in fol.) p. 577,

"MEVIVS MAXIMINO CONIVCI DVLCISSIMO
CVM QVEM VIXIT ANNOS LX MARCIA
MAXIMINA FECIT."

where, after noticing the solecism, "cum quem," of which he mentions another example at p. 305 (No. 299) of his book, he adds: "Nil aliud præterea hæc inscriptio continet, præter literas *m, q,* et *u, recenti scribendi usui conformes:*" whence I am led to conclude, that Fabretti was in some degree imbued with the common notion, that the Romans of ancient classical times were unacquainted with genuine minuscule writing. And this, indeed, seems to have been the belief of Buonarruoti; for, though he furnishes us with the above numerous specimens of minuscule letters, he considers them, as we have seen, to be, in great measure, corruptions of the ancient Roman characters; originating in the ignorance or carelessness of the individuals by whom these inscriptions were written or sculptured.

We have also, twice, the true minuscule *q,* in the monumental inscription of an early Christian, perhaps a martyr, of the illustrious name of Gentianus; which was found in the cemetery of S. Agnese, and is copied of the full size, in fac-simile, in the above work of Marini, (p. 362), who was in possession of the original: and this inscription has, besides, the round cursive *d,* the round ϵ, the round *m,* the v rounded on one side, as we often have it in manuscripts, and the monogram of Christ, ☧.

I find this other inscription in Fabretti, p. 547:

"D N [M?] AVRELIAE DICTORIAE QVAE DIXIT ANNVM ET MENſEſ OCTO;"

where the *d,* the *b,* and the *s,* are minuscule letters; and where, in two instances, the *b* is used instead of *v*. This substitution of *b* for *v* is very common in early inscriptions, where it sometimes has a strange effect; as in "*Bi*bas (vivas) in pace dei" (Buonarr. tab v.): "*Bi*bas in deo" (Murat. 1855. 7. Boldetti, 417): "Credo quia redemptor *bi*bit" (Fleetwood, 520. Murat. 1841. 5): "Conjugi bene *bi*benti que vixit" (Fabrett. 546. iv.) I take these references from Ulr. Frid. Kopp ("Palæographia Critica,") vol. iii. p. 498; in which volume (p. 514), I also find the following Latin inscription, written with a singular mixture of Greek and Roman characters; among the latter of which we have several times the minuscules *m, n,* and *r,* as well formed as possible. See our Plate V. No. 15.

" Αυχεnθιω· PHIλιω· DVλKICCImω· εBε
nε · mερεθι . ACθιAnYC · nAθ · BInDελικYC
DεκYΓιω · CKYθAΓιωrYm · ε · εYDœKIA · nIKε
PArεnθεC · m · PAKε · YικCιθ· Ann · L · m · I ·"

Kopp says that this inscription has been read thus: " Auxentio filio dulcissimo et benemerenti. Astianus natione Bindelicus [Vindelicus ?], decurio scutatorium et Eudocia Nice parentes in pace. Vixit ann. L. mens I." With respect to the age of the son, however, he observes: " Quum enim videret, Græcis Latinisque literis promiscue usum esse in inscriptionis auctorem; L et I pro λ et i, Græcis numerorum notis accipere, ideoque vertere ei licebat annos xxx. menses x."

I have before mentioned the having looked into the extensive work, entitled "Le Pitture Antiche d'Ercolano;" and have sufficiently noticed the line of Euripides, which was found on a wall at Resina, written in Greek minuscules with accents, and is spoken of in the second volume of that work. I have now to add, that in the vignette to the description of plate ix, in the same volume, we have an ancient painting, in which are represented, a double inkstand, perhaps for holding black and red ink, with a reed pen, a rolled volume, partly open and written on, and a book of tablets, also open. In speaking of this vignette, in a note at page 328, the illustrators of this work observe as follows:

"On the roll," say they, " are several lines of writing, which appear to be in Roman characters. In the first line, we think we read *quisquis*[f] (see this word carefully copied from the engraved vignette, in our Plate IV. No. 19); in the last but one *maxima*; and in the last *cura*: and it is to be observed, that the *q*, the *u*, the *r*, and the *s*, are *minuscule characters*. We might here not improperly speak of the epoch of minuscule characters in Latin writing; . . . . . but we shall defer what we have to say on the subject, till we have come to the volume treating of the papyri; where these paintings, and the inscriptions upon

[f] At first sight, the first letter of this word *Quisquis*, struck me as being much more like an A than a Q. I have since learned from Kopp that it is in fact the Tironian Q of the ancients. See this character three times employed in an Inscription of the time of Marcus Aurelius, (Plate V. No. 16) which I have had the good fortune to find at page 106 of the first volume of the "Palæographia Critica" of this learned writer.

them, and whatever else pertains to ancient writing, will be examined in detail. &c..... Suffice it for the present to observe, that negative arguments ought but little to be relied on; and that it is dangerous, upon them, to found a system concerning matters of fact...... It has been observed that minuscule characters are not commonly found on medals or marbles, nor in manuscripts" (supposed to be—the writers might here have added—), "of the first centuries of the Christian era; and it has hitherto been the fashion, on this account, to fix the introduction and use of them at a very late period....... It cannot, however, be denied that traces of cursive or minuscule writing are to be found on medals; not only of the third century, but even of times prior to Augustus: and, on the whole, there seems reason to conclude, that the Ancients had two kinds of writing: the more ancient, formed of majuscule characters, which was used in public works, and adopted by those who desired to write magnificently; the other, of cursive letters, of somewhat different shapes, and less elegant."

The Dissertation upon the writing of the Ancients, promised in the above note, has not yet made its appearance; although two thin folio volumes of the Papyri have been published at Naples, the last in 1809; besides a third volume, entitled, "Dissertationis Isagogicæ, ad Herculanensium Voluminum explanationem, Pars prima," in 1797. This, I find from the Introduction, is to be followed by two other Parts; in the last of which the information I am in search of is promised to be given. Meanwhile, at the end of this first part, we have a few plates of fac-similes of Inscriptions, the originals of which are said to have been written, in black or red with a brush, upon the walls of buildings in Pompeii; and which, though generally written in capitals, contain here and there a minuscule letter. (See Plate IV. Nos. 4—16.) The small *b*, for example, occurs several times; once or twice we have the minuscule *k*; we have also a good cursive *f*; the v is often rounded at bottom, like our u; and in the following inscription, in which one Pothinus, a seller of the tunny-fish, salutes the Ædile Postumius, we have, besides the small *b*, the minuscule *e*, exactly formed as we now use it in writing: (Plate IV. No. 7.)

POSTUMIUM PRObUM AED. POTHINUS ROG.
FeR TUNNUM.

To which I may add, that a friend of mine, who visited Pompeii about ten years ago, remembers having remarked the following inscription on the front of a house of debauch, near the barracks of the soldiers, which he thinks was written in red, in minuscule characters:

" eic abitat voluptas:" for " heic [hic] habitat voluptas."

Since writing the above, I have looked into the elegant work entitled " Les Ruines de Pompeii," by Mazois, Paris, 1812, in fol.; where, in a vignette prefixed to the second part, or volume, I find several of these painted inscriptions, engraved in correct imitation of the originals. As he observes in the previous volume, (p. 48, note 3,) the characters are commonly very tall in proportion to their width, and in consequence the letters I, T, and L, are often with difficulty to be distinguished from each other: but this appears to have been in some degree occasioned by the writer having been required to put a good deal of matter into a small space. In one of them (See our Plate IV. No. 4), the minuscule *b* occurs three times; though all the other letters are capitals. In another, the *d*, in the name *Popidium*, (No. 15), is a minuscule or cursive character. But the most interesting parts of this plate of Mazois, are the fac-similes of a few words in *ancient cursive*, which are not very easy to decypher; though some of the letters are sufficiently well formed. (See Nos. 14, 17, 18.)

" These three fragments," says Mazois, " exhibit letters of the highest interest; as they are the only examples we have of the cursive of the Romans of the first century of the Christian era. The letters of the first two fragments were written with a large red crayon on the wall of a tomb. I should," says he, " have doubted of their antiquity, if I had not been present when the monument on which they were written was discovered, and if I had not been obliged to remove a thin coating of ashes in order to read them. No sense is to be made from them, nor have they ever made part of a continued inscription. Some passer-by has, for his amusement, written his name, or copied perhaps part of the inscription of a neighbouring tomb. We read," says he:

" *Atmetus*   Cemellu . . .
   cum P. Po.   . . . tanine
                   SAL.

" The third specimen, where we read the letters *vtilitiss.* was found written upon white stucco; and made part of an illegible inscription of one line."

I will not stop to express my doubts as to the French writer's having read these scrawls correctly. A few of the letters, the minuscule t for example in all of them, and the double s in the last, appear very clear; whilst others remain equivocal. I think it evident that the first two inscriptions were written by the same individual; and that, as a scribe, he was but half instructed; whence—and not upon the supposition that the complete minuscule alphabet had not yet been invented—I am disposed to account for his having used in every instance the capital M, and the N, instead of the small letters proper in cursive writing; and also for the rude manner employed by him in making a small e, so unlike that in the above-mentioned inscription of Pothinus.

To these, let me add the following short inscription, written on a painting in a tavern at Pompeii, for which I am indebted to the "Museo Borbonico," vol. iv. (1827), p. 5, at the end:

M. Fpilᴀ· M. Tᴠtillᴠᴍ

This the editors read: "Marcus Furius Pila Marcum Tutillum;" and suppose to be a salutation addressed by the tavern-keeper, M. F. Pila, to one M. Tutillus. Most of the letters in this inscription may fairly be termed minuscules. See our Plate IV. No. 1. a.

By the bye, I have found no notice of these cursive inscriptions, or of these minuscule characters, in Sir William Gell's "Pompeiana." Not only do they appear to have entirely escaped his observation, but, in that number of his Appendix which treats of the papyri, I find a passage which leads me to conclude that, in accordance with the old opinion, he took it for granted that the ancients had no other way of writing except that in majuscules. For he says: "There is a suspicion, that in one of the papyri, have been observed not only contractions but accents: but this, which would certainly prove a treasure to critics and philologists, is probably an imaginary discovery, and contractions seem impracticable, even in the most corrupt species of writing, with *detached capitals*." What, if this papyrus should turn out to be in fair minuscule writing!

The particular difficulty that has been experienced in unrolling the Latin manuscripts has already been noticed. In consequence of this, the fragments of only one Latin manuscript have yet been published; and this happens to be a poem, and is written in capitals; so that it can be of little use in the present argument.

The words in this manuscript are all divided from each other by points, as we often see them in ancient inscriptions. (Plate IV. No. 3.) The letters appear to have been rapidly written, the whole in strokes of nearly the same thickness; and the tops and bottoms of them are without those thin horizontal strokes, which are sometimes called the bases and capitals of the letters, and which we commonly find in finished majuscule writing.

Indeed, several of the characters may be not improperly styled cursive capitals; especially the F, the S, and the V. The E is constantly the round capital, (Є), such as we find it in manuscripts written, in what it is the fashion to call *uncial* characters; and, on the whole, this papyrus, had it been known when the authors of the "Nouveau Traité de Diplomatique" published their enormous work, might have furnished those gentlemen with a new set of rules for judging of the dates of manuscripts written in capitals; or, what would have been better, have caused them to perceive that the great variety which is to be observed in the forms of the same letter in ancient manuscripts and inscriptions, rendered it unsafe to insist, so much as they have done, upon any rule whatever, drawn from such accidental circumstances. It is remarkable that the *h*, save its angularity, is of the same form as is used in minuscule writing; the perpendicular stroke, on the right hand, rising only so high as to meet and form a right angle with the cross stroke of the letter; as is sometimes the case with this character (used as a capital) in a celebrated ancient manuscript of Terence, ornamented with drawings, in the Vatican library. This manuscript, a late writer, D'Agincourt, has been pleased to place many centuries later than its probably true date; chiefly, I suppose, in consequence of the text being written in well-formed minuscules: for the names of the dramatis personæ are written over the figures, and inserted, throughout in the dialogue, in capitals very like those employed in another very ancient manuscript of Terence in the Vatican, and in the Medicean Virgil. (See Plate VI. Nos. 1, 4, and 5.) As far as I can judge, from the prints given of the figures in this manuscript, in the edition published of it at Urbino, in 1736, and from the specimens given in outline by D'Agincourt, (for I do not wish to express myself as confidently upon this point, as perhaps I might feel justified in doing, if the manuscript itself were before me), I should say that, both in respect of the style of art and the costume, they accord better with a period antecedent to the time of Constantine, than with a later.

I may add, upon the subject of this *h*, that it also occurs in two words, in the latter part of the inscription of Pupus Torquatianus, spoken of in our note at page 84, and in part engraved in Plate V. No. 16, upon the authority of Kopp. For, since that plate was done, I have found that Kopp has given only the beginning of this inscription; which consists altogether of fourteen lines, and is given entire in the before-mentioned work of Marini (page 268); from whose plate I have caused the above two words to be copied, under the lines before taken from Kopp. I find it also in the Arvale Table, No. xxxvi. supposed to be of the age of Commodus or Marcus Aurelius (page 490 of the said work) in the words "honorariam" and "honoravit," in the first and last lines; and in Tab. xli. (p. 523), said to be of the year 218, where it appears, in the word "hæc," exactly formed as it is in the Herculaneum manuscript. Indeed, these Arvale tables, although professedly written in majuscules, contain, here and there, other letters, which bear a near resemblance to cursive and minuscule characters; though in several of them the letters are so very rudely and unequally formed, as to render their perusal a matter of extreme difficulty, and sometimes, as Marini confesses, little less than impossible: which circumstance, by the bye, causes me to suspect, that the members of this most ancient priesthood (for it dated from Romulus) were more careful, upon the occasion of their annual solemnities, that the costly refections, of which Marini speaks, should be skilfully cooked, than anxious as to the well sculpturing of the inscriptions recording them.

The inscriptions which have been produced, taken together, furnish, I think, abundant proof of the *existence* of the Latin minuscule alphabet in ancient Roman times: and if it should be argued, as making against our belief of its general *use* in those times, that, (considering the great number of ancient inscriptions existing) minuscule letters are of very rare occurrence in such monuments; it may be answered, that their being found in them at all, is to be considered as accidental; and to be chiefly, nay perhaps solely, ascribed to the carelessness of the individuals who wrote or sculptured the inscriptions in which they appear, and who, sometimes forgetting the nature of the task they were employed on, here and there inadvertently introduced a letter, such as they were accustomed to use on common occasions: for it appears certain, that in ancient, as in modern times, it has always been the custom, in inscriptions intended for the public eye, to employ only majuscule characters. But the occasional occurrence of minuscule letters in inscriptions, appears at no time to have attracted general notice, even among the learned; and hence, in great measure, the prevalence of the opinions which I combat.

The Authors of the " Nouveau Traité de Diplomatique," begin their third volume with an account of the different historical systems, (as they call them), which previous writers on the subject had sought to establish; in order to account for the various changes, which they supposed to have been introduced, at different times, and in different parts, in writing; beginning from the time of the ancients. I shall concern myself only with the first and oldest of these systems; which I find still prevails in this country, and was, indeed, in part adopted by Mabillon; though he admitted the use of minuscule and cursive writing, of some kind or other, by the ancient Romans.

" This system," say they, " gives the Latin mode of writing, as anciently universal in all Italy, Gaul, Spain, England, and that portion of Germany which was conquered by the Romans, &c. The irruptions of Barbarians changed the aspect of the Western Empire in the fifth and sixth centuries. The Goths first introduced their writing into Italy, and substituted it for the Roman. The Visigoths" [or Ostrogoths] " did the same in Spain; the Franks in Gaul; the Saxons in England. Lastly, the Lombards, having made themselves masters of the country which bears their name, banished the characters of the Goths, to replace them with those which were used by their own nation; and soon this sort of writing became commonly adopted throughout Italy.

" Hence, the beautiful and dignified Roman writing became at length transformed into *cursive* of various kinds, which it is often almost impossible to decipher. Hence the Gothick writings of Italy, Spain, Lombardy; hence the Saxon, and the Franco-Gallican, or Merovingian. The rigid defenders of this system deny that the ancient Romans ever used writing in minuscules, or running hand. All that is said by ancient writers of *minute writing* refers, they think, only to *capitals, formed of very small dimensions,* &c. All ancient Roman writing, in their opinion, ought to resemble that found on medals and on marbles, where they suppose no essential and considerable changes have ever been observed."

The celebrated Marquess Maffei first boldly denied the truth of all this, in his " Istoria Diplomatica," printed in 1727, (pp. 113, 114). " The study," says he, " of the forms of the characters, and their varieties, is very essential to diplomatic criticism ; and it appears by all to be thought, that this knowledge is now carried to such perfection and certainty, that nothing remains to be desired, to enable us to judge of written documents with accuracy. But it appears to me that we are in great want of new observations, and, what is more, of a change of system. I well know how strange this opinion may appear; but I ask only of the learned, that they will suspend their judgment of it till they hear my reasons. So far as deciphering the most difficult writings, there have always been persons, in Italy especially, who were fully competent to do this. The copies which we find in our archives, written in proximate centuries, prove it; and also the first printed editions of ancient authors; which were often taken, as the editors sometimes mention, from manuscripts called Gothic, or Lombardic. Mabillon, with the fine engravings introduced in his work, where writings are represented with the forms of their characters, and accompanied sometimes by their interpretation, which had also been done by Papebroch in the Propylæum to the "Acta Sanctorum" (for May), facilitated this study to all; and, as well for this as for his numerous learned observations, merits the highest praise. But, inasmuch as he has confirmed the old vulgar belief, nay magnified the deceit, by determining *five kinds of ancient Latin characters,* viz. *Roman, Gothic, Lombardic, Saxon,* and *Franco-Gallican,* I cannot subscribe to his doctrine: for I shall hereafter shew by incontrovertible evidence, that these supposed Gothic, Lombardic, Saxon, and Franco-Gallican characters, never had existence; and the same may be said of other fanciful names, arbitrarily introduced. This is very important to our subject, and to enable us to form a sober judgment of such documents as present themselves to us. May I be permitted to say, with all humility, that of what concerns the middle ages, notwithstanding the immense numbers of writings which have been collected in various provinces and published, we know but very little ; and that of Italy, especially, in those times, the idea which we have had for a long course of years, is so erroneous, so different, so distant from the truth, that it sometimes seems to me, as if by the force of witchcraft we had hitherto been deluded, and made to see every thing the reverse of what it is. But it shall be my fault, if I do not make this appear in the clearest manner, should the Giver of all good continue me in life and health. There will not, I am aware, be wanting those, who, for the sole gratification of opposing, will take every pains to discredit these propositions: one person, desirous to make a name, may come forward with fanciful and unheard-of opinions, little caring that they are repugnant to reason, and unsupported by truth: another, incapable of making a book, except out of other books, putting on the right side that which before stood on the left, and rendering those things unintelligible in his compilations which others had expressed with clearness, hates, with deadly hatred, every new discovery, especially if it does not come from afar off; and with a sardonic smile, pronounces, without examination, every opinion, which from ignorance he was himself incapable of originating, to be fantastic and extravagant. I flatter myself that I am none of these. The first, nay the only object of him who studies, ought to be the discovery of the truth; if this should sometimes happen not to have been before observed or known, I feel that there is no disgrace in discovering it; and I consider that the being silent respecting it, rather than oppose the current of public opinion, is cowardice, and not modesty."

The above promise was afterwards performed by Maffei, in the following masterly argument, in the first volume of his "Verona Illustrata," printed in 1732, (col. 321, et seq.); which I give the more willingly, as it does not appear to have been so generally read as it deserves. Indeed, fifty and sixty years ago, the Italian language was not so much studied, out of Italy, as it is now: and, besides this, the title of the work might naturally lead to the supposition that it treated only of matters of local interest, and thus deter many curious persons from perusing it.

After having spoken at length on the Italian language, to the formation of which he shews that neither the Goths nor the Lombards contributed; he proceeds to prove, that there is no ground for the opinion, that those barbarous people occasioned changes in the writing of the Italians.

"When, in the fifteenth century," says he, " the new art of printing caused early manuscripts to be sought after and scrutinized more diligently than heretofore, some were occasionally met with, written in characters which appeared very confused and difficult to read: and, as it was observed that this kind of writing was very unlike the simple kind found in ancient Roman inscriptions on stone or marble, and in certain ancient manuscripts, it was immediately believed to be barbarous; and such writings were termed Lombardic. We find this term several times in Poliziano; and Matteo Bosso says, in a letter addressed to him, that he sends him a manuscript of Ausonius, *written in Lombardic characters*: and indeed, Biondo notes the circumstance of the Lombards having thought of inventing a new kind of writing, in order to use it instead of the Roman, as a singular trait in their character. This opinion continued in the century following; save that this strange and confused kind of writing was not always denominated Lombardic, in our parts; but more frequently Gothic. In the last century, a third name was put forth beyond the Alps, that of Saxon, or Anglo-Saxon: till at length Mabillon came; who, in his great work on this subject, affirmed, that the four *genera*, into which Latin writing was then commonly divided, that is Roman, Gothic, Saxon, and Lombardic, were not sufficient; and, therefore, added the Franco-Gallican, which he also called Merovingian. Hence a system became established and embraced every where, the result of which has been, that our books are filled with these terms. But, ... I must make free to say, that this system is false in all its parts, and that this Gothic, this Lombardic, this Saxon, this Franco-Gallican writing, never had existence; that, moreover, these false notions have given rise to many important errors; and that in consequence many questions have been warmly debated by learned men, whose arguments, on the one side and on the other, have been founded in fallacy. . . . .

" I must in the first place observe, that the above four genera of writing, ascribed to foreign nations, are not in reality four different kinds, but one only. Full proof of this may be found in the very examples which Mabillon gives of these supposed different kinds of writing, in his plates. For it is easy to see that a person who has acquired the ability to read, for example, the long documents on Papyrus, which are all in the same kind of writing, will without difficulty read all those termed Gothic, Lombardic, Saxon, and Franco-Gallican. The ground-work of the writing and of the ciphering is always the same; and the differences are either accidental, as between large and small, thick and slender; or consist only in a very few letters, and in here and there some particular stroke, such as always distinguish the hand-writing of different individuals: so that we often find much greater variety in the writings of our notaries of the present day, than are to be discovered in the documents and manuscripts christened with so many different names. . . . . .

"When Mabillon came to the papyrus in the Imperial collection, he at first doubted what kind of writing it was; though he afterwards called it *Italo-Gothic*, which he said was used in Italy before the arrival of the Lombards: and yet the style of writing is quite the same as that of the other papyri; and also of documents on parchment possessed by us of the last years of Desiderius; and in the same sort of character are many documents of the ninth, and even of the tenth century, and later. Mabillon, indeed, well saw this uniformity; and therefore he once says, that the Gothic character *approximates* to the Lombardic; and upon another occasion, that the Saxon *bears affinity* to the Gothic; and again, that the writing in the papyri of Ravenna is *not very unlike* the Franco-Gallican. . . . . .

"In some instances, in consequence of the resemblance which he observed in these supposed different kinds of writing, he calls the writing of the same manuscript sometimes by one name and sometimes by another: and he confesses (p. 364) that he at first considered a particular manuscript (of Gennadius) to be written in the Lombardic character, and afterwards judged it to be in the Merovingian. He who will be at the pains to compare, here and there, different specimens, given both in the body of his work, and in the supplement, will sometimes observe that two, attributed to the same nation, differ more from each other, than they do from others, given elsewhere, under other names: and he who carefully examines numerous manuscripts, will sometimes find those particular forms in the same letter to occur, indifferently, in manuscripts called under different names, which are supposed to characterize one particular kind only. And so it is in inscriptions on marble. We have one at San Stefano, in which the letter M appears several times, formed in three different manners, which it is customary to call by different names, and to consider as indicating ages very distant from each other; and the same may be said of the N, the V, and the E. In fine, nothing is more certain, than that all these kinds of writing have the same origin, and that the differences which have been observed in them are not such as to constitute distinct genera."

Maffei next proceeds to shew that the above barbarous nations could not have corrupted the old Latin mode of writing, by introducing their own characters; for that, if they were not entirely ignorant of writing of every kind whatever, it is certain that it could have been known and practised but by a very few of them. "What," says he, "is the reason why we know nothing of so many different nations? because they had no writers, no records: and why this? because they had no letters. . . . . . Irenæus attests that, in his time, many barbarous people, who had become Christians, were unacquainted with the use of paper and ink; but preserved their traditions written in their hearts. . . . . .

"We have many reasons to believe that the northern nations were quite ignorant of the use of letters, till they fell under the dominion of the Romans; and that they" [in whose countries the Romans had not previously a fixed residence] "did not practise writing until the introduction of Christianity among them. . . . . . The Goths, who were more civilized than the other barbarians, remained until the end of the fourth century without characters. . . . . . It is stated by Socrates, that the Bishop Ulphilas was the first who introduced writing among them; and that he invented letters in which he wrote a translation of the Scriptures in the Gothic language: but, as we learn from Isidorus, his invention consisted only in bringing the Greek alphabet from Constantinople, and in adding, perhaps, a letter or two, expressive of particular sounds peculiar to the language. I shall not here stop to inquire if the characters of the famous manuscript in letters of silver, be, or be not, those of Ulphilas. We learn from Tacitus, that in Germany, which was the country of the Saxons, the Franks, and the Lombards, the people were ignorant of the use of letters; and that they continued so in the time of Ammianus Marcellinus, is remarked by Reinesius. The German language, indeed, does not appear to have been committed to writing, till the ninth century. . . . One of the first who did it was Otfridus, a monk, who translated the Gospels into German; premising that, as that language heretofore had not ever been polished, by using it in writing, he, in first attempting this, had adopted the Latin characters. . . . . .

"And, as it happens that the term Lombardic is applied, more frequently than any other, to documents of the middle ages, I must here observe, that so far is it from being true that the Lombards brought into Italy new characters, with which they transformed ours, that, on the contrary, it may be certainly affirmed that when they came among us they were ignorant of every kind of writing and of every sort of character whatever. This is clear from the words of

King Rotharis, who having been the first, in 643, to put together a code of the Lombardic laws, declares, at the end of his edict, that *he had been careful to record the ancient customs, and the laws of their fathers which had not before been written.* . . . . And of the Hunns, who came after the Lombards, Procopius, in the time of Justinian, assures us, that they had no knowledge of writing; and that certain ambassadors who were sent by one of their Kings to Constantinople, carried with them no letter or other written document; but stated all they were instructed to say, by word of mouth, and from memory. The same Rotharis, reciting in the proem to his work the names of the kings his predecessors, says that he had learned and received them from aged men: so that even these had not been before written down.

" In the course of time, it is true, the Lombards became naturalized among us; became Italians: and then writing was commonly practised by them. But as they had learned among us, they could only write in the same manner as their masters; and as was here practised. And so, on the coins and inscriptions of the Gothic Kings, and of the Lombards, by whatsoever artist they were executed, we always find the Latin language, and Latin characters; and these, in both cases, are commonly majuscules, and sufficiently well formed. . . . . .

" Now, as it is quite evident, that the above barbarous nations had no characters of their own; where, then, it may be asked, and with whom, originated this kind of Latin writing, which has hitherto been ascribed to them, and is so different from the Roman ? To this I answer, without hesitation, that it had its origin at Rome; and that it was no less used by the Latins than other modes. Great error has been occasioned in these matters, in consequence of people having observed the distinct and dignified characters which the Romans used in their inscriptions on marbles, and in their most noble and sumptuous manuscripts, and having thence concluded that this was the only kind of writing that was practised by them; and that the other kinds of Latin writing owed their origin to foreigners. But it was exactly the same error into which, in the present day, any person would fall, who, observing our inscriptions on stone, and the books which issue from the presses of our finest printers; and who, afterwards taking up the written documents of some of our notaries, and the familiar letters of many of us, which are often extremely difficult to read, should judge the former to be in the Italian character, and the latter in that of other nations.

"Strange, that it should never have occurred, that it must have been absolutely impossible for the Romans to transact the multifarious business of their numerous tribunals, and of their commerce, by the slow operation of writing in capital letters! Besides, many written communications were sometimes required to be dispatched at the moment, as Symmachus observes. It was therefore a natural, nay an inevitable consequence, of the frequent necessity for quick writing, that the Romans should soon begin by making their letters smaller; next, that they should modify their shapes, so that each might be made by one stroke of the pen; and, lastly, that they should seek out a way of joining them together, so that a word might be written, without taking off the hand. A prodigious number of professed scribes were employed in Rome, and every magistrate had his own; we know the different classes into which they were divided, and the names by which they were distinguished, and how many different kinds of instruments and public acts were written by them every day. And those men who were constantly occupied in important affairs; who were often called upon to write, or dictate long addresses, and quantities of letters; is it to be believed that such persons could have got through their business with writing in majuscules? For, not only are we to consider the size of the characters, but also that it was necessary to make each by a separate stroke of the pen; nay, that some, the A and the E, for example, required three or four strokes: let any one who is employed in a great public office, or is accustomed to keep up an extensive written correspondence, ask himself, how he would get on, if he were obliged to make all his characters like what are used in printing. It is therefore certain, beyond all doubt, that a smaller character and cursive writing were also used at Rome."

After shewing that all these varieties had been previously used by the Greeks, in writing their language, Maffei goes on to say, that: "In diminishing the majuscule characters, and, then, seeking to join several letters together, two new sorts of writing were produced; the *minuscule*, and the *cursive*. Of the first, as the most distinct and elegant, the scribes began to avail themselves in manuscripts, substituting it for the *majuscule;* more especially after the Christian church began everywhere to produce so many written works: and from the most even and best-formed writing of this kind, which was much practised in the fifteenth century, the character used in printing was taken. The second was used in epistolary correspondence, and in notarial acts and other documents; and, in order to save time and labour, some persons also wrote books in this kind of writing, which, as we have said, has since been called, sometimes Gothic, sometimes Lombardic, Saxon, and Franco-Gallican."

Our Author next speaks of the specimens of *minuscule* and *cursive* letters, observed by Buonarruoti in ancient inscriptions, and which have been already noticed in this Paper. After which he brings to his support the authority of ancient writers.

"Ancient writers also," says he, "bear testimony to what I have said, when they make mention of *minute*, and *very minute* writing; as Vopiscus, Suetonius, Seneca, Plautus, and others. Martial speaks of the works of Virgil, and of those of Titus Livius, written on a small-sized parchment," [or rather, according to the opinion of Schawrzius, before produced, in a small-sized parchment book,] "which written in larger characters" [on rolls] " would have filled his library or book-case: it does not seem possible that majuscule characters could ever have been reduced to such small dimensions. The younger Pliny relates of the elder Pliny his uncle (lib. iii. epist. 5), that, independently of the many works which he had published, he left at his death one hundred and sixty commentaries on various subjects, written by him on both sides the paper or parchment, in *a very minute hand*. To a man constantly occupied, as he was, in weighty affairs, an age would scarcely have sufficed to write all this with separate majuscule characters. We read in Plutarch, that Cato gave to his son a manuscript of his 'Origines,' written by his own hand in *large letters;* by which expression he seems to denote the largest sized characters, and that this was not the common mode of writing. . . . . .

"But no one informs us more distinctly that people commonly wrote in cursive, than does Quinctilian, (lib. i. ch. 1,) where he blames the neglect of teaching people to write, at the same time *well* and *rapidly*, as being so essential in *epistolary correspondence:* hence, after children have learned their letters, he recommends that they should be taught to form *syllables*, that is, those groups of joined letters which are expedited by one stroke of the pen; and so, in teaching them to read, he recommends that they should not be made to go on at a quick rate, *except where the joinings of the letters are so clear as to be subject to no doubt:* ('nisi cum inoffensa atque indubitata literarum inter se coniunctio'). Who does not clearly see that this passage relates to *cursive* (or minuscule) writing, in which alone it was proper to join one letter to another?

"But, to remove all doubt on this subject, it is sufficient to cast our eyes upon those ancient documents, written in Italy, wherein, more than in others, we recognize this sort of writing that has been called by so many barbarous names; all of which are on papyrus. They may be seen in our 'Istoria Diplomatica:' among them are five of the sixth century, with the date of the year, which are all anterior to the entry of the Lombards into Italy, and are yet in this same difficult character: how therefore can this character be attributed to the Lombards? And should any one be therefore disposed to say that it was introduced by the Goths, even this refuge is taken away from him by the famous papyrus in our possession, which is in exactly the same kind of writing; as that document furnishes indubitable proof that it was written immediately after the year 444, during the reign of Valentinian III. and almost fifty years before the arrival of Theodoric, the first Gothic king in Italy. . . . I may add, that three of the other papyri, given by us in the above work, which are without date—viz. the second, the third, and the fourth—furnish strong grounds for the opinion that they are more ancient than the above, and written either at the beginning of at the fifth century, or the end of the fourth. Indeed, Ponticus Virunius, in his introduction to the Greek grammar of Guarino, asserts that in his time (that is at the end of the fifteenth century), a document on papyrus, in an unknown character, was preserved at Ravenna, which was of the time of the Emperor Adrian; nor is the fact to be deemed incredible. . . . . .

"Mabillon tells us (p. 64), that he was for some time doubtful what was the true Lombardic character; but that at last he found it in the ancient bulls of the Popes. How could he ever suppose that Lombardic writing should have especially fixed itself at Rome, where the Lombards never came? and that the Roman way of writing should have been abandoned, more than elsewhere, exactly in that Court and by that Church, which has ever been the jealous preserver of Roman traditions, and of the Latin language? . . . .

"It is astonishing that a person who had turned over so many manuscripts as Mabillon, should not have seen in them clearly, that all the different kinds of Latin writing had the same origin, and were all practised by the same persons: for it is by no means uncommon to find these different kinds of writing in the same manuscript; to find the body of the work in cursive, and the titles, and sometimes the first verse also, in majuscules. Such is the case with one of ours at the chapter-house, which contains the canons of Cresconius. Will any one, therefore, say that here a Lombard and a Roman scribe worked in company? But it sometimes happens, that we see a manuscript begun in *capitals*, then decline into *minuscule*, and lastly fall into *cursive*, and so continue to the end. We have, among ours, the work of Isidorus 'De Summo Bono,' where, after five leaves of large characters, it passes to smaller, almost as neatly formed as printing types, and afterwards by degrees falls into decided cursive: and although certain chapters again begin with majuscule writing, and continue it as far as seven verses, the cursive then recommences. What can be a more certain proof, that these varieties were not occasioned by the difference of centuries or nations, but by the laziness or hurry of the writer; which occasioned him to abandon that kind of writing which was the most laborious and required the most time, and take up that which was easier to him and quicker done? . . . . From all which it is very clear, that minuscule and cursive writing are neither to be styled Merovingian, nor Franco-Gallican, ancient Lombardic, more recent Lombardic, Semi-gothic, nor by any of those names which we find given to them in the large Diplomatic work of the above author.

"We shall conclude this argument," says Maffei, " by observing, that under the terms *majuscule, minuscule,* and *cursive,* all kinds of Latin writing are comprehended; save that occasionally we find a mixture of two or more of these, especially of the two last, in the same writing; whilst on the contrary, by the five genera, and the many names hitherto used, the greatest confusion is occasioned. . . . .

"By viewing the subject as we have here recommended, many errors, otherwise easy to fall into, will be avoided; as people will not be so ready, upon light grounds, to deem a piece of writing discordant in itself, or to doubt of the antiquity of those manuscripts or documents, wherein, in the same word, letters occur, perfectly formed, mixed with others that seem strange and confused: knowing that the whole are Roman characters, and that not all the letters in cursive writing are different from those in minuscule, but only a few of them with their joinings; the rest being distinct and well-formed. Nor will they, because they find the letter *r* of a certain shape, which occurs in a great number of our manuscripts in minuscule or in mixed characters, at once style the writing Saxon. Neither will they so confidently pretend to determine the precise century of a manuscript or other monument; knowing that at the same time, and by the same person, various modes of writing were employed: in fact, many documents exist, subscribed by numerous persons with their names, on the same day and in the same place, some in *majuscule*, some in *minuscule*, others in *cursive* writing, and others, again, in *mixed characters*, according to the various hand-writings of the parties. The author of the 'Diario Italico,' (Montfaucon), in consequence of having believed a certain document, written at Rieti, to be in the Lombardic character, judged it to be of the eighth or ninth century; though it happened to bear the date, which we afterwards discovered, of the year 557; that is, eleven years before the Lombards marched into Italy. . . . .

"I cannot conclude," says Maffei, "without adding a few words upon the *Franco-Gallican* character; a name which has been given to what we call the *minuscule*. If we are to give credence to the common notion, which is spoken of and approved by Mabillon, it was Charlemagne who first polished this kind of character, and caused the four above-mentioned barbarous genera to be abandoned; substituting, instead, that clear and distinct manner of writing, which, therefore, it is said, the French did not take from the Romans, who then had only the Lombardic character, but the Romans afterwards took from the French. That a manuscript therefore is of the age of Charlemagne, is sometimes argued from the neatness of its minuscule writing; and it is asserted that the Italians learned it from the race of Charlemagne, quitting for it the Lombardic; that the Spaniards, learning it in like manner, left the Gothic; the Germans, the Teutonic; and the English, the Saxon.

"Now, this is an error, no less fanciful and extraordinary than all the rest. . . . . The famous 'Medicean Virgil' has interlineary notes and observations in this character, which are believed to be of the same age as the text. As soon as the advance of the Christian religion made so much writing necessary, not only for the sacred books to be used in churches, but also on account of the great number of synods and acts, and the treatises of different authors, which were every where produced, more especially at Rome, the minuscule character was very frequently used in manuscripts. Of this kind, numerous manuscripts are every where to be found; which were written in Italy, long before Charlemagne was born. Among the examples given in Mabillon's work, the two Pope's Bulls of the seventh century are in this sort of writing, although a little altered by an affected extravagance in the forms of a few particular letters. Of the same kind are several manuscripts forming part of the remains of our ancient library at the Chapter-house of Verona, which there is every reason to believe are of a still earlier date. I shall mention only one, which of itself is sufficient to settle this point; and to show how much the world has hitherto been deceived concerning it. It may contribute, at the same time, to our Veronese history; as it furnishes the name of a studious clerk of this diocese. A manuscript, therefore, is preserved, as above, *written in perfect minuscule,* which contains the works of Sulpicius Severus, excepting his history; and which we believe to be the only manuscript existing, of such high antiquity, that bears so precisely, the time when, the place where it was written, and the name of the writer: for at the end of it we read, that it was written (that is finished) at Verona, on the first day of August, Agapitus being Consul, in the tenth Indiction, by Ursicinus, reader of the Veronese church. This note of the time indicates the year 517 [see our Plate VI. No. 9]: so that we find that this kind of writing was current in Italy two hundred and fifty years before the arrival of Charlemagne, and practised in 517 at Verona, where he and his Franks did not come until 774.

" This kind of writing was indeed called Italian, and more especially Roman: though, it is also true that in distant provinces it was sometimes styled Gallican; because the people of those provinces, residing nearer to France than to Italy, had it from France: but, without doubt, it was originally carried to France from Italy. It is possible that the first example the French had of it, was in those manuscripts which Pope Paul the Second, as we learn in his epistles, sent from Rome to King Pepin,[a] the father of Charlemagne; among

[a] I venture here to differ from Maffei. Good minuscule writing was certainly practised long before in England; as may be seen in various original charters in Aug. A. II. in the Cottonian

which there were, particularly, some on grammar and on orthography. Charlemagne, who with his vast mind and enlightened views sought to inform himself upon various sciences, did not, nevertheless, know how to write, till an advanced period of his life; when he attempted to learn to do so, with little success, as Eginardus informs us in his history; though Lambecius and another writer strive to give to his words the forced interpretation, that he was ignorant only of the art of writing in large characters and in chancery hand. . . .

"The monk Engolismensis, who lived at the time, and wrote the life of this great Emperor, relates that the Pope, at his request, gave him certain professors of church music, and the Antiphony, written in Roman musical characters; and that he conducted these singers to France, where they taught their art, and where these Roman notes (exactly as happened to the Roman letters) were afterwards called Gallican. He also relates, that he conducted thither from Rome, at different times, masters of the art of grammar, among the requisites of which was anciently included the art of writing well and distinctly: so that it is easy to see from what source France, in the time of Charlemagne, got that kind of writing, and how the knowledge of it became thence propagated in other provinces. The above writer and others cited by Du Cange, assert that, before the time of this prince, every grammatical study, as well as all the liberal arts, which had flourished there under the Roman Empire, had been lost in France: and it is therefore evident, that the new life which this great man succeeded in giving to all of them, after he had visited Italy, is to be ascribed to the ideas he had acquired at Rome, and to the professors which he invited or took with him from that capital."

I think that Maffei, in this luminous argument, has clearly made out his case, and mine; and that he has left us no fair ground to doubt, that the ancient Romans were the real inventors of all those different kinds of writing, which, for these last two or three centuries, it has been the fashion to attribute to the barbarous nations, and to call, as he says, by so many fanciful names.

It is very possible that Casley, when in 1734 he published his "Catalogue of the Manuscripts of the King's Library," had not seen the above argument

Collection; and I cannot doubt that it was practised at the same time by the French, and other people, who, like us, had in ancient times learned it from the Romans. It may, indeed, have been but little used in writing books, during one or two of the ruder centuries: but it could never, I think, have been entirely lost, in any country where it had once been known.

of Maffei; which, as has been said, first appeared in the "Verona Illustrata," only two years before: and, indeed, I conclude from his preface, that he was quite unacquainted with the before-mentioned work of Buonarruoti, and several other foreign publications on the subject of antiquities, which might have been of use to him, had he taken the trouble to look into them.

Speaking of certain *criteria*, by which the ages of old MSS. are to be known, he says (p. vii.) : " *Saxon characters* were in use in England from the seventh century down to William the Conqueror's time. *A small alphabet seems to have been first contrived in the seventh century* ; and the writing whole books in capitals was left off not long after. See the word ' *manentium* ' at the end of the first plate." Now this single word happens to be written in very fair *Roman minuscules* at the back of a Saxon document in the Latin language, of about the year 670, which, with the names of the parties to the instrument, this word only excepted, is written in what are called *uncials* (Cottonian Coll. Aug. A. II. No. 29): it was, I suppose, the earliest specimen that Casley had chanced to meet with, written in England in minuscules, and therefore, without hesitation, he concludes, that the minuscule alphabet, of which this word contains some of the letters, was invented (I suppose he means in England) in the seventh century. The reader will find this word *manentium* carefully copied from the original document in our Plate VI. No. 8.

One would almost think that Casley could not even have seen the great work of Mabillon, although it had been published several years before. If he did see it, he certainly employed but little care in examining it ; as the sixth plate of that work contains a specimen of five lines, in very good *minuscules*, traced from a celebrated MS. of St. Hilarius in the Vatican ; which, it appears from a marginal note, written at the time in the book itself, was collated at Kasulis in Africa, in the year 510, and which Mabillon thinks may have been written at the close of the fifth century (see a copy of this specimen in our Pl. VI. No. 9): and in the seventh plate he might have seen two other considerable specimens of the latter part of the sixth century. Any one of these, had he examined it, ought to have prevented his saying, that "a small alphabet seems to have been first contrived in the seventh century."

We have something more of Casley's opinions on this subject, in the twelfth and following pages :

" St. Jerom," he tells us, " in his Prologue to the book of Job, says: ' Habeant qui volunt veteres libros, vel in membranis purpureis auro argentoque descriptos, vel *initialibus*, ut vulgo aiunt, literis, onera magis exarata quam Codices; dummodo mihi meisque permittant pauperes habere Scedulas, et non tam pulchros Codices quam emendatos.' From whence it is manifest, that there were in his days some old books very pompously written, in parchment of a purple colour in characters of gold and silver, and the whole books in such large letters as were commonly used at the beginnings of sentences, &c. . . . .

"But," continues Casley, "I am obliged to take notice, that in the above quoted sentence from St. Jerom, is commonly read '*uncialibus*, ut vulgo aiunt, literis': and so it is printed, and always quoted in print: and not *initialibus*, as I have put the word, by the authority of several MSS. and by the known way of reading such ambiguous words, which is, to take that reading which agrees best with common sense. By *initialibus literis* it's obvious to understand such letters as are wont to be put at the beginnings of books, or chapters, or paragraphs: wherein if a whole book should be written, it would be indeed rather a burden than a book, as Jerom says. And several such old books are still remaining. But what can be made of *literis uncialibus?* Letters of an inch in length? Who has ever read of the Ancients writing books in such monstrous characters? . . . .

"This same single sentence of Jerom," he continues, "has been very fruitful of errors. For besides the *literae unciales*, which first sprang from it, and have passed muster so long and so universally; the *literae minutiæ*, or small letters, have been found to be couched in it. For by *literis initialibus* (or *uncialibus*, if you please) they would have *capitals* to be meant, in opposition to *small letters*, which the *pauperes scedulæ* were supposed to be written in; and which were imagined to differ as much as the great and small letters do now: whereas it's obvious, to all who are conversant in books and inscriptions as old as to Jerom's time, that *small letters were not then found out;* and that there were no other characters made use of in writing, but *capitals*. This being matter of fact, it is a sufficient proof, to shew, that all the old books and inscriptions of those times, which happen yet to remain, are in capitals; and that there cannot be produced one single instance to the contrary. . . . .

By *literis initialibus*, therefore, Jerom can mean no more than *a larger sort of capitals:* for his *pauperes scedulæ* were written in capitals too; but of a smaller sort; and, abating for the difference of several hands, differed from the other only in size.[b] . . . .

"But," says he, "it is still objected, that those characters are so inconvenient for dispatch, that it cannot be imagined that so many volumes as were published by some of the Ancients, could be written in them: and that they could not miss the finding out a quicker way of writing for ordinary business. This supposes, that they had such pens and ink as we have. But I answer, when a useful thing is first found out, men generally wonder, that it was not found out sooner," &c. &c.

Casley's opinion, or rather assertion, as to the late invention of minuscule writing, has been so fully disproved in what has gone before, that I should not have thought it worth noticing, had I not reason to believe the common opinion here to have been mainly formed on it; and had he not coupled with it the above remarks on the well-known passage of St. Jerom; which, I believe, contains the only ancient authority we have for the use of the term *uncial*, as applied to letters. Even here, his opinion, as to the proper reading, though given so confidently, appears to be wrong. The authors of the "Nouveau Traité," informs us (vol. ii. p. 510) upon the authority of Blanchinius ("Vindic. Can. Script." p. ccxcviii.), that several men of letters of Italy requested the learned M. Assemani to consult the best MSS. in the Vatican, in order to determine fairly the true reading of the text of St. Jerom; and that the learned prelate, after having well examined them, attests that they all contradict the supposition of Casley. Among these MSS. are several of the seventh and eighth centuries; and they all, without exception, have the passage: ' *uncialibus,* ut vulgò aiunt, literis.' "

The remarks of the writers of the 'Nouveau Traité' upon this interesting passage from Jerom, are much to our present purpose: "When," say they, " St. Jerom prefers to MSS. written in *uncials*, his own, which had no other merit than exactness, he seems to mean to say, that *uncial* letters were only employed for rich people, and in writing books for the use of churches. *We*

[b] Strange as it may seem, this appears also to have been Mabillon's notion of Jerom's meaning: notwithstanding, as has been said, he insisted that the ancients were acquainted with minuscule and cursive writing.

may thence conclude, that in the fourth and fifth centuries, the use of minuscule and cursive writing was much more general than was that of uncials, or capitals. The same continued to be the case till the middle of the sixth century. But, ignorance and barbarism increasing continually, *the monks and clerks wrote little* (any longer) *in minuscule,* and *still less in cursive.* These two kinds of writing required too much ability. . . . . If we except persons employed officially as secretaries (excepté les gens d'affaires), no one wrote any more during the latter part of the sixth, the whole of the seventh, and the first half of the eighth century, unless in *uncials.* In the eighth century, the use of cursive writing became again more frequent; because studies were resumed. We indeed are of opinion, that the practice of writing, though not the study of orthography, had in some degree been renewed," [I take it they mean in France,] " before the time of Charlemagne. *The general use of uncial writing,* therefore, which requires but little capacity, though a great deal of patience, *belongs to the barbarous centuries.* Thus we see, in the MS. No. 936, of the Abbey of S. Germain des Pres, that after the middle of the sixth century, the scribe abandoned minuscule writing, a little mixed with cursive, and kept to uncials."

I shall take this opportunity of saying a few words upon the improper use (as I consider it) of the term *uncial,* as applied by the writers of the 'Nouveau Traité,' to a particular kind of writing, very unlike that which Jerom intended to describe, not only in the last quoted passage, but throughout their whole work.

They tell us (vol. ii. p. 506) "that by *uncial writing* they mean *writing in round majuscules,* which is distinguished from *writing in capitals* by certain elements. The term *uncial,*" they admit, " strictly speaking, and *according to the ancient acceptation of the word,* (Struv. ' de Criter. MSS.' § xi. p. 15,) means writing in *letters of an inch in height;* and they add that the term *semi-uncial,* was, in like manner, applied to characters of half that height."

Now there can be no doubt that Jerom spoke of books written magnificently in capital letters; and that by the term *uncial,* he intended to denote the *large size* of the characters; though we are surely not bound to conclude that they measured a full inch in height. But the term has evidently no reference to the particular forms of the letters; and, as the most ancient MSS. that we have, written in capitals, are generally in what, for the sake of distinction, may be styled *square or angular majuscules,* and not in the *round majuscules* above mentioned, (which round majuscules, by the bye, have always some minuscule characters mixed with them,) it surely would have been wiser, if the term uncial was to be used at all, to apply it only to writing in large capitals. The knowledge, too, that this term was used by Jerom, and its present application to writing in round capitals, naturally lead people to suppose that this sort of character prevailed in the fourth century; whereas the fact appears to be that it was not introduced, or at least not much used, till afterwards.

Again, the term *uncial,* they tell us, was anciently given to letters an inch high, and the term *semi-uncial* to such as were *half that size.* But they, throughout their book, use both these terms, with scarce any reference at all to the magnitude of the characters: for sometimes their *uncials* are above a quarter of an inch high, and sometimes less than an eighth; and what they call their *semi-uncials* is no other than minuscule writing, in which, perchance, a few capital letters, the N for example, are here and there mixed: and as ancient minuscule writing is seldom or never quite free from this mixture, we, in consequence, find the same writing sometimes called by them *minusculo,* and sometimes *semi-uncial.*

Besides, some writers, as they themselves observe, have used the term *uncial* to denote writing in capital letters of every kind; and, in point of fact, it is applied to the text of Hyginus in our MS. by Wanley in the Harleian Catalogue, although it is written throughout in square capitals; so that, on the whole, great confusion has resulted from the introduction of this term, and its vague and inaccurate application to different sorts of writing: and one cannot but regret, that the learned men who since Maffei's time have written on the subject of ancient diplomas and other MSS. (the authors of the ' Nouveau Traité de Diplomatique' more especially) were not satisfied to adopt the simple mode, recommended by him in the foregoing dissertation, of comprehending all ancient writings under as small a number of classes as possible.

Maffei, after he had been at the pains to refute, as we have seen, the erroneous notions which had before prevailed, upon the origin of minuscule and cursive writing, flattered himself that in future the world would hear no more of the *Italo-Gothic,* the *Lombardic,* the *Saxon,* the *Merovingian,* or *Franco-*

gallican, &c. &c. But in this he greatly deceived himself: for, although the writers of the " Nouveau Traité de Diplomatique" admit, in the fullest manner, that he has proved all he contended for; still, they not only retain all these terms, but add others to their number; among them the *Caroline* and the *Capetian*, as they are pleased to call them : besides which, they divide, and sub-divide each of these supposed *classes*, into so many minor *classes*, *genera*, and *species*, that there seems no end to them ; and one is almost tempted to suspect that they adopted this complicated machinery for the laudable purposes of swelling out their book and puzzling their readers.

As the best illustration of their system that I can think of, I give, in the note below,[c] the *titles* of some of the first *chapters* and *plates* of their third

[c] "NOUVEAU TRAITÉ DE DIPLOMATIQUE," vol. iii. p. 34, et seq. "CHAP. II. WRITING IN CAPITALS, in Manuscripts of Italy, France, Germany, England and Spain. ARTICLE I. *Roman Capitals* in Mss.: First Subdivision, included in plates xxxiv. and xxxv."

The title of the first of these two plates is thus : " Writing taken from Mss , including the first five genera of Roman Capitals, appertaining to the First Division of the Second Class ;" that of the second : " Writing taken from Mss , containing the sixth, seventh, and eighth last genera of Roman Capitals, written in an unfinished and negligent manner (or Rustic Capitals), appertaining to the first division, first subdivision, of the Second Class." And, then, in the margins of the pages explanatory of these two plates, we read : 1st DIVISION, 1st SUBDIVISION : 1st Genus, 1st Species, 2d Species : 2d Genus, 1st, 2d, and 3d Species ; and so on : the 3d Genus having 4 Species ; the 4th Genus, 3 Species ; the 5th, 4 Species ; the 6th, 3 Species ; the 7th, 2 Species, and the 8th Genus, 3 Species.

Then comes : " ARTICLE II. Writing in *Lombardic Capitals:* exposition of plate xxxvi. containing the Second Subdivision of the first Division of writing found in Mss." The title of the plate itself is nearly the same ; and in the margins of the accompanying text, we have, in the same way as before : "SECOND SUBDIVISION :" of which the 1st Genus has no less than 10 Species; the 2d Genus has 5 Species; the 3d Genus—writing in *Lombardic Capitals*, mixed with *minuscules*—has 2 Species ; the 4th Genus—ancient *Lombardic Capitals* and *Uncials* mixed—has 7 Species ; the 5th Genus—*Lombardic Capitals* of different kinds—has 3 Species ; and the 6th Genus has 8 Species.

Then " ARTICLE III. Writings in *Visigothic*, *Anglo-Saxon*, and *Gallican Capitals* in Mss. Explanation of plate xxxvii. which contains the third, fourth, and fifth Subdivisions, appertaining to the first Division of the Second Class of Latin writings." The title to the plate is the same. "SECT. I. Writing in *Visigothic Capitals* of Spain and *France*. THIRD SUBDIVISION." The 1st Genus has 5 Species ; and the 2d has 9 Species. " SECT. II. Writings in *Saxon Capitals* of *England* and *France*. FOURTH SUBDIVISION." The 1st Genus has 4 Species ; and the 2d has 4 Species. " SECT. III. *Ancient Gallican writing, in Capitals*. FIFTH SUBDIVISION." The 1st volume (which is more especially devoted to a description of early manuscripts), with a list of their *classes, divisions, sub-divisions, genera*, and *species*. The perusal of it may seem tedious; but I thought it incumbent on me thus Genus has 5 Species; and the 2d Genus—*Gallican rustic Capitals*. or such as are executed in a negligent manner—has 8 Species.

Now comes "ARTICLE IV. Writing in *Capitals* employed in *Merovingian* Mss., also *Teutonic* and *Modern Gothic*: explication of plates xxxviii, and xxxix, wherein are contained the sixth and seventh subdivisions of the first division of Latin writings of the second class. SECT. I. *Merovingian* or *Franco-Gallican Capitals*. SIXTH SUBDIVISION." The 1st Genus gives 6 Species; the 2d Genus, 10 Species; the 3d Genus, 10 Species; the 4th Genus—*Rustic Merovingian Capitals*—6 Species; and the 5th Genus—*Merovingian Capitals* mixed with *Uncials*, &c.—has 8 Species. "SECT. II. Writings in *Teutonic* or *German Capitals*. SEVENTH SUBDIVISION" The 1st Genus has 4 Species; and the 2d has 3 Species. "SECT. III. *Modern Gothic Capitals*." 1 Genus only, which gives 3 Species.

We have now "ARTICLE V. Writings in *Caroline* and *Capetian Capitals*: explanation of plates XL. and XLI. which contain the eighth and ninth subdivisions of writings in *Capitals*, &c. SECT. I. Writing in Mss. in *Caroline Capitals*. EIGHTH SUBDIVISION." The 1st Genus produces 11 Species; the 2d GENUS—*Semi-rustic Capitals*—gives no less than 12 Species; the 3d Genus—*Rustic Caroline Capitals*—has 5 Species; the 4th Genus, 5 Species; and the 5th Genus—*Caroline writing in Capitals*, in *English* Mss.!!—has 4 Species. " SECT. II. Writing in Mss. in *Capetian Capitals*; NINTH SUBDIVISION." The 1st Genus has 4 Species; and the 2d Genus—*Capetian Capitals mixed with uncials and minuscules*—has 9 Species.

Now upon counting them up, I find that these pretended distinct Species of *majuscule writing* only, found in Latin Mss., amount to no less than one hundred and eighty-nine in number. What are we to say of such a system?

CHAPTER III. (p. 141), treats of *Uncial writing; Roman, Gallican, Merovingian, Lombardic, Caroline, German*, and *Gothic*; that is, of what they call "the Second Division of the Second Class of Latin writings in Mss." ARTICLE I. treats of *Roman Uncials*, describing the specimens in plate XLII. They are divided into 7 Genera; the different Species of which amount together to 20. ARTICLE II. describes plate XLIII., which gives specimens from Mss. written in *Gallican Uncials*. It is divided into 6 Genera, which together produce 27 Species. ARTICLE III. describes plate XLIV, which contains specimens of *Franco-Gallican* or *Merovingian* writing in *Uncials*. It is divided into 7 Genera, which give 23 Species. ARTICLE IV. Treats of *Lombardic, Visigothic, Caroline, Anglo-Saxon, Teutonic*, and *Modern Gothic* writing, in *Uncials*; explaining plate XLV. They have 10 Genera, which give 37 Species; *Uncial writing*, altogether, furnishing 107 Species.

CHAPTER IV. (p. 204). This chapter treats of *Semi-Uncial* writing. ARTICLE I. Explains plate XLVI. under 9 Genera, which produce 32 Species. ARTICLE II. Is explanatory of plate XLVII., and has 7 Genera, which give 28 Species.

CHAPTER V. (p. 232). Treats of *writings of a mixed kind* in ancient Mss., explaining plate XLVIII, under 9 Genera, which give 33 Species.

to expose the quackery of these learned writers; though at the same time I willingly admit that their work abounds in curious matter, and is therefore highly valuable.

Upon adding them up, we find no less than *one hundred and eighty-nine* species of *majuscule writing* in Latin manuscripts; *one hundred and seven* species of *uncial writing*; *ninety-three* species of *demi-uncial writing*; and *two hundred and thirteen* species of *writing in Latin minuscules*: to say nothing of the different *species* into which they divide *cursive*, or *running-hand*, which I have not been at the pains of counting. It is evident, that if, at the present day, any one were to apply the above system in this country, the handwritings of the members of our Houses of Lords and Commons, with those of their wives, sons, and daughters, would, of themselves, furnish him with an abundant harvest of *classes, divisions, subdivisions, genera,* and *species*.

But it is curious enough, that the writers of the Nouveau Traité, themselves, now and then, inadvertently, volunteer confessions, which at once prove the unsoundness of their own and Mabillon's system, and fully justify Maffei's condemnation of it; as in the following passage (vol. iii. p. 13), which, strange as it may seem, forms a part of their introduction to the above absurdities:

CHAPTER VI. (p. 252). Treats of ancient *minuscule* writing. ARTICLE I. Illustrates plate XLIX., and gives 3 Genera, containing 12 Species. ARTICLE II. Continuing the explanation of plate XLIX., and giving also that of plate L., produces 5 Genera, comprising 28 Species. ARTICLE III. which is explanatory of plate LI., furnishes 3 Genera, which give 12 Species. ARTICLE IV. Explains the remaining part of plate LI, and the first part of plate LII., and gives 4 Genera, which comprise 27 Species. ARTICLE V. Explains the remaining part of plate LII., under 2 Genera, which give 11 Species. ARTICLE VI. Describes plates LIII. and LIV., which contain examples of what they call the *Caroline minuscule*. The writers begin this article with an argument in which they attempt, unsuccessfully I think, to defend Mabillon's system against the animadversions of Maffei, in the before-given dissertation in his "Verona Illustrata." This article is divided into 8 Genera, which produce no less than 54 Species. ARTICLE VII. Describes plate LV., under 10 Genera, which give 40 Species. ARTICLE VIII. Is explanatory of plate LVI, and gives us 6 Genera, which are productive of 29 Species. So that this chapter, on the whole, describes no less than 213 Species of *minuscule* Latin writing.

The VIIth CHAPTER (p. 401-459) treats of *Cursive* writing, *Roman, Gallican, Merovingian, Lombardic, Caroline, Visigothic,* and *Saxon*. I have spared myself the trouble of counting the number of Genera and Species which this chapter is productive of.

"The supposition," say they, " that the ancient Romans had no other letters but such as were elegantly formed, and that all that appears otherwise is to be ascribed to the barbarous nations, has occasioned the origin of minuscule and cursive writing to be attributed to these last. To be convinced of the contrary, it will suffice to compare *Visigothic, Merovingian, Lombardic,* and *Saxon* writings, with *Roman cursive. They will then no longer appear to be so many distinct kinds of writing,* having little affinity to each other. It will be seen that *all the pretended barbarous kinds of writing were derived from the Roman,* but especially the *Merovingian* . . . . . indeed THE ROMAN MAY BE REGARDED AS IDENTICAL WITH THE MEROVINGIAN; the difference consisting only in such changes as from century to century all kinds of writing underwent. *The Merovingian, therefore, is but a branch of the Roman, used in the Gauls in the fifth and sixth centuries, and continued in the seventh and eighth. The Lombardic is another branch of the Roman character of Italy,* formed upon that used in the sixth and seventh centuries, which had acquired *an established character* in the eighth century; and continued to the twelfth, when we see it still employed in the Bulls of the Popes." [The reader will remember what Maffei has said, upon the absurdity of supposing this pretended Lombardic writing to have been patronized at Rome, where the Lombards never came.] " For the rest, *the conformity between the cursive Merovingian and the Lombardic* is so striking, as naturally to lead to the conclusion that both had one common origin; namely the *Roman cursive.* The *Saxon* equally draws its origin from the Roman, whether that which had been preserved in Great Britain (learned originally from the Romans), or that which was carried into England by the monks, disciples of St. Gregory the Great. We find it already formed in the seventh century, and we discover its most singular characters from the fifth and sixth." [The French writers, perhaps, here intend to refer to one or two characters invented by the Saxons, to express particular sounds of their own language, the character denoting *th* for example.] " For the rest, it is less derived from the *Roman cursive,* than from the *minuscule.* The *Saxon* prevailed until the tenth century in England, and sustained itself to the end of the twelfth; notwithstanding the introduction of Norman writing, or French, into this kingdom, under the reigns of Edward the Confessor and William the Conqueror. The *Visigothic* may perhaps have distinguished itself from the Roman, from the sixth century; but we have not seen it anterior to the seventh: it lasted until the thirteenth. THE CAROLINE IS BUT A CONTINUATION OF THE MEROVINGIAN. [They have said, above, that '*the Roman is identical with the Merovingian.*'] "Commencing in the eighth century, it continues to alter until the twelfth, when it is lost in the *Roman minuscule.* Later *cursives* are but emanations."

After having confessed all this, what could induce these learned men to mystify their work, by the introduction of the above pretended *classes, divisions,* and *subdivisions,* &c. &c. unless, as I have said, they did so for the purpose of swelling it out, and of puzzling their readers. I can think only of one other motive which may have actuated them; namely, that they retained these French names, the *Gallican,* the *Franco-Gallican* or *Merovingian,* and added to them the *Caroline* and the *Capetian,* in order to flatter the vanity of their countrymen. Admitting these, it of course became necessary, in order to avoid the accusation of undue patriotism, to retain the *Visigothic,* the *Lombardic,* the *Saxon,* and the *Teutonic;* and thus their work became an immense jumble of truth and error, of erudition and absurdity.

For, although they introduce all these *classes, genera,* and *species,* it is not to be supposed that they are always able to determine to which of them a particular piece of writing really belongs: for, as we have seen, in speaking of the curious MS. made of the barks of trees, before-mentioned, they say, "they found in it *twenty-two lines of Merovingian writing,* and consequently different from that of the rest of the MS. This writing," say they, "is at least as early as the seventh century: *but it may be more ancient, as, in fact, our Merovingian characters are the same as those used in the cursive writing of the Romans.*"

But this is not all; for *different specimens* of the *same writing,* taken from the *same identical MSS.* occur, over and over again, in different plates and chapters of their work, as examples of *distinct genera,* and *species.* I could produce abundant instances of this; but shall satisfy myself with noticing the following: In plate 46, therefore, which is devoted to examples of what they call *semi-uncial* writing, *Roman, Gallican,* and *Merovingian,* we have a specimen from the MS. No. 766 of the library of St. Germain des Prés, beginning: "Causa ergo," &c. which is described at page 211, as *semi uncial Gal-*

lican writing, of the 2d Subdivision, 1st Genus, 1st Species. In plate 48, we have another specimen of the same writing from the same MS., "Porro autem," &c. which, at page 238, is described among *various mixtures of different Roman cursives*, as of the 2d Genus, 1st Species. The same plate gives another specimen of the same, beginning, " Quam similia," &c. which at page 242, is called a *melange of Gallican writing*, 1st Genus, 6th Species ; and at plate 49, which, in the title, is said to be devoted to *Roman* and *Lombardic minuscule* writing, we have again another similar specimen, from this same MS. beginning, " Interia Roma," &c. which in the text, p. 266-7, is described as *Roman minuscule* of the 2d Genus, and the 3d Species. From all which we become let into the secret, that *semi-uncial Gallican, mixed Roman cursive, mixed Gallican,* and *Roman minuscule* writing, are in reality all the same. What can be said of such a system as this? is not one constrained to apply to it the words of Maffei, and to pronounce it false and deceitful in all its parts?

I must add a few more words upon minuscule and cursive writing; in order to obviate certain objections, which might otherwise still occur in the minds of persons who have not, perhaps, sufficiently considered, either the different degrees of *resemblance*, or of *variety*, which it is reasonable to expect to find between different specimens of legitimate *minuscule* and *cursive* writing, whether ancient or modern. I consider this the more necessary, as it has been stated by one of my friends, as among his chief reasons for not believing in the antiquity of our MS. of Cicero's Aratus, that the minuscule writing in that MS. is so very unlike that of the interesting *papyrus,* which is hung up in the manuscript room at the British Museum; and which, though it is in Latin, he told me he found himself unable to read.

I thought it a sufficient answer to this objection, and I think so still, that this document is not in genuine *minuscule,* but in *cursive;* and moreover that, being a notarial act, it probably does not give us a fair sample even of the common cursive of the time when it was written; and certainly not of the kind of writing which an author or a scribe would have employed in writing or copying a manuscript.

For it ever appears to have been a primary consideration in writing MSS. (if we except such as, with a view to magnificence, were written in very large characters), to put as much matter as conveniently could be in a moderate space; and, besides, to make the writing as regular and distinct as possible; so that it might at all times be easily read: and therefore we commonly find the lines in MSS. at a moderate distance, only, from each other; care at the same time being taken, that the tails or bottoms of the letters, in one line, should never reach so low as to touch any of the letters of the line under it. Whereas, on the contrary, many of the ancient notaries (I speak more especially of those of Italy and France) appear to have been ambitious to make their writing fill as much space as possible: for which reason they wrote their diplomas, as in the case of the one I am speaking of, in a large scrawling hand; and moreover affected numerous flourishes, or other extravagancies of the pen, which were perhaps intended to throw an air of mysterious importance over their performances, and at the same time to render them so difficult to read, as to oblige the person holding them to have again recourse to some one of their own body, whenever, for legal purposes, it might in future become necessary to refer to and examine their contents.

But, besides that a great part of the letters in this papyrus are in reality fair minuscules, although obscured by the above flourishes, the document is of a later date, by seventy years, than the MS. of St. Hilarius in the Vatican, and fifty-five years later than the Sulpicius Severus of Verona, beforementioned; both of which are written in good regular minuscules (see our Plate VI. Nos. 9, 10); and therefore any argument, that might otherwise be drawn from the writing of that document being unlike that of our MS. can have no force. It is true that papyri, written in this kind of character, exist of a much earlier date. Maffei, as we have seen, was the possessor of one of about the year 444, and speaks of others, which he conjectures to be still older: the curious antiquary may read the contents of them all, in his "Istoria Diplomatica;" where, at page 163, he will find, under No. ix. the specimen in the British Musuem, which formerly belonged to a Monsignor Fontanini, and is no other than a deed of sale of certain lands in the territory of Rimini, written at Ravenna in the year 572.

The authors of the "Nouveau Traité," (vol. iii. p. 258,) put a somewhat similar objection, and answer it in the following manner: " If *minuscule writing*, say the objectors, was in usage amongst the ancient Romans, it must have been so different from ours, as not to be now read without great difficulty.

(Allatius, " Animadv." p. 66.) Might we not, in like manner, say: if *writing in capitals* was used by the Romans, the letters must have been very different from ours, and therefore not to be read without a great deal of trouble? But the objection, and the evidence upon which it is founded, apply only to *cursive writing*, or *running-hand*, in which the letters are joined to each other, and which the objectors have confounded with *minuscule writing*."

Now the first part of this answer is to the purpose; but the last, inasmuch as it seems to say that *the letters in minuscule writing were never meant to be joined to each other*, is not, I think, true: for it appears evident that they were invented for this express purpose; that so the writer might save time, by being enabled to write an entire word without taking off his pen. Were it not that minuscule characters are so constructed, as readily to admit of this, as well because of their freedom from angularities, as of the fine strokes, rising upwards, with which most of the letters terminate, little or no time would be gained by the use of them. It is true that, in MSS. written in minuscules, we often find letters which are not joined to those that precede, or follow them: but more frequently they are; and, where they are not, it is evident that the scribe has omitted the joinings, only from a fear of blotting, and in order to insure to his writing the greater appearance of neatness: for good *cursive writing*, I should say, is no other than good *minuscule writing*, written more or less expeditiously.

On the whole, I see no room to doubt, that the complete Latin minuscule alphabet existed at least as early as the *first* century; and I am of opinion, that the men of those times, who had been thoroughly instructed in the art of writing, such persons for example as Quinctilian and the elder Pliny, used it in writing their compositions; joining the letters together much in the same way as we do now, and occasionally availing themselves of abbreviations, in order to economize their time and paper.

Nor do the paucity of minuscule characters, found in the scrawls on the walls of Pompeii, and the frequent mixture of capital letters with minuscules, which we see in MSS. and diplomas of later centuries, shake this my belief. In the time of Quinctilian, as he himself tells us, (lib. i. cap. 1) few, even among persons of consequence, took the pains to write a good hand. The *majuscule alphabet* existed, no doubt, many centuries before the *minuscule*; and would, consequently, long after the invention of this last, continue to be more generally known than the other by the common people. General customs do not change rapidly. Schoolmasters, especially in distant provinces, would go on teaching children their A B C upon the *majuscule alphabet*, and perhaps on that only, for a long time after the *minuscule alphabet* had come into use among men of letters; and even among these last, some of the more aged, who had been taught to write before the advantage of the minuscule character had become well understood, would be likely to mix the two kinds of letters together. This mixture, therefore, in the few specimens which we are enabled to produce of ancient cursive or minuscule writing, cannot be considered as good evidence against the existence of the complete minuscule alphabet at the time when they were written; nor against the use of it, in those times, among well-educated persons: for besides that many, nay perhaps all of these specimens were written by individuals of small literary attainment, and several of them probably by persons of the lowest classes, it will be observed that the ancient inscriptions which we have collected, taken together, furnish us with *all the minuscule characters.*

There is, on the whole, abundant reason why the specimens which we meet with of *ancient cursive*, or *running hand*, should in many cases be very unlike ours, and difficult to read; it having commonly for its foundation (for the reasons given) more or less of the above *mixture of majuscule and minuscule* characters; whilst with us the sole foundation of our cursive writing is the genuine *minuscule*. With all this, I think I could produce writings in modern cursive quite as difficult of perusal as most or any of the ancient cursives; for, as for *the genuine minuscule alphabet, it appears to have been, from the first, very much if not quite the same as we now use in writing;* save that in recent centuries the tall s (ſ) has been considered applicable only to typography; and that we put a dot over the *i*, and commonly give a certain degree of inclination to the letters, in writing, which the ancients did not; and that besides, we are more careful than they were to leave proper spaces between our words, and to separate one sentence, or member of a sentence, from another, by marks of punctuation.

I SHALL here briefly enumerate the specimens contained in the three Plates, IV. V. and VI. intended to illustrate the foregoing Dissertation ; adding references to the pages in which they have been spoken of: besides which, I shall occasionally offer a few additional remarks upon some of them.

The entire contents of Plate IV. are from the Antiquities of Herculaneum and Pompeii, and are therefore all of the first century.

No. 1. *The title, in Greek, of a painting of the Muse Erato,* in the Herculaneum Collection; remarkable for the form of the letter *psi*. See p. 49.

1[a]. *A short inscription,* written on the wall inside a tavern at Pompeii; see p. 87. All the letters, except the initials and the A and M, are fair minuscule characters.[d]

2. *A sentence from Euripides,* in Greek minuscules, with accents, found, written on a wall, in the excavations at Resina, and which has been sufficiently noticed at p. 50.

3. *Six lines of the only Latin MS. of the Herculaneum Collection that has yet been published;* from the 'Herculanensium Voluminum quae supersunt,' tom. ii. 1809, and which has already been briefly mentioned at pp. 87-88:

"*Obterere adnisi* portarum *claustra per* urbem,
Opsidione tamen nec corpora moenibus arcent,
Castraque pro muris, atque arma pedestria ponunt.
Hos inter coetus falisque ad bella paratus
Utraque sollemnis iterum revocaverat orbes
Consiliis nox apta ducum, lux aptior armis."

---

[d] As I have before said, I am obliged for this specimen to the "Museo Borbonico." I would not willingly speak disrespectfully of this work, which I have been assured is edited by men of learning. But I am obliged to say, that the heterogeneous mixture which it contains, of ancient with modern pictures, &c., and the very imperfect idea which its meagre engravings in outline convey of the various styles and merits of the originals they are intended to represent, render it a publication of *a very inferior class* to that entitled "Le Pitture Antichi, I Bronzi, &c. d'Ercolano," whereof so many fine volumes in folio were formerly given to the world, under the patronage of the King of Naples, and of which I, for one, lament the discontinuance more than I can express. Would that this note might meet the eye of his present Sicilian Majesty; and that he might be induced to take into consideration the suggestion the author would humbly make, that a publication so full of interest, and so honourable to the taste and liberality of his Majesty's August Family, should be resumed; or rather, perhaps, that the paintings, sculptures, bronzes, &c., which the excavations of Pompeii have furnished so abundantly, should be engraved in the same finished manner, and form the subject of another work upon the same scale of magnificence.

supposed to be of the 2d or 3d century. 119

All that remains of this MS. are the fragments of eight columns of text, of which this is the last. The letters printed in italics are supplied by the Neapolitan editors. In the second line, we have *opsidione*, instead of *obsidione*; and in the fifth, *sollemnis*, with a double *l*, according to the ancient orthography; of which indeed the other columns furnish interesting illustrations. Thus, in the third line of the first column, we have *adsiduus* for *assiduus*, (the preposition being maintained in its original form), and in the fourth line *opsessis* instead of *obsessis*. In the third line of the fourth column, we read *exsiguas* for *exiguas*, according to the ancient mode of putting an *s* after an *x*. Thus the ancients sometimes wrote *vixsit Alexsander*, *dexstero*, &c. The sixth line of the same column reads:

" Hic *igitur* partis *animum* diductus in omnis."

partis in omnis, for *partes in omnes*. The ancients wrote *parteis* and *omneis*, but the *i* was often used in these cases for both the letters. In the fifth column, and the third line, we have, again, *instantis*, for *instantes*. In the seventh line of the sixth column, we have *Intersaeptam animam*; the first word being written with a diphthong: in the Medicean Virgil, we find it, sometimes written in one way, and sometimes in the other. I have thought it well, so far to notice the orthography in this ancient papyrus, as similar peculiarities occur in our MS. of Aratus.

The characters in which these fragments are written, may not improperly be styled cursive capitals. The alphabet, which is added in the plate, under the above six lines, exhibits some trifling varieties in particular letters: the ɪ, when intended to represent *ei*, has sometimes a little distinguishing mark, joined to it on the left. The ʜ, as has been before observed (pp. 88, 89) is very remarkable.

Nos. 4 to 18 inclusive, *exhibit various Inscriptions*, or parts of inscriptions, in which *minuscule* or *cursive letters* occasionally occur, and which have been found on the walls of buildings at Pompeii, written with a brush, or with a crayon, in black or red. All, except the four last, will be found in the plates at the end of the volume published at Naples in 1797, entitled ' Dissertationis Isagogicae ad Herculanensium Voluminum Explanationem, pars prima.' And I have spoken briefly of them at pp. 85-87.

Of the first inscription, No. 4, our plate omits the first two lines, which are in much larger characters than the rest, and the seven initial letters at bottom. I here give the whole in ordinary type, as the original, in consequence of the L and the I being scarcely at all distinguishable from each other, is not very easy to read: the above Dissertation may be consulted as to its supposed meaning; for I believe some doubt exists as to the true interpretation of parts of it. The most reasonable supposition seems to be, that the 'nongentum tabernae pergulae,' &c. therein mentioned, were tents or booths, which it was customary to use upon the occasion of public festivities.

IN . PRAEDIS . JULIAE . SP . F . FELICIS
LOCANTUR
BALNEUM . VENERIUM . ET . NONGENTUM . TABERNAE . PERGULAE
CENACULA.EX.IDIBUS.AUG.PRIMIS.IN.IDUS.SEXTAS ANNOS.CONTINUOS.QUINQUE
S . Q . D . L . E . N . C .

The *b*, in this inscription, as has been already observed, is in every instance a minuscule; as it is, also, in No. 8.

I have before noticed the inscription, No. 7. "POSTUMIUM PROBUM AED(ILEM) POTHINUS. ROG(AT) FER TUNNUM ; in which we have the minuscule *e*, exactly formed as we now make it in writing.

In the name *Popidium*, in No. 15, the *d* is a minuscule, or cursive, character; and so are the *f* in No. 12, the *g*, in No. 10, and the *k*, in Nos. 6, and 11.

No. 13, represents two words of the following short inscription: "POPIDIO RUFO INVICTO MUNIFICO III DEFENSORIBUS COLONORUM FELICITER." The way in which the N is joined to the s in the word *defensoribus* is remarkable; this joined *s* is such as we now use in writing; and in the following word, *colonorum*, we have a curious example of abbreviated writing in capitals.

The small specimens of cursive writing, given under numbers 14, 17, and 18, have been already spoken of (pp. 86, 87), and are exactly traced from the plate in the work of Mazois: they give us very clearly the minuscules *t, u,* and *s*. But, as I before observed, they must not be considered as samples of the cursive writing used in the first century by well educated persons and men of letters, but as the scribblings of individuals of an inferior class of society.

No. 19, exhibits the first *four lines of the writing (or rather the pictorial imitation of writing) which appears on a rolled volume, represented partly open, in one of the paintings of the Herculaneum collection.* The painting, as has been said (pp. 84, 85), is introduced, as a vignette, in the second volume of ' Le Pitture Antiche d'Ercolano,' and the learned illustrators of that work observe that this writing appears to be in great part in minuscules. In the fourth line, the minuscule *a* may be perceived; and in the first we have the word *Quisquis*, all the letters of which appear very clear, except the initial; and this singular character, as has been observed, proves to be the *Tironian Q of the ancients.* (See this character, three times employed in the inscription, Plate V. No. 16.) As far as it goes, therefore, this word *Quisquis* (and we may join with it the short inscription given under No. 1ª) furnishes as satisfactory evidence of the use of Roman minuscules, in the first century of the Christian era, as can be desired. Perhaps the reader will agree with me, that the writing of this word bears considerable resemblance to that of the " Ceruus Silvie," in Plate VI. No. 3, which occurs, among other inscriptions, chiefly in capitals, upon one of the drawings in the Vatican MS. No. 3225, containing the celebrated fragments of Virgil, already spoken of at p. 51-53, and concerning which I shall have occasion to remark further.

No. 20. The specimen of Greek writing, here given, is taken from a papyrus published in the same volume as the above Latin fragments; and I was induced to introduce it here, because of the resemblance that some of the letters, especially the A and the Є, bear to those of the Latin MS.; which is such, as might almost lead to the supposition that both these MSS. were written by the same hand.

The contents of Plate V. are all taken from Buonarruoti, except the two last inscriptions, which are from the ' Palæographia' of Kopp. I have sufficiently spoken of those from the former writer, at pages 79-84; and have observed, that, taken together, they furnish us with all the letters of the minuscule alphabet, except the *h* and the *q*, both of which I shall now produce in other ancient inscriptions.

This last character, therefore, (the *q*,) occurs, as has been said (p. 83) in the inscription of *Mevius*, given in Fabretti, and in that of *Gentianus*, which is engraved in the work of Marini, and which, had I seen it in time, I should willingly have caused to becopied accurately, though of reduced dimensions, in this plate. As it is, I think it well here to give this inscription in type, distin-

122   *On a MS. of Cicero's translation of Aratus,*

guishing, as I have done before, those letters, which may in some sort be termed minuscule or cursive characters, from the others; besides which, I have caused two or three words of it to be engraved in exact imitation of the original, under No. 17.

gentianus fidelis in pace qui uix
it annis xxi menss viii dies
xvi et in o [a bird 𝔓 a bird] rationis tuis
roges pro nobis quia scimus te in ☩

Here the *d* is the round cursive character; the *e* is always round; the *g*, instead of rising up at bottom, has a tail, as in Plate IV. No. 10, though shorter; the *m* is round; the *q* is decidedly the minuscule letter, being formed like the *p* turned in an opposite direction; and the *v*, except where it is used as a numeral, is rounded on one side and perpendicular on the other, as we see it in MSS.

Lastly, the minuscule *h* occurs in the inscription of Pupus Torquatianus, which has been mentioned at pages 84 and 89, and which I here insert entire, as the first four lines only, and the two words *Eucharis* and *hoc*, are copied in our plate under No. 16.

"D   M   S
pvpvs torqvatianvs
filivs bonvs qvi semper
parentibvs obseqvens
vixit annis viii. m. viiii. d xiii.
item alivs pvpvs laetianvs qvi
idem fil bonvs et obseqvens
idem parentibvs vixit annis
n. v. m. vi. d. vi. posvervnt ga
ianvs et evcharis parentes
filis dvlcissimis sed non hoc
merentes a vobis qvi sibi sense *(sic)*
rvnt. iii. idvs. sept. exqvibvs. vnvs. vixit. in.
xi. kal. oct. et. alivs. in. iii. kal. easdem."

The four lines of this inscription, given in our plate, will, as far as they go, convey a correct idea of the strange forms of the letters composing it. A considerable number of them bear more resemblance to cursive or minuscule characters than to capitals. The *b* is always the minuscule; the *e* is so oftener than not (I mean it is the round *e*, thus ϵ), and so the *f*. The *h* in Eucharis, in the tenth line, is exactly the minuscule of the present day, and so would be that in *hoc*, in the line following, but that the lower part has an angle where it ought to be rounded. The *p* has a remarkable appearance, and seems in most cases to have been formed by a single stroke, but whether commenced from the bottom or from the top, it is difficult to say; and so I find it in the Arvale table, No. xxxviii. in Marini (p. 497), of the time of Caracalla. The *q*, as has been observed, is the ancient Tironian character; the *r*, as in the word "parentibus," in the fourth line, is sometimes more like the minuscule than the majuscule character; and so is most frequently the *s*. Kopp, from whose 'Palæographia Critica' (vol. i. p. 106), as has been said, I took the four lines given in the plate, states this inscription to be of the second century, and of the time of Marcus Aurelius; but I do not find that Marini, from whose work (vol. i. p. 263), he copied it, asserts this: all he there says of it (speaking of the sur-name Laetianus), being that this inscription, engraved in semi-cursive characters, afterwards coloured red (as was often done in inscriptions), is in his own collection. Possibly, however, he may have mentioned it again, in some other page, which has escaped my observation.

If the curious works of Marini and Kopp had been known to me earlier, I might perhaps have made more use of them than I have done. I will only add, from the preface of the former writer, a remark or two upon the forms of the characters found in some of the Arvale tables, and in other ancient inscriptions: "Having now," says he (p. xxxv.), "to speak of the quality of the writing, I must observe, that the characters in inscriptions differ exceedingly, and are scarcely ever regular, and well-formed, even in the time of Claudius: .... and that it may be considered as indubitable, that *nothing is more fallacious than the idea of being enabled to determine the ages of ancient inscriptions from the particular forms of their characters; and that it is mere folly, upon such grounds, to attempt to build any solid argument. The whole, whether they chance to be majuscules or minuscules, are still ancient Roman characters*, and their forms are more or less perfect, in proportion to the ability, the diligence, the hurry, of the individual who sculptured them, and perhaps the price stipulated for his work; besides which, much depended on the quality of the instrument used in sculpturing them, and the nature of the stone itself: whence, every one may readily understand that inscriptions with ill-formed letters, may often happen to be much more ancient, than others in which they are well-formed, and *vice versa*. And so, in our Arvale tables, it will be seen that tab. xxxvi. is much more rudely written than tab. xxxviii.; that in tab. xl. and xli. the characters are as bad, as confused, and undetermined as possible; whilst in tab. xlii. xliii. and xliv. they are well formed and very easy to read: and indeed there exists in the College of Rome, a celebrated inscription, sculptured in the xiiith Consulate of Augustus, that is, in the first year of the Christian era, in which the letters are as rudely and irregularly formed as in the worst of the Arvale tables." Great part of what Marini has here said is, perhaps, to the full as applicable to manuscripts, as to inscriptions.

In the remaining Plate VII. are exhibited a few examples of the writing found in certain very early MSS. in libraries on the continent; beginning with two or three specimens of writing in capitals, which, it will be seen, very much resemble the text of Hyginus, written within the figures, in our ancient manuscript.

No. 1. gives the following two lines, in small capitals, from a celebrated MS. of Terence in the Vatican (No. 3226), supposed to be of very high antiquity:

"O FORTUNA! O FORS FORTUNA! QUANTIS COMMODITATIBUS
QUAM SUBITO MEO (H)ERO ANTIPHONTI OPE VESTRA HUNC ONORASTIS"
(*diem*)! Phormion, Act. v. Scen. v.

This specimen, which I wish had contained a greater number of lines, was, I believe, first given in the work of Mabillon, whence it was copied by the authors of the "Nouveau Traité;" who observe, naturally enough, that the *h* is of a very remarkable form. For my part, I suspect some inaccuracy in the person who originally made the tracing, and that the letter *h* in this MS. may in reality be of the same shape, or nearly so, as that in the Latin papyrus, of which specimens are given in Plate IV.

No. 2. exhibits three lines from the celebrated fragment of a MS. of Virgil in the Vatican (No. 3225), in which are the drawings which were engraved by Bartoli:

" AT REGINA GRAVI JAM DUDUM SAUCIA CURA
VULNUS ALIT VENIS ET CAECO CARPITUR IGNE
MULTA VIRI VIRTUS ANIMO MULTUS QUE RECURSAT."
Æneid, lib. iv.

This MS. as has been shewn (p. 51-53), was judged by three of the most learned antiquaries of the end of the seventeenth century, to be as early as the time of Septimius Severus: I shall now give my reasons for believing it to be still more ancient.

Besides the prints by Bartoli, we have, in the Lansdowne collection of MSS. in the British Museum (No. 834), a copy in fac-simile of great part of the text of this MS., together with the drawings, carefully done by him in 1677, in colours, in imitation of the originals, by order of the Cardinal Massimi. These copies, although they were perhaps not traced from the originals, are of the same dimensions; and have the appearance of having been done with great attention to accuracy. Being entirely executed with a brush, they are exempt from that hardness in the outlines of the figures, and in the foldings of the draperies, which characterise the engravings of this artist; and they have much of that looseness and freedom of execution, which we so commonly observe in the paintings of the ancients. Judging of the originals from these copies, I should certainly say with Schelestrate, that there is *nothing in them unworthy the best era of ancient Roman art.* I may add, to what he has said of the costume, that the ships, introduced in several of these drawings, agree, in a most remarkable manner, and in all their details, with those in two of the Herculaneum paintings (vol. ii. pp. 91 and 97), each of which represents the abandonment of Ariadne by Theseus; so as very much to favour the supposition that this celebrated MS. may be of the same century.

The drawings in this MS. having strongly impressed me with an opinion of its high antiquity, it afterwards occurred to me, that, if that opinion was well founded, the text itself might, if examined, chance to furnish further testimony in support of it; and I therefore resolved to compare these fragments (or rather the Lansdowne MS.[e] containing correct copies of them,) line by

[e] I find upon looking at the printed edition of these fragments, published at Rome in 1741, that the Lansdowne MS. above mentioned, does not give the whole of the remaining text of this MS., but only as far as verse 309 of the fourth book of the Æneid; and that the Vatican

line, with the fac-simile of the Medicean Virgil, printed at Florence in 1741, and carefully to mark the differences between them.

The first page of these fragments begins with the Georgics, lib. iii. v. 1, and in the sixth verse, in the Vatican MS. I found, " *Quoi* non dictus Hylas," &c.; whilst the Medicean MS. has, " *Cui* non dictus," &c.

The second fragment begins with v. 146 of the same book; and here again, at v. 147, I found the same difference; the Vatican MS. having, " Plurimus alburnum volitans *quoi* nomen Asilo," and the Medicean, ... " *cui* nomen Asilo."

Another page begins with v. 209 of the same book; and at v. 211, I read in the former MS. " Sive boum, sive est *quoi*," &c. and in the latter, " Sive boum, sive est *cui*," &c.; and at v. 347 (in a following page) the Vatican MS. has " *quom*," and the Medicean " *cum*."

Another fragment commences, Georg. lib. iv. v. 97, which line in the former MS. is " *Quom* venit, et terram sicco spuit ore viator:" whilst the other has: " *Cum* venit," &c.

Again, v. 103, begins " At *quum* incerta, &c. in the Vatican MS., and " At *cum*," &c. in the other; and in the verse following, the last word, in the Vatican MS. is " *relinquont*," and in the Medicean, " *relincunt*." Again, the last three words in v. 113, are ... " *quoi* talia curae," in the Vatican MS., and in the other, ... " *cui* talia curae."

Another fragment begins with v. 153 of the same book; and at v. 154, the last two words are ... " legib. *aevom*," in the Vatican MS., and in the Medicean, ... " legib. *aevum*."

At v. 171, I, for the first time, find " *cum*" in the Vatican MS. as well as in the other; both having, " cum properant," &c.: and the same occurs in another fragment in v. 487, where both have " cum subita;" but at v. 523 we have " Gurgite *qum* medius portans," &c in the Vatican MS. and " Gurgite *cum* medio portans," &c. in the Medicean.

MS. contains, besides, considerable portions of the fifth, sixth, seventh, and eighth books. It is remarkable that the editor (Bottari) takes no notice whatever, whether in his preface or his notes, of the numerous examples of ancient orthography which this MS. furnishes: nor are they mentioned by Foggini, in the learned preface to his edition of the Medicean MS.; notwithstanding he speaks of Bottari's publication, which had made its appearance whilst his own was in hand.

In the fragments of the Æneid, which begin, lib. i. v. 185, the orthography no longer differs in this striking manner from that of the Medicean MS.: we have always "*cum*," in both the MSS.; and in lib. ii. v. 677 and v. 678, we have in both, "*Cui* parvus Julus, ... *Cui* pater et conjunx," &c. and so this dative pronoun is written, whenever it again occurs in the fragments of the Æneid. I say nothing of certain other peculiarities in the orthography of the Vatican MS. which might also perhaps be insisted on as evidences of its great antiquity; because I wish chiefly to confine my remarks to the use of the words *quom*, *quum*, and *qum*, in that MS. and to the dative *quoi*, which we have seen is used constantly in the fragments of the Georgics, instead of *cui*.

Every one knows that in the works of Virgil, as we now have them, the word *quum* never appears; but, that in every case we read *cum*. So, as far as I have examined, I have always found it to be in the earliest printed editions, and so it is in those of the present day. Upon looking into several MSS. of this poet, of different centuries, in the British Museum, I have invariably found the same; and after having gone through Foggini's fac-simile edition of the celebrated Medicean MS., which some of the most learned men of Europe have judged to be as old as the second century, I have been unable to find *quum*; though I once, at p. 157, v. 14, find, by error, *qum*, instead of *quem*, the *e* having been afterwards added at top by the corrector of the MS.; and in two instances, in the first book of the Georgics, (viz. at page 27, v. 12, and page 29, v. 20,) *quom*; which in both cases has been anciently altered to *cum*, by a scratch of the pen through the letters *q* and *o*, and the insertion of of a *c* at top.

Were this *quom*, thus altered to *cum*, of frequent occurrence in the Medicean MS. and did we know it to have been certainly written in the second century, we should then, I think, have fair reason to believe that that MS. had been copied from one of very nearly the age of Virgil himself, which, by chance, had escaped the emendations of grammarians of any later period: since *quom*, which is very ancient Latin orthography, had much fallen into disuse, before the second century; and it appears certain that the grammarians, real or pretended, whom the ancients employed to correct and punctuate their manuscripts, after the labour of writing them letter by letter had been performed by slaves [f] or other menials, were accustomed, very unceremoniously, to expunge and alter whatever they considered as obsolete; and to change the orthography according to the usage of their own times.[g] As it is, the appearance of *quom*, although only twice, in the Medicean MS.[h] is something in favour of its antiquity; and when taken in conjunction with the *quom* and *quum*, in the Vatican fragments, furnishes, I think, very good evidence that when writing the Georgics, at least, Virgil occasionally used that word, as well as *quum* and *qum*.

In the fourth book of the Georgics, as has been said, we have sometimes *cum* in the Vatican fragments, as in the Medicean MS.; and in the fragments of the Æneid, which are very considerable, we have always *cum*, and never *quom* or *quum*;[i] and always *cui*, instead of the archaism *quoi*, which is of constant occurrence in the Georgics.

Now I am very much disposed to argue from all this, that the use of *cum* instead of *quom* and *quum*, began to be introduced before the death of Virgil, and that in fact he constantly employed the former word when writing the

[f] I do not, however, here mean to admit, that in very ancient times *all* MSS. were copied by persons of this class, or in this kind of character. Lovers of Literature, who could not afford to buy MSS. would often copy them themselves, and of course in a more expeditious sort of writing; in short, in cursive and minuscule: and of this kind, it is probable, many very ancient MSS. still exist, in the library of the Vatican and elsewhere, which, in consequence of the old prejudice against the ancient use of minuscule writing, have even until now been termed " Manuscritti in carrattere Lombardico," and considered not earlier than the ninth or tenth century.

[g] I shall presently insist further upon the truth of this observation; which is also, I believe, generally applicable to the copiers and correctors of MSS. in later centuries, as well as to original writers. If it be true, it follows, I think, that a careful study of the dates of the different changes which took place in Latin orthography, is likely to do more towards enabling us to judge of the ages of early MSS. in that language, than any other *criteria* that may be mentioned, excepting, perhaps, the drawings and illuminations which are found in some of them.

[h] I have also once found *quoi* in the Medicean MS.; viz. in the first book of the Georgics, page 26, v. 24. It had, like the above *quom*, we may conclude, escaped the notice of the grammarian who had been employed to correct the MS. from which it was copied; and in consequence the writer of the Medicean MS. put it in. It is corrected by a pen stroke across the *q* and the *o*, and the insertion of a *c* over the former letter, in the same way as the two *quom*.

[i] In the printed edition of these Vatican fragments, we have (p. 56) at verse 680 of the second book of the Æneid, " *Quum* subitum," &c.; but I consider it an error of the press, as in the Lansdowne MS. before mentioned, it is " *Cum* subitum."

Æneid. Or, if this should be going too far, I would say, that the use of *cum* having come into vogue about the time of Virgil's death, his friends, to whom he left the task of revising his last poem previous to its publication, thought well to adopt it, as also the *cui* instead of *quoi:* and, further, that very soon after the great reputation of Virgil occasioned his former works to be collected together, and the whole to be inscribed, with the Æneid, in one large book, it was thought advisable, for the sake of uniformity, to expunge the words *quom, quum,* and *quoi,* wherever they were found in the Bucolics and the Georgics, and to substitute *cum* and *cui.* It appears very doubtful if the Vatican MS. ever contained the entire works of Virgil: I incline to think that it never did; as it still has a sort of frontispiece, filling the whole page, and containing six coloured designs, which Bartoli has not engraved; and as this frontispiece is immediately followed by the *First* verse of the third book of the Georgics. The Lansdowne MS. has a copy of this frontispiece, of which one or two of the designs are very beautiful.

I may also observe another circumstance which goes very far, in my opinion, to shew the great antiquity of this MS. and that it may have been written soon after the death of Virgil; viz. that the grammarian who was employed to correct it, has left the above archaisms in the Georgics unaltered, thereby, I think, shewing that he performed that office at a time when, as yet, none of them were become obsolete.

I may add, in proof of the above preference having been given to *cum* in the first century, that in the fragments of the only Latin MS. of the Herculaneum collection hitherto published, and of which I have already spoken (pp. 87, 88, and 118, 119) we have seven times *cum,* and in no instance *quum.*

And this seems to be further proved by Quinctilian, in the first book of his Institutes, cap. vii. "De Orthographia;" where, speaking of certain niceties formerly insisted upon by grammarians, he says: "Illa quoque servata est a multis differentia, ut *ad,* cum esset praepositione, *d* litteram; cum autem conjunctio, *t,* acciperet. Item *cum,* si tempus significaret, per *q*; si comitem, per *c*; si vero causam, per *q,* ac duas sequentes *u u,* scriberetur. . . . . Verum haec jam inter ipsas ineptias evanuerunt." So that when he wrote, these, and other nice distinctions of this kind, were out of date.

He does not expressly mention *quom*; but other instances of the ancient use of the *o* instead of *u,* are noticed by him in the following passage:

"Quid dicam *vortices* et *vorsus*, caeteraque ad eundem modum, quae primo Scipio Africanus in *e* litteram secundam vertisse dicitur? Nostri praeceptores *cervom servom*que, *u* et *o* litteris scripserunt; .... nunc *u* gemina scribuntur," &c. And again, at the end of the same paragraph: "Illud nunc melius, quod *cui*, tribus, quas proposui, litteris enotamus; in quo *pueris nobis*, ad pinguem sane sonum *qu* et *oi* utebantur, tantum ut ab illo *qui* distingueretur."

I think it will be admitted that Quinctilian here speaks, as if the use of *quum* and *qum* had for some time gone out of fashion; and as if *quom* and *quoi* had become obsolete. Now changes of this kind are only adopted by the public by slow degrees. *Quoi* and *quom* were, no doubt, the most ancient Latin orthography; and a long series of years must have elapsed between the first introduction of *cui*, and *cum*, and their coming into such general use as to cause the former modes of writing those words to be entirely discontinued, and as it were forgotten. But they were so, it appears, when Quinctilian wrote as above, which we may suppose to have been soon after the year 80 of the Christian era; and, therefore, as the Vatican MS. has these archaisms,[h] it must, I think, have been written previously.

But it was lately objected, by one of my friends, that the circumstance of the archaisms *quoi* and *quom* being now found in the works of Plautus, is at variance with the position above assumed by me, (and on which my argument in proof of the high antiquity of the Vatican MS. in question, mainly rests) that it was really the custom of the ancient grammarians to alter the orthography of the MSS. confided to them for correction, according to the usage of their own times: for, if they always did so, how comes it that these examples of ancient orthography now appear in the plays of the above writer, and also in the poems of Catullus, &c.?

This objection certainly requires an answer. Upon its being first made to

[h] If I except the accidental occurrence, before-mentioned, of *quoi*, in one instance, and *quom*, twice, in the Medicean MS., no MS. of Virgil, as far as I can learn, except the one I am speaking of, has these archaisms. I do not find them once, among the numerous examples of the orthography of the celebrated Vatican MS. No. 3867, which Bottari has given in the Supplement to his edition of these Fragments: and yet this MS., which is written in capitals of the largest size, has always been considered one of very high antiquity; and indeed some writers appear to have thought it more ancient than any other. See the "Nouveau Traité de Diplomatique," vol. iii. p. 61.

me, I replied that, upon examining Plautus it would, I thought, be found, either that these words had been left occasionally in the dialogue, in order to mark, perhaps, the broad pronunciation of people of the lower classes; or else, that they had been introduced about the period of the invention of printing, by the Italian critics; who employed great pains at that time in the study of the ancient Latin language, and endeavoured, as is said in the prefaces to some of the first editions, to restore the orthography of the ancient Roman poets, as far as possible, to what it was originally: taking for their guide in this attempt, such early MSS. as happened still to exist, in addition to the authority of ancient inscriptions, and passages collected here and there upon the subject from the works of the early grammarians: in proof of which I may refer the reader to the prefatory address of Georgius Alexandrinus, to Jacobus Zeno, Bishop of Padua, prefixed to the first edition of Plautus himself; in which the writer, after descanting in no very measured terms upon the ignorance and presumption of the numerous critics and grammarians, who in former times had corrupted the text of his author, in their silly attempts to amend it, congratulates himself, very complacently, upon the better success of his own labours in the same way.[1]

[1] For the satisfaction of the reader I here give an extract or two from this preface to the "Editio Princeps" of Plautus:

"Nam Plautinæ viginti Comœdiæ quæ ad hoc ævi duntaxat extant, Latinæ scilicet linguæ deliciæ, rerum atque verborum venustate, et festiva sermonis elegantia, legentium animos mira voluptate afficerent; nisi pluribus in locis dimidiatæ haberentur: Et tum temporum injuria, tum litteratorum negligenti arrogantia, et librariorum inscitia depravatæ forent, &c. .... Adeo ad ejus percipiendos sensus necessaria erat multiplex, varia, et exquisitissima quædam eruditio: Quam rem tum Varro ad Ciceronem scribens, tum Donatus Terentium explanans, testantur. Quod si quispiam nostro isto sæculo, ubi plæraque veterum scriptorum aut interierunt, aut fracta et mendosa habentur in tanta librorum inopia, & bonarum litterarum egestate, opus quod prisci viri, macti ingenio & omnifaria doctrina præstantes, cognitu difficillimum existimaverunt, recognoscere et corrigere; immo abdita et pluribus ignorata aperire temptaverit: is, si cœpti sui aliqua ex parte compos evaserit, nimirum quid magnum effecit. Nam ut de octo prioribus taceam, *quis duodecim Comœdias quadraginta ab hinc annis repertas*, lectionis tum confusæ tum falsæ, duodecim Herculis ærumnis apud Poetas famigeratis jure non comparaverit? In quibus corrigendis operam atque studium insumere velle, &c. .... Porro cum nec tantum dictiones examinandæ, sed litteræ atque syllabæ pensitandæ fuerint atque enumerandæ; ut ex earum positu atque figura aliquid vel verum vel vero proximum aucuparemur: ...Verumtamen numerosa hæc et impudens grammaticorum turba non æreo tinitu, quemadmodum stymphalices paludis olim volucres, abactæ fuerunt; sed vera ratione et multiplici veterum auctorum

My first supposition had no foundation; but I was right in the second. For, having looked, for the sake of facility of reference, into the Index of the Delphin Plautus, and having noted down twenty passages in the eight first plays, in which the word *quoi* is said to appear in that edition, (for, as will be shewn, it is not found in all the places referred to), I collated those passages with *ten manuscripts* of various ages in the British Museum, and also with the *Editio Princeps* of Plautus, printed at Venice in 1472, by Jo. de Colonia and Vind. de Spira, and the *Aldine* edition of 1522; when the result was, as is contained in the following statement:

The MSS. which I distinguish by the letters A, B, C, D, &c. were these:

A. *Royal MS.* (No. 15. C. XI.) Sæc. x. (Casley); B. *Harleian MS.* 2476 (on paper), Sæc. xiv.; C. *Harl. MS.* 2776, Sæc. xiv.; D. *Harl. MS.* 5285, with date M.CCCC.XV.; E. *Harl. MS.* 3439 (on paper), Sæc. xv.; F. *Harl. MS.* 4704, Sæc. xv.; G. *Harl. MS.* 2634, Sæc. xv.; H. *Arundel MS.* 338, Sæc. xv.; I. *Burney MS.* 227, Sæc. xv.: all the above MSS. contain the first eight plays of Plautus, and no more; and these were all that were known in modern times, till about the year 1434, when, as we are informed by the above Georgius Alexandrinus, the remaining twelve were discovered. But the MS. K., No. 228 of the Burney collection, contains all the twenty plays of Plautus; and we shall find that this MS. (which is of course of a later date than most, perhaps than any of the others), has no want of the above archaisms.

The passages collated were these:

No. 1. Delphin Edition *Amphitruo*. Prol. line 72.... "*quoi duint.*" MS. A. (leaf wanting); B. has *cui*; C. (leaf wanting); D. *cui*; E. *cui*; F. *coy*; G. *coi*; H. *cui*; I. *cui*; whilst the MS. K. alone has *quoi*. The edit. 1472, has *cui*; and the Aldine *quoi*.

2. Delph. Edit. *Amph.* Act. i. Sc. 3, line 22. " *Quoi ego.*" The MS. A. is still wanting. All the other MSS. as well as the edition of 1472, have *Quo lego:* the Aldine has *Quoi lego.*

3. Delph. Ed. *Asinaria.* 1: 1. 65. " *quoi concrederet.*" The first nine MSS. A. to I. have all of them *cui*; but the MS. K. and the two printed editions, have *quoi.*

testimonio absterrebitur, immo fugabitur atque preteritur. Deluctari cum Antæo est ea cognitione, eaque eruditione, quæ per hæc tempora exigua haberi potest; velle in reconditos et penitissimos Poetæ sensus penetrare, et priscarum atque ignotissimarum vocum interpretamenta indagare," &c. &c. From all which, I think, it is easy to account for our finding various examples of very ancient orthography in this printed edition, which do not appear in MSS. written long before it was published.

4. Delph. Ed. *Asinaria.* 3 : 2. 43. *" quoi rei ?"* The MSS. A, B, C, D. have *cui :* E. has *qui ;* F. *cui ;* G. *coi ;* H. and I. have *cui :* and the MS. K. and the two printed editions, as before, have *quoi.*
5. Delph. Ed. *Asin.* 3 : 3. 3. *" quoi tu abiens,"* &c. All the MSS. except K. have *cui tu abiens,* &c. : but the MS. K. and the two printed editions have *quoi tu abiens.*
6. Delph. Ed. *Captivi.* 1 : 2. 54. *" Quoi obtigerat."* The MS. A. is here injured. All the others, together with the edition of 1472, have *Quod obtigerat :* in the Aldine, the words are wanting.
7. Delph. Ed. *Captivi.* 2: 2. 98. *" Neque adeo quoi."* All the MSS. have *cui ;* except the MS. K. which, with the two printed editions, has *quoi.*
8. Delph. Ed. *Capt.* 4 : 2. 7. . . . . *" quoi verba data sunt."* Again, all the MSS. except K. have *cui ;* but, as before, that MS. and the two printed editions have *quoi.*
9. Delph. Ed. *Curculio.* 4 : 2. 45. *" Quoi homini dei sunt propitii,"* &c. The MS. F. has *coi ;* but all the others, except K. have *cui.* The MS. K. and the two printed editions have *Quoi.*
10. Delph. Ed. *Curcul.* 4 : 3. 6. . . . *" quoi nihil debeo."* All the MSS. except K. have *cui ;* but that MS. and the two printed editions have *quoi.*
11. Delph. Ed. *Curcul.* 4 : 3. 11. *" Scire volo quoi reddidisti."* As before, all the MSS. except K. have *cui reddidisti :* but that MS. and the two printed editions have *quoi.*
12. Delph. Ed. *Curcul.* 4 : 4. 1. *" Quoi homini dii sunt propitii."* Again, all the MSS. except K. have *cui,* but that MS. and the two printed editions have *quoi.*
13. Delph. Ed. *Cistellaria.* 2 : 3. 32. *" Quoi illam dedisset."* All the MSS. as well as the two printed editions have *quo illam dedisset.*
14. Delph. Ed. *Cistellaria.* 4 : 2. 27. *" quoi haec excidit,* &c. Again, all the MSS. except K. have *cui ;* whilst that MS. and the two printed editions have *quoi.*
15. Delph. Ed. *Epidicus,* 1 : 2. 57. *" cui* (sic) *potissimum,"* &c. All the MSS. have *cui,* except the MS. K. which has *quoi.* The Ed. of 1472, has *cui ;* the Aldine *quoi.*
16. Delph. Edit. *Epid.* 3 : 1. 8. *" tibi cui divitiae,"* &c. The MS. G. has *coi ;* all the others have *cui,* except, as before, the MS. K. which, with the two printed editions, has *quoi.*
17. Delph. Ed. *Epid.* 3 : 4. 17. *" meas cui praedicem,"* &c. In this instance the MS. G. has *quoi,* like the MS. K. ; but all the other MSS. and the edition of 1472, have *cui.* The Aldine has *quoi.*
18. Delph. Ed. *Epid.* 3 : 4. 19. *" cui centones,"* &c. All the MSS. have *cui,* except the MS. K. ; that MS. and the Aldine edition have *quoi.* The edition of 1472 has *cui.*
19. Delph. Ed. *Epid.* 4 : 1. 2. *" cui multa in unum,"* &c. Here again the MS. G. has *quoi,* like the MS. K. All the other MSS. have *cui ;* but the two printed editions have *quoi.*

20. Delph. Ed. *Epid.* 5: 1. 12. "*cui libertas in mundo sita 'st.*" All the MSS. except K. have *cui*: that MS. and the Aldine edition have *quoi*; but the edition of 1472 has *cui*.

Now, if we throw aside three of the above passages, in which none of our MSS. have either *quoi* or *cui*, and which therefore do not affect our argument one way or the other, the result of our examination of the readings of the MSS. in the remaining *seventeen passages* will be thus: viz. that the four oldest MSS. A, B, C, D, have always *cui*; that the MS. E, has once *qui*, and sixteen times *cui*; the MS. F, once *coy*, once *coi*, and fifteen times *cui*; the MS. G, three times *coi*, twice *quoi*, and twelve times *cui*; that the MSS. H, and I, have always *cui*; and lastly, that the MS. K,[k] which was, perhaps, the last written of the whole, has invariably *quoi*; which is also, in most instances, the reading of the two printed editions.

I think I need say no more in defence of the position I set out with, that the ancient grammarians (and so, I believe, those of the middle ages) were accustomed to alter the orthography of the MSS. confided to them for correction, according to the usage of their own times; and that the archaisms, *quoi, quoius, quom*, &c. which we now find in Plautus, were not inserted in the first printed editions upon the authority of any very ancient MSS. of that poet, which chanced to exist in fifteenth century; but were put in by ingenious critics of that time, who, in so doing thought to restore the original expressions of this ancient author. Whether or not they were right in this belief, is another question: for it does not follow that, because Virgil used this orthography,

[k] It would be amusing enough, to compare more generally this *Burney MS.* 228, (K.) with the *Royal MS.* 15. C. XI. (A.), which, as I have said, is thought to be of the tenth century. I shall give only one specimen, in addition to the above: In *Amphitruo*, 3: 2. 1. the *Delph. Ed.* has "*cui est servus Sosia,*" the MS. K. has "*quoius est servos Sosia*;" whilst the MS. A. reads in the ordinary Latin of the tenth century, "*cuius servus est Sosia.*"

But though the MS. K. is full of old words, such as *quoius* for *cuius*, *quoiquam* for *cuiquam*, *quom* for *quum*, *architector* for *architectus*; and had *conmemorare*, *conmutavero*, *adsimulavit*, *conmovent*, &c. I find in it also, several times, *cui, ouius*, and *cum*; and *comminisci*, *commemores*, *aggrediar*, &c.; as if the writer of this MS. had sometimes forgotten the task he had imposed on himself, of keeping throughout to the above ancient mode of writing; for I believe it to be certain that, in writing compound words, the most ancient way was to maintain the preposition in its original form, and in no case to change its last letter into the initial of the word joined to it.

which we learn from Quinctilian continued still in use in the early part of the first century; it does not, I say, follow that exactly the same was practised by Plautus, who flourished two hundred years before the birth of Christ. But I merely hint this doubt, as one worthy the consideration of those who are better conversant than I am in the antiquities of the Latin language, and the numerous changes which during several centuries it is said to have undergone.

No. 3. It appears that Bartoli, when engraving the drawings in this MS. omitted certain inscriptions of the names of the personages, &c. represented; which in the originals are written in small characters, chiefly capitals, over, or by the side of the figures.[1] A few of these inscriptions are here introduced, copied from the plates in outline, which d'Agincourt has given of some of these drawings, traced from the originals. In the fourth inscription, on the first line, the *u*, the *l*, and the *i*, are minuscules; and in the second line we have the inscription, *Cervus Silvie*, which, from want of room to write it in capitals, the artist has written in small minuscule characters between the feet of the animal.

D'Agincourt's boasted tracings are, in these and many other instances, not such as to convey a very high idea of the merits of the originals from which they were taken. It is proper, therefore, that I should here state, that the person, who was commonly employed by him in this way, was not an artist, but a very good kind of man who acted for him, during many years at Rome, as a sort of factotum, and was so fully aware of his own incompetency in drawing, that I have more than once heard him join with Piroli (who etched the best of d'Agincourt's plates) in laughing at his own performances. When the figures in a drawing, besides being of sufficient dimensions, are drawn with a decided outline, an ignorant person, if he employ due diligence, may trace them with tolerable accuracy. But it is quite otherwise when, as in the case of the drawings in this MS., little or no outline is apparent, and the forms of the figures are defined only by lights and shadows, and broad masterly touches of the pencil; which, though productive altogether of the effect desired, it must at

---

[1] I find that these inscriptions are added to the plates, in the above edition of Bottari; but this is done without any attempt to imitate the forms of the characters, which are all represented as ordinary majuscules.

all times require the hand of a skilful artist to *translate* properly into an outline.

No. 4, gives three lines of the celebrated *Medicean MS. of Virgil*, traced from the specimen given by Foggini, in the preface to his edition of that manuscript, which was printed in 1741, at Florence, with type cast on purpose, in imitation of the characters in which it is written:

PROTINUS HINC FUSCIS TRISTIS DEA TOLLITUR ALIS
AUDACIS RUTULI AD MUROS. QUAM DICITUR URBEM.
ACRISIONEIS DANAE FUNDASSE COLONIS.

This MS. is of the form and dimensions of a square quarto, and is written throughout in capitals, without the usual separation between the words. The first part of the Bucolics are wanting; but it has all the Georgics, and Æneid. The first three lines of each book are in vermilion. Lucas Holstensius thought this MS., written towards the end of the fourth century; but other eminent critics, and among them Hensius and Card. Noris, have considered it to be much more ancient; and I incline to their opinion. It was examined and corrected by Turcius Rufus Apronianus Asterius, who was Consul in the West in the year 494; as appears from an inscription of eleven lines, closely written, at the end of the Bucolics. The first three lines of this inscription are in small capitals; but all the rest is written in minuscules; or rather, I ought to say, in a mixed character, in which minuscules preponderate.

At the end of the Bucolics, we have also:

P. VERGILI MARONIS
BUCOLICON. LIBER EXPLICIT
INCIPIT GEORGICON LIB. I. FELICITER.

the second line in red, and the other two in black; and in the space between, and above and below these lines, the above inscription of Apronianus is inserted. The different books of the Georgics and the Æneid are terminated and prefaced like the Bucolics, with the usual terms *explicit, incipit feliciter*, &c.

Upon the ancient use of the term *explicit* in MSS. the writers of the "Nouveau Traité," observe as follows, (tom. iii. p. 37): " The word *explicit*, placed at the end of a work, is not strictly Latin: it is but the abridgment of the word *explicitus*, meaning *sermo*, or *liber absolutus*. Martial (lib. xiv. 1.) says, in this sense: ' Versibus explicitum est omne duobus opus ;' and (lib. xi. 107.)

' Explicitum nobis usque ad sua cornua librum
Et quasi perlectum, Septiciane, refers.'

It was customary in the time of St. Jerome, to employ the word *explicit*, or *feliciter*, or some other similar term, to mark the end of a work, and to distinguish it from that which followed. We find in the Jurisconsults, ' explicitus est articulus.' This formula, which properly belonged to rolled volumes, passed into usage for books composed of different gatherings bound together."

No. 5. Under this number, I have given specimens both of the drawings and of the writing of a very celebrated MS. of Terence in the Vatican, No. 3868; the whole carefully copied from plates xxxv. xxxvi. of the work of d'Agincourt. The writing bears the appearance of being a good fac-simile of the characters employed in this manuscript; but I would not say so much for the figures; which, notwithstanding d'Agincourt's assurance that they were accurately traced, have, I am satisfied, lost much of the spirit of the originals.

The text of this MS. is written in minuscules, very like those in our Aratus ; but the names of the different characters who take part in the dialogue, or the first three letters of them, are written, for the sake of distinction, in capitals, before the speech of each; besides which, the names of the personages represented in the drawings are inscribed at full length, in capitals, over the figures. In addition to the drawings, which illustrate the text throughout, we have the portrait of Terence himself—a fine characteristic head—introduced within an architectural ornament, on the second leaf of the MS.; and prefixed to each drama, are representations of somewhat a large size, of the particular masks to be worn by the different characters. This MS. until d'Agincourt was pleased to ascribe it to the end of the eighth, or the beginning of the ninth century, was always thought to be one of considerable antiquity; and had it not been written in minuscules, would probably have been judged to be at least as old as the time of Constantine. I think it has been shewn that this circumstance is not against it; and as the general style of the drawings, and the costume of the figures, appear (as far as I can judge from the prints) to accord extremely well with such a period, I see no reason for placing it later.

D'Agincourt is of opinion, that these drawings are copies, done by an unskilful artist, after very ancient originals of great excellence. " The figures," he observes, " are of too short a proportion ; . . . the rude contours, done with straight lines, give none of the articulations; and we never trace the naked under the draperies. These faults, he is persuaded, were not in the originals, for the following reasons : The action of the figures is almost always in accord with the intention; the movement of the head, conformably with that of the hands, gives them a precise signification, so that they appear to speak; and the spirit of the dialogue is never wanting. The difference between the action of him who speaks, and the repose of him who listens, is always justly marked; . . . the masks themselves have surprising truth of expression, notwithstanding their extraordinary forms; and this truth causes the defective proportions of the figures to be forgotten, whilst it adds to the energy of the action : so that, notwithstanding the heaviness of the touch, the crudeness of the pencil, and the habitual incorrectness of the copyist, we still feel the merit of the original artist, and recognize in these drawings primitive compositions, which no doubt were admired for their faithful imitation of nature.

"These paintings," he adds, "make us acquainted also with the dresses of the time," [that is, of the time when the originals were done, or, perhaps he means, of the time of Terence himself,] " and of the different ways in which they were put on. We see also the particular colours worn by each of the characters. They are applied by the copyist with but little ability ; but it is to be presumed that he has faithfully preserved the kinds: these are green, blue, and red, mixed with yellow, and with certain grey tints : the hair of the male characters is black; and that of the female for the most part blond. We discover, moreover, the traces of many ancient usages, some of which are continued even at present; as that of the handkerchief, or *sudarium,* round the neck, which is still worn at Rome, by servants, and others of the laborious classes," &c.

Now there is nothing in all this that at all militates against the supposition that these drawings are really ancient ; though they may, or may not, be repetitions, or copies, done from still more ancient and better originals. Had they been copied, as d'Agincourt supposes, in the time of Charlemagne, they would not exhibit, as they do, the costume of classic times ; and as to the short proportions of the figures, on which he so much insists, he ought to have borne in mind, that the masks of the ancients, unlike ours, enclosed the whole head; and that, in consequence, persons wearing them would necessarily appear to be of short proportions. As I feel that I cannot sufficiently depend either upon the outlines given of a few of these figures by d'Agincourt, or upon the shaded prints, given of the whole, in the edition of Terence printed at Urbino in 1736, I will not remark further upon their style as works of art: we find among the paintings discovered at Herculaneum and Pompeii, a small number which are of a high class of excellence; but the greater portion are chiefly to be admired for the invention and expression, as, we are told, is the case with the drawings in this manuscript. Should any one still be disposed to think these drawings of the time of Charlemagne, let him compare d'Agincourt's prints of them, at plates xxxv. and xxxvi. with those representing the figures in a magnificent Bible done for Charlemagne, at plates xl. xliii. and xliv.: let him compare, especially, the gothic portrait of the prince, with the fine head of the Roman poet; and I think he will perceive that, in point of style, the decorations of these two MSS. have nothing in common; that the one is a work of classical times, the other a performance of a barbarous age.

D'Agincourt, after all, appears to have formed his idea of the age of this MS. not from the figures, but from the writing; which he says, "furnishes him with sufficient *criteria* to induce him to fix the epoch when the drawings were done, in the ninth century, at the latest." Now, without going into other details upon this head, I will merely observe, that *the Y in this MS. appears never to have a point over it;* and that the authors of the "Nouveau Traité," vol. ii. p. 398, assure us, among their other rules for judging of the ages of MSS., that "the more seldom we find in a MS. the letter Y surmounted by a point, the more ancient we ought to esteem the MS.:" and they add, in a note, that "those MSS. in which the Y is never, or scarcely ever, with this point over it, *bear the mark of the highest antiquity;* of the fifth century at the least," [m] &c.

---

[m] The pompous title of "Histoire de l'Art par les Monumens," is calculated to mislead the unwary into the belief that in matters of date, at least, the work of d'Agincourt is a good authority. But this is very far from being the case. What would Mabillon, Bottari, and the writers of the "Nouveau Traité de Diplomatique," have said, to any critic of their own time, who, in utter contempt of the opinions of all the best judges of such matters, beginning from the

No. 6, represents specimens of the writing in the curious MS. before spoken of (pp. 59-61), in the collection of St. Germain des Prés, which the authors of the "Nouveau Traité" believe to be made of the inner barks of trees. The writing, which is in large bold minuscule, they consider to be at least as early as the fifth century: a word, here and there, is clear enough, but so many parts are obliterated, that the general sense intended to be conveyed is beyond the reach of conjecture. The derivation of the minuscule e, from the round ϵ, which we so often find in ancient MSS. and inscriptions, (or rather the identity of the one with the other) is here clearly shewn, in the manner in which that letter is joined to letters following it; as it is also in two words in the cursive inscription, Pl. V. No. 4, spoken of at pp. 79-80, and in the word *manentium*, Pl. VI. No. 8; besides which, it is once found in our MS. of Aratus, in the word *repente*, in the line beginning "Non pauca e caelo," &c. (See our Plate XXIV. No. 5.)

No. 7. This specimen of capital and minuscule letters mixed, which the authors of the "Nouveau Traité" term uncial writing, is copied from plate xlii. of their third volume; and is from a very celebrated MS. of the Gospels, said to have been written by the hand of St. Eusebius, Bishop of Vercelli, in the middle of the fourth century:

"Dixit autem quidam illi, Domine, si pauci sunt qui salvi futuri sunt. Qui dixit ad illos, Intrate per angustum ostium, quoniam multi dico vobis quaerent nec poterunt introire."

No. 8. The word *manentium*, in minuscules, on the back of a Latin document, written in England about the year 670. See p. 104.

fifteenth century, had ventured to ascribe the celebrated MS. of Virgil in the Vatican, No. 3867, to the twelfth or thirteenth century; that MS. which is all written in the largest sized capitals, and has always been considered at least as early as the Medicean MS.! And yet this is what d'Agincourt has been pleased to do, upon the sole ground that the drawings which it contains are ill done; as if at all times there had not been bad artists as well as good. The *costume* in these drawings is decidedly ancient, and the MS. has all the other marks of genuine antiquity. See numerous specimens of its orthography, in the supplement to the "Antiquissimi Virgiliani Codicis Fragmenta," &c. edited by the above-mentioned Bottari, in 1741; in which work, among the plates engraved by Bartoli from the admired drawings in the MS. No. 3225, are a few taken by him from this MS. 3867, which was probably not written more than a century or two later than the other.

No. 9, represents five lines of excellent minuscule writing, from the celebrated *MS. of St. Hilarius, in the Vatican*, which has already been mentioned, and is, I believe, written throughout in this character. It appears from a marginal note of the time, that this manuscript was revised at Kasulis in Africa, in the year 510; so that it was probably written, in part, at the close of the preceding century, and possibly earlier :

" Non sum nescius difficillimo me asperrimoque tempore scribere et haec adversum vesanā inpiorum heresim dī *(dei)* filium creaturam esse adfirmantem adgressum fuisse, multis iam per omnes ferme romani inperii provincias" *(ecclesiis morbo pestiferae huius praedicationis infectis.)*

No. 10. I close these specimens of early minuscule writing with two passages from the MS. of *Severus Sulpicius*, spoken of by Maffei in his " *Verona Illustrata*," (see our p. 102), and which, as he observes, and as appears from the last extract, was written by a clerk of that city, who completed it on the first day of August, in the year 517:

" Explicit dialogus de vitâ beati Martini episcopi et confessoris per Severum Sulpicium monachum Massiliensem."

" Obsecro quicumque haec legis, ut Hieronymi peccatoris memineris : cui si Dominus optionem daret multò magis elegeret tunicam Pauli cum meritis ejus quam Regum purpuras cum meritis suis.

" Explicit vita beati Pauli monachi Thebei. Perscribtus codix hec Veronâ de vita beati Martini episcopi et confessoris et beati Pauli. Suprà scribta sub die kalendarum augustarum Agapito viro clarissimo Consule indictionis decimae per Ursicinum lectorem ecclesiae Veronensis."

I do not think that I need add anything further, in proof of the ancient use of writing in minuscules. The inscriptions in our Plate IV. (all of which are certainly of the first century) furnish examples of almost all the minuscule or cursive alphabet: the *a* being found in No. 2, and No. 19 ; the *b* in Nos. 4, 7, and 8 ; [the *c* I need not insist upon, as the majuscule letter is of the same form as the minuscule] ; the *d* in No. 15 ; the round ϵ, which may be considered as identical with the minuscule, in No. 3, and the cursive *e* in No. 7 ; the *f* in Nos. 3, and 12 ; a near approximation to the *g* in No. 10, and to the *h* in No. 3; the *i* in Nos. 1ª, 2, 17, 18, and 19 ; the *k* in Nos. 6, and 11 ; the *l* in No. 1ª, and No. 4 ; [the *o* I need not speak of, as it is the same in large and small writing]; the *p* in No. 1ᵃ; the *q* in No. 19; the *s*, in all its various shapes, in Nos. 3, 14, 17, 18, and 19; the *t* in Nos. 1ᵃ, 14, 17, and 18; and the *v* and *u* in Nos. 7, 14, and 19. I think I have proved the Vatican fragments of Virgil to be fully as ancient as the above, and this further gives us the minuscule *r*. (See Plate VI. No 3.)

The precise age of several of the inscriptions in Plate V. is not known, but they are all ancient Roman; and I think that their contents, super-added to the above, and taken in conjunction with the remarks of the erudite Marini, in his work upon the "Arvale Tables," (see our p. 123) ought to be considered as furnishing ample evidence in proof of what I have contended for.

I need add nothing concerning the specimens given from MSS. in our Plate VI. unless to request the reader to compare the minuscule writing from the Vatican Terence, given in No. 5, with the engraved specimens of the writing in our MS. of Aratus.

I shall, however, take this opportunity of stating that, since this Paper was read at the rooms of our Society, I have had the pleasure of inspecting at Leyden, a MS. much celebrated by Grotius, of the translation of Aratus's Poem by Germanicus. This MS., which has the good fortune to be in as perfect preservation as if it had been written and decorated only ten years ago, appears certainly to be of very high antiquity, and has numerous classical figures of the constellations painted in body colours, which Grotius caused to be engraved by Jac. de Gheyn, and published, with the text itself, in the year 1600, in his well-known work, entitled "Syntagma Arateorum." The text in this MS. is written, opposite the drawings, in capitals not very unlike those of the Medicean Virgil, but perhaps a little larger, and more freely and loosely executed: among the letters which struck me as remarkable, I remember noticing several instances of the H, formed exactly as it is in the word HOC, in the last line of the inscription of *Vero*, in our Plate V. No. 5; and I may add, that the words in this MS. are to the full as well divided from each other by spaces, as they are in the poem of Cicero in our ancient MS. But the principal cause of my here mentioning this Leyden MS. is that it has a beautiful planisphere, evidently done by the same artist as the other drawings, and of which an engraving may be seen in the work of Grotius, opposite page 36; and that *this planisphere is illustrated throughout by inscriptions in very small minuscule of the greatest beauty, carefully written within the different circles, marking the orbits of the heavenly bodies,* in the way represented in the said plate, and that I think there is not the smallest doubt that they were written at the same time as the rest of the manuscript. I may add, that the *palimpsests* of Cicero and Fronto, published by the learned Mai, furnish further evidence of the ancient use of cursive and minuscule writing.

I HAVE been under the necessity of making this Dissertation a long one. When first I undertook the task of proving the antiquity of the manuscript, which chance had thrown in my way, all those who, from the nature of their avocations, were the most likely to be well practised in determining the dates of early MSS., were, for the reasons before given, decidedly opposed to me in opinion; and it, therefore, became incumbent upon me, to go at some length into details of proof, touching the ancient use of minuscule writing; and to introduce long extracts from eminent foreign writers, shewing their opinions on the matter; in the hope that that respect might be willingly shewn to their judgment, which I did not flatter myself with supposing would be paid to my own.

I have been also actuated by another consideration: for, besides that IT IS SOMETHING FOR A PUBLIC LIBRARY TO POSSESS A CLASSICAL MS. OF THE SECOND OR THIRD CENTURY, *the question touching the ancient use of minuscule writing is one of great importance, upon general grounds. For I cannot but suspect, that the genuineness of* SOME *of the earliest English charters and other documents, in the Cottonian volume, Aug. A. II., was doubted by the author of the catalogue of them, for the sole reason that they are written in good cursive or minuscule characters; and I think it extremely probable, that the prejudice against the antiquity of that kind of writing, which, until now, has been so firmly rooted among us, may have, and has, occasioned various MSS. in our collections to be placed several centuries later than their true date.* [n]

I suspect that the same, though in a smaller degree, has happened on the

[n] Several MSS., written entirely, or in part, in beautifully formed minuscules, are indeed attributed to the eighth century, in the catalogue of the Harleian Collection; and these MSS. every way correspond with known MSS. of the time of Charlemagne, at Rome and elsewhere: and, besides these, the British Museum possesses other MSS. written in minuscules, some of which, upon a nice examination, would probably be found to be considerably older.

continent, where this opinion prevailed almost universally till the beginning of the last century, and where I have reason to believe it in some measure prevails still.[o] We have seen that in the middle of that century, notwithstanding all that had been said in its confutation by Maffei and others, the authors of the " Nouveau Traité de Diplomatique," still thought it necessary to write against it; as they were aware that numerous adherents of the old school still existed every where. Indeed, even they themselves, if two very early MSS. had been put before them, the one written entirely in capitals, the other entirely in minuscules, or part in capitals and part in minuscules, would, I think, in the absence of other evidence on one side or the other, have at once ascribed the greater antiquity to the former; notwithstanding that they admit, in the fullest manner, that minuscule writing was well known to the ancient Romans and every where taught by them to the people whom they conquered.

I entirely agree in opinion with these learned writers, that the *pauperes schedulae*, which St. Jerom contrasts to the magnificent volumes written in large capital letters of gold or silver, were no other than copies of the Holy Scriptures, written in minuscule characters. It cannot be doubted that this unostentatious kind of book was much more common in Jerom's time than the other; and, on the whole, I think, we have the best reason to conclude, that for manuscripts done for ordinary persons, and more especially for treatises, histories, &c. minuscule and cursive writing had, long before, been much more commonly used than writing in capitals; although this last, as the most dignified mode, continued for some centuries afterwards to be occasionally adopted in transcribing the works of eminent poets, and in copying books of devotion, especially the Psalter and the four Gospels, for persons of exalted rank, or for the use of churches. I shall only add, that when we come to the sixth century, the number of Latin MSS. written in different parts in this character, appears to be so considerable, as to leave, I think, no doubt that this sort of writing had been commonly used long previously throughout the Roman empire.

[o] Angelo Mai, for example, betrays this in his Prefaces; and Kopp, in various parts of his Palæographia; especially, where he speaks of the ancient cursive inscriptions, given by Buonarruoti, (see our Plate V. Nos. 3, 4.) as being in *uncial* characters : but I write this note from memory, without having before me the particular passages in these writers from which I infer this, and feel no desire to re-enter upon the controversy.

ΕΡΑΤω ΤΑΛΤΡΙΑΝ   ΛΛ Fρ Π ΛΛ ΤVΤΙLLVM

ὡς ἔνσο δὸρ βέλευμα τὰς πολλὰς χεῖρας νικᾶ

POR V AUSTR E URBEM
OPSIDIONE·TAMEN·N C·CORPORA·MOENIBUS·A NT·
CASTRAQUE·PRO·MURIS·ATQUE·ARMA·PEDESTRIA·PONUNT·
HOS·INTER·COETUS·ALISQUE·AD·BELLA·PARATUS·
UTRAQUE·SOLLEMNIS·ITERUM·REVOCAVERAT·ORBES·
CONSILIIS·NOX·APTA·DUCUM·LUX·APTIOR·ARMIS·

A A·B·C D E E·F F·G G·H H·I I I·L·M·N·O·P P·Q·R R·S S·T I·U U U V·X X·

BAINFVMVINERIVMHNONGENTUM TABERNAE PERGVLAE   DVOBVS·ELB IIS·FELI
CENACVLA·EX·IDIBVS·AVG·PRIMIS·IN·IDVS·AVG·SEXTAS·ANNOS·CONTINVOS·QVINQVE   PVG·N·V·IIII·III·PR·K·DEC·VENAT

POSTVMIVM·PROCVM   M·HOLCONIVM·PRISCVM   M·CERRINIVM
                           C·GAVIVM·RVFVM·IIVIR   AED·SALVIENSES
AED·POTHINVS·ROG   PHOEBVS·CVM·EMPTORIBVS   ROG·
FER TVNNVM   SVIS ROGAT
                                                      VNIVERSI·ROG
V·APRIL VENATIO ET VELA ERVNT   MESSIVS
                                                      DEFEMORIBVS·COLONI·

Gellius   POPIDIVM   V TAELIVS
Cymplod   ANATEΛΛωNANATEI
                       GEMELLV   GESTANICHE   NONTECEICTOMEPOCTHC
                                                      ΠΑCHCΠEH COYMET·
                                                      BHMENEKTOY TO TH
                       Valens   Sal   ΜΙΝΔΤΟΜΕΝΟCΦΑΙ
                                                      NETAIOTPEΠOΛMN
                                                      ENIO TETΛNYT ΠΠMC
                                                      EBHKOCIN Λ
                                                      ΤΟΤΟΤΚΕ ΝΑΥΤΥC

Plate V Vol XXVI p 144

N° 1
ZINNVMLOCI·QVIITINI·ET
MARTVRIAE ☙

2
DIOGENIA FILIAE
BONAE QVAE VIXIT
ANNOS (EX)ı ıoX
DIOGENES PATER IN F ELIX

3
OPUS ΑΤΤΙΣΙΟΝΙΣ ΑΦΡΟΔΙΣΙΕΝΙΣ

4
ωτζωπυραττη ηατ ετ ψιδυτπουbωb υρσοτρολ ϭmjο ϲϡϥ

5
VERO DULCISSIMO FILIO PARENTES
QUI BENE MERENTI INSECULO VIXIT AN
NUM ENSIIII ET DIES XIII EX KOC DEFUNCTEST XVIII KAL MAI

6
POSVIT · TABVLA MA
GISTER DISCENTI
PANPINO BE NEM
ERENTI

7
D·   M·
Q·TERENTI·PRISCIANI
VIXII·ANNIS·IIII·MEN
SI DVS·VII ·FRVMENTVM
PVBLICVM·ACCEPIT·MEN
SI DVS· VIIII·
TERENTIA·SABINA
ALVMNO· FECIT·

8
ASINDRPRE

9
TROΛΟΛS

10
SARINA VIXIT AN
NOS XVIIII MENSES VI DS XIII
SERNA FECIT SE GIBO

11
DOMITI
IN PACE
ΧΕ Λ FECIT

12
INNOCENTIA CONIV NXLSSI GVARIS
QVAE CVM EVM VIXIT BEATE
ANNIS X OIES DVODECIM
QVAE DES AECVLO EXIBIT
I DIBVS AVG GALLICANO CONS·

13
EVAGRENI·FILIAE·CARISSIME·BENE
MERENTI QVE VIXIT AN·XVIIII·M·VII·DXXIII
MAXINVS ET·P·ALAME·PARENTES·FECERVNT
DECES·IIII·NON·OCTO

14
RINCENTIVS KARO FILIO KA
RISSIMO BENEMERENTI POSVIT
TABVLA QVI BIXIT ANNOSIII
ET DIES XXII·

15
ΑΣΧΕΝΘΙωΡΚΙΛΙω·ΔΥΛΚΙϹϹΙΤΙω·EBE
πεπερεθι·ΑϹΘΙΑΠϹΕΠΛΘ·BΠΔΕΛΙΚϹϹ
ΔΕΚΥΠω·ϹΚϹθΑΤΠωΤϹΠΗ·ΕΕΔωΚΙΑ·ΤΗΚΕ
ΠΑΤΕΠΘΕϹΙΠ·ΠΑΚΕϹΙΚϹΙΘ·ΑΤΠ·L·Π·I
ϹΕΝΤΙΑΠΥΣ FISELIS QVIASCIMVSTEINΣ

16
D   M   S
EVEVSTOR NATIANVS
FILIVS BONVS VIS EMPER
PARENTIBVS OBSEQVENS
EVCHARIS   hoC

Published by the Society of Antiquaries of London April 28 1836

A O FORTUNA OFOR; FORTUNA QUAN
QVAM SUBITO MEO FROM TIENON

PROTINUSHINCEUSCISTRIS
AUDACISAUTULIADMUROS
ACRISIONEISDANAEFUNDA

GALESUS	TROIANI	LATINVS	MU li
AGRESTES	ANCHISES	CREVSA	Cornu silue
AENEAS	FAMULA	LAOCOON	ANGVES	CENTAVRI

MYSIS

DIXIT AUTEM
QUIDAM ILLI
DMES IPAU
CISUNT QUI
SALUIFUTU
ERISUNT
QUI DIXIT AD IL
LOS INTRATE
PER ANGUS

TUM OSTIUM
QUONIAM MUL
TI DICO UOBIS
QUAERENT
NEC POTERUN
INTROIRE

miseram me quod
uerbum audio

TUM

anums....   mangritium †

CH difficill, mo me capere, mo que
ere et hue ea duersum uerana
PROJE sim dispiscum creatur amerre
n ad zr errum sunt re multi ICM
PH mero man in perup prouinctus

DEMI PHOGEIA

oz ur deuit a beati
et conressions p reuenum
monachum martgen rem
cumq, haec lez ir uthieronrm
mem in enir cum dnr optionem
tomaz ire le zenet
aul cum menti resur
m purpur ar cum menti erruir
a. beati pauli monachi che be
btur. Co dix hec. de uita beat

dichazio HEG oro er pi et confser beati paul, SS
CRI mene undem da u'z'j azapiro uc c Indi de cimae
ABCDEFGHNILMNOP léct, ecclesiae ueronen sir

I now come to describe our ancient manuscript of Cicero's translation of Aratus; and, in doing so, shall speak also, as I have said, of the two others, which were copied from it, one in the tenth century, and the other, perhaps, considerably earlier. It may seem strange that, although all the three MSS. contain ten lines of the Poem, in addition to those hitherto known, and furnish improved readings throughout, they have until now escaped the researches of every editor of it. But this is in some measure to be accounted for, by the way in which they are spoken of in the catalogues.

In the catalogue of the Harleian Collection, vol. i. p. 397, our ancient MS., which consists of only twenty-one leaves, is thus described, under No. 647:

"FRAGMENTS OF A VERY ANCIENT MANUSCRIPT IN SQUARE FOLIO.

1. "A leaf written in *Anglo-Saxon characters*, in which is treated of the celestial signs: *Scorpione, Sagittarius, Aquarius, Pisces*, &c. (fol. 1.)

"Then follows, in *Gallican* writing, about a thousand years old:

2. "De claris stellis post Orionem sub signo Geminorum positis, &c. (fol. 2.) and

3. "A prayer of the author or compiler of the work to the Holy Trinity, imploring that his labours may be beneficial to others.

4. "Then follow representations of the Constellations, elegantly painted in the Roman manner; the accounts of them by Julius Hyginus being written within the figures in capital letters. Metrical explications, also, from the Phaenomena of Aratus, are added underneath the figures, written in minuscule characters, which, from a note on the margin of the first page, we find to be from " *Ciceronis de Astronomia*," (fol. 2, *verso*, to 13.)

5. "The heads of Jupiter, Sol, Mars, Venus, and Mercury. (fol. 13, *verso*.)

6. "Then follow verses of Cicero from Aratus, without figures. (fol. 14, 15.)

7. "Part of the work of *some astronomical poet*, with a marginal commentary in prose, written more than 700 years ago, containing prognostics, and observations concerning the clouds, fire, water," &c. &c. (fol. 16, 17.)

Here the remaining lines of Cicero's poem are considered as the performance of an unknown author; whilst the *Prognostics*, from the eighteenth book of *Pliny*, which are written in the margin, are treated as the notes of a scholiast. The first of these errors may be thus accounted for. It happens that the writing on the *verso* of fol. 15, terminates abruptly in our ancient MS. half way down the page, with the 340th line of the poem,

"*Signifero ex orbi sex signorum ordine fultum :*"

the rest of the page is left blank; the leaf which should come next is wanting; and, as what follows is written in a somewhat smaller hand, the writer of the Catalogue too hastily concluded that it was the composition of some other poet. The remaining contents of the MS. beginning on the verso of fol. 17, immediately under the last line of the poem, comprise extracts upon astronomical subjects, from the works of *Macrobius*, and *Felix*, or *Martianus Capella*; the *recto* of the last leaf having no writing, but presenting on the other side a planisphere, by a monk of the name of Geruvigus, a fac-simile of which is given in our Plate XXII.

Both the Copies contain other matter, besides the entire contents of the ancient MS. The oldest of the two, as I think, is in the Harleian collection, and will be found under the title of *Julius Hyginus*, in the second volume of the Catalogue, page 697, No. 2506, where it is thus described :

"A MANUSCRIPT ON PARCHMENT, IN WHICH ARE CONTAINED:

1. " *C. Jul. Hygini* ad M. Fabium Astronomicum, &c.
2. " Anonymi opusculum Astronomicum," &c.

And now follows the description of what is taken from our ancient MS.:

3. " An Anonymous treatise on the twelve Zodiacal Signs, and the other Constellations, beginning : ' Domine Deus Omnipotens, Sancta Trinitas,' &c.
4. " *An Anonymous Poem*, describing the heavenly bodies, with figures, and an enumeration of the stars in each constellation, &c.
5. " A small anonymous tract, entitled, ' De concordia Solaris cursus et Lunaris,' " &c.

We need not go further : in the fourth article, Cicero's juvenile performance is treated as the work of an unknown poet; and in the fifth, the Prognostics of Pliny are also styled anonymous.

The Poem in this MS also, is illustrated by figures of the Constellations ; but here they are outlined with a pen, and lightly shaded with bistre, and without any colouring : besides which, the designs, though they represent the same constellations, and occupy the same situations in the Poem, are different.

The other Copy makes part of a very thick MS. in the Cottonian Collection, Tiberius, B. v.

The Poem is spoken of in the Catalogue, under article 39 of the MS. to this effect: " The Constellations and other heavenly bodies represented in elegant figures, with prose explications of them from Hyginus; and others, in verse, from the Phaenomena of Aratus, which Cicero in his youth translated into the Latin language; and of which the first verse is:

"A quibus hinc subter possis cognoscere fultum."

In the sequel of the description of this MS., also, the prognostics of Pliny are spoken of as the work of an unknown writer. This inadvertency will readily be pardoned; but one cannot but feel surprised that neither of the learned writers of the above two catalogues, should have thought it worth while to look into one of the printed editions of Cicero's Aratea; by which he would immediately have discovered, that the MS. before him contained, at the end of the poem, nine lines not heretofore known, and a tenth in another place.

I have already mentioned a leaf being wanting in the ancient MS. A second also is deficient in an earlier part of the poem; and at the beginning of the volume, two leaves are lost, which had been doubtless prefixed by the first Christian possessor of it, (most probably the above-mentioned Geruvigus), and on which he had piously written a Christian account of the wonders of the heavens, and, condemning the fables of the Pagans, ascribed the glory of them to the only true God. It is this treatise which ends on the *recto* of the second leaf, with a prayer to the Holy Trinity. (See the lower part of this page carefully imitated in our Plate XXIV. No. 2.) The first leaf of the MS., so unlike all the rest, as well in the quality of the parchment and the colour of the ink, as in the forms of the characters, is the second of two leaves, whereon, in the eleventh century perhaps, the contents of the two lost leaves were copied from some other MS. by a Saxon scribe, in order to make good the deficiency. It is remarkable that this person so miscalculated the space which their contents would occupy, as to complete his task before he had got to the middle of the fourth page (that is, the *verso* of the first leaf of the MS. as it is at present); for we find, from both the copies above described, (which were made before the ancient MS. had suffered mutilation), that the passage ending, "*tempus ostendunt occasu hiemem*," with which the writing on that page terminates, is immediately followed by the passage, "*Item claras stellas post Orionem*," &c. with which the page following (now the *recto* of fol. 2,) commences. The two first paragraphs of the first page of fol. 1, and the three concluding lines on the *verso* of that leaf, are accurately copied in our Plate XXIV. No. 3. I ought to mention, that, in both the copies, the prayer to the Holy Trinity is *prefixed* to the above Christian account of the constellations; whilst in the ancient MS. *it is placed at the end*. Upon a careful perusal of the entire page which contains it, in the ancient MS., my friend Mr. Prevost (to whom I am also indebted for his learned observations on the readings in the poem, to be produced hereafter,) could discover no error, no barbarism, in the Latin; and he is therefore of opinion, that I am justified in considering this part of the MS. as, properly speaking, original. As a compilation, the MS. is certainly original: the first part of the poem of Cicero, as far as fol. 15, having been written by one hand; its continuation by another; the passages from Macrobius and Felix Capella, by a third; and the above Christian treatise by a fourth writer: whilst in each of the two copies, on the contrary, the entire contents of the ancient MS. are in the same hand-writing.

The most ancient part of this MS. when first executed, must have had a very gay appearance; as well from the painted figures, as from the different coloured inks, used, for the sake of ornamental variety, in the text. It was doubtless for the sake of this variety, that the poem was written under the figures in minuscules, and the text of Hyginus, within them, in small capitals; this last kind of writing having been preferred for the figures, because of the regularity in the heights of the letters, and the means it afforded of making the lines of the writing very close together and at the same time distinct from each other; so that by it a certain evenness of tint might be obtained, which was desirable in the writing within the figures, but might be dispensed with in the verses below. The MS. appears originally to have commenced on the *verso* of the first leaf of a gathering of eight leaves (now the second leaf in the book), with the figure of the constellation *Aries*, and the verses of Cicero underneath, commencing with the line,

"E quibus hinc subter possis cognoscere fultum."

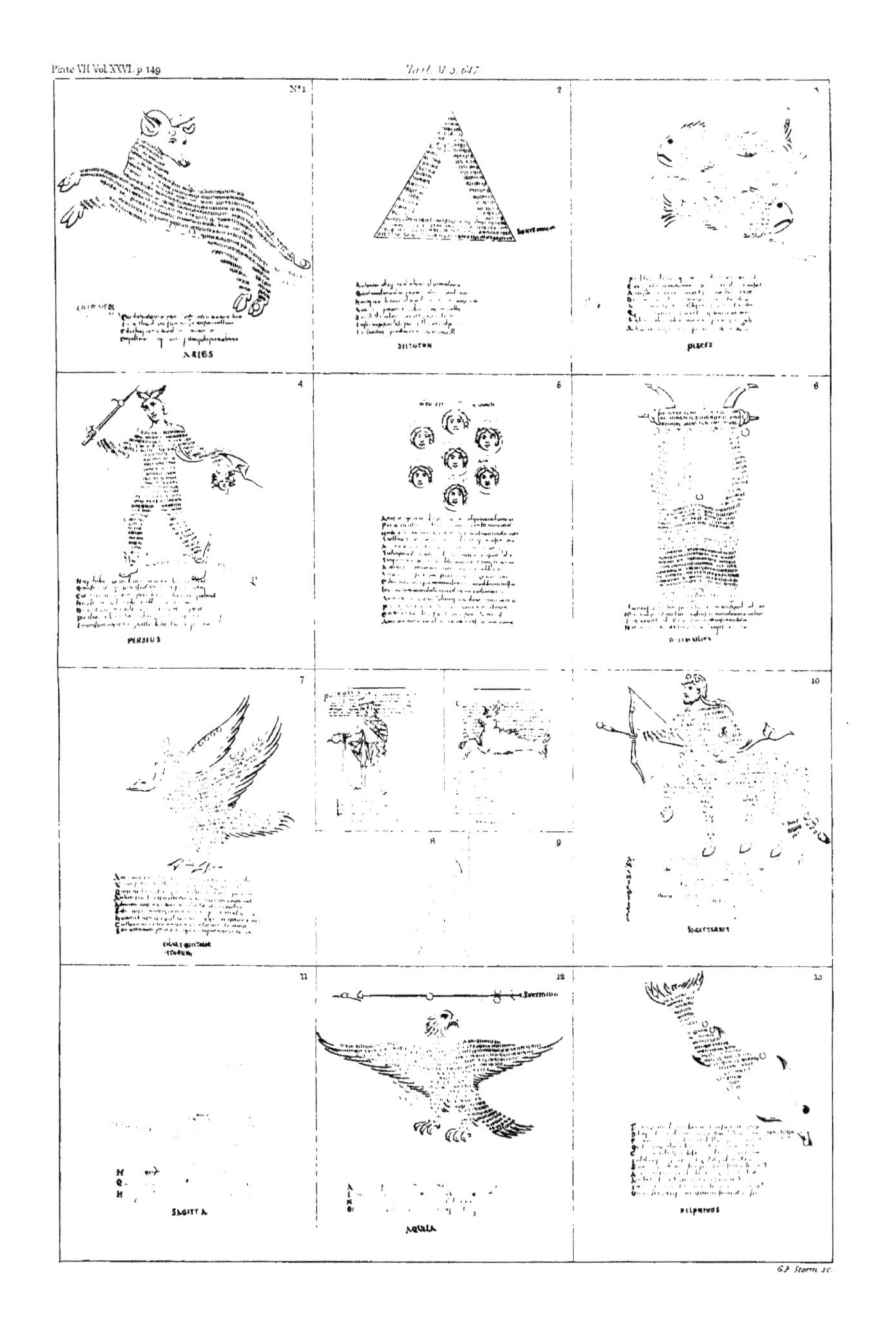

As far as I can learn, all the MSS. of Cicero's Aratea existing, begin with this same verse; two hundred and thirty-four previous verses being wanting, according to Grotius;[p] and there therefore seems some reason to doubt if Cicero ever translated the entire poem.

It appears to have been customary, from the first, to illustrate the Phaenomena of Aratus with drawings; and in doing this the artists employed are said to have sometimes taken unwarrantable liberties with the text, in order to make it accord with their figures. Grotius speaks at length on this subject, in his notes on the translation by Germanicus, page 2, and there may be some ground for the accusation. On the other hand, it may be doubted whether the preservation of the poem at all (I speak as well of the original as of the different Latin translations) is not mainly to be attributed to the same cause: since, in the most barbarous times, those persons who were incapable of appreciating the writing, may still be reasonably supposed to have attached some value to the decorations. Another circumstance operated in favour of this poem with the early Christians; namely, that St. Paul had quoted part of the fifth verse of it, in his discourse to the Athenians; as appears, chap. xvii. ver. 28, in the Acts of the Apostles.

I have caused all the pages in our ancient MS. that are ornamented with drawings, to be engraved, upon a reduced scale, in Plates VII. and VIII.; and the copies in the Cottonian MS. Tib. B. v. in Plates IX. X. and XI.; besides which, the last mentioned plate contains two specimens of the figures in the Harl. MS. 2506, the designs of which, as I have said, are different from those in the other two manuscripts. These plates, though small, shew distinctly the distribution of the writing in the ancient MS. and the Cottonian copy, and the number of verses introduced under each figure; and will even convey to the reader a sufficiently accurate idea of the strange differences that occur between some of the Saxon copies and the classic originals; though, for this purpose, I have also caused a few pieces of both series to be engraved of the full size.

[p] "Syntagma Areteorum," p. 8. The MS. fragments at Leyden, which Grotius used, and which I lately examined in the library of the University of that city, begin with this line, upon the *verso* of a leaf, the *recto* of which has been left blank, as appears to have been originally the case in our ancient MS.

So perfect an idea of all the different kinds of writing employed in this MS. is given in Mr. Storm's fac-similes, that I need say little or nothing of the forms of the letters; and I shall therefore chiefly confine my present remarks to the figures; in enumerating which, I shall avail myself, as I go along, of the observations of Spence, in that chapter of his Polymetis wherein he describes the figures of the constellations, as they appear sculptured upon an ancient celestial Globe, supported by a figure of Atlas, in the Farnese collection of antique statues; a monument unique in its kind, and which is commonly known under the title of *the Farnese Globe.*

No. 1. ARIES, or the Ram, "turning his head backward:" Spence observes that he is so represented, also, on the Farnese Globe, and so described by Manilius, in several places. Under this figure are the first four lines of the poem, beginning, "E quibus hinc subter," &c.; in the margin, on the left, we read; "CICERONIS DE ASTRONOMIA;" and at bottom, we have the name of the constellation in capital letters, in minium, as is the case with all the others. Both the text within the figure, and the verses below, are written in a light brown tint; the initials of the poem are written with minium throughout the volume. Near the tail of the animal, we read: SUNT STELLAE. XVII.

2. DELTOTON; with seven lines of the poem underneath. The text of Hyginus, which in the ancient MS. is written in the figure, is inserted behind it in the Cotton MS. and so with the other figures: the part occupied by the writing in the original MS. is moreover filled with interlaced ornament by the Saxon copyist. The text within the figure in the ancient MS. is written with minium, and the verses with the same brown tint as the last. SUNT STELLAE. III.

3. PISCES; with eight lines of the poem; but, as I have said, the small plates shew correctly the number of verses under each figure; and I shall not in future state them. Both the prose text and the verses are written with the above-mentioned brown tint.

"The river," says Spence, "which has its source from the urn of *Aquarius,* goes in some of its windings to *Pisces.* . . . The poets mark both their places (viz. of the two fishes) very exactly, and their being turned different ways."

"Dissimile est illis iter, in contraria versis." (Manilius, 2. v. 164.) And so they appear in our manuscript.

4. PERSEUS. The text within the figure is written with minium, and the

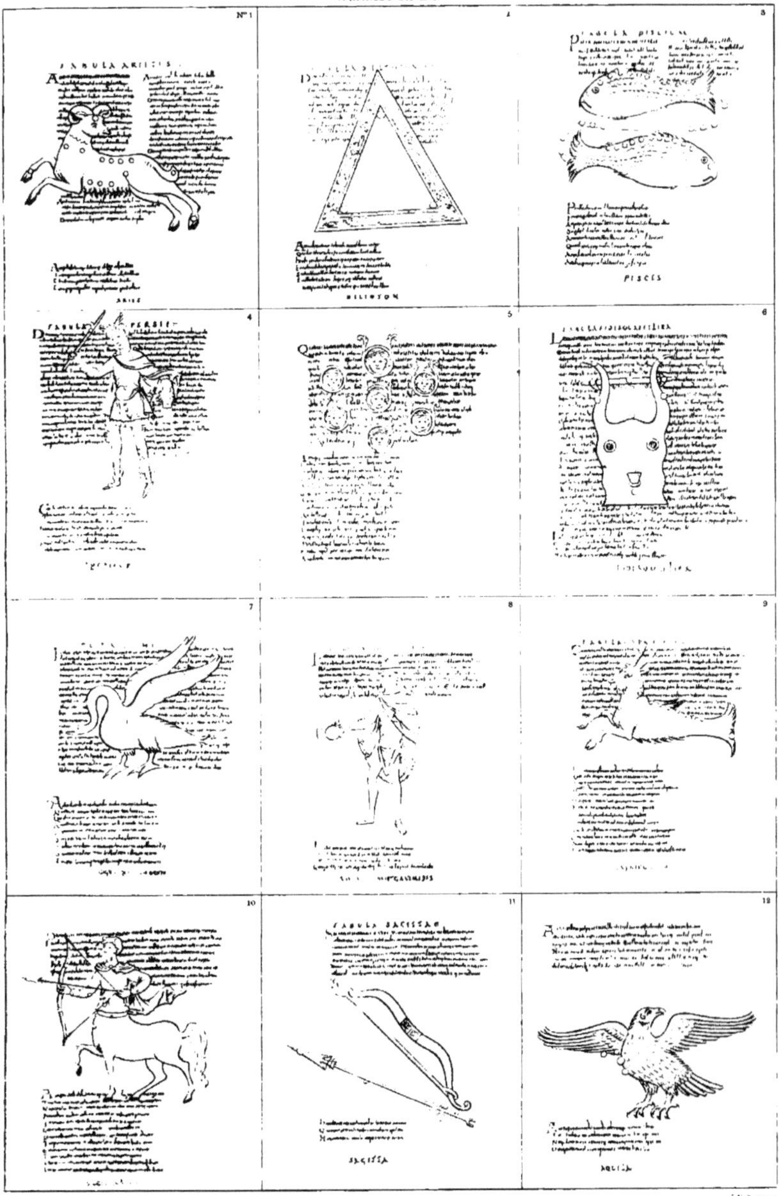
Nº 1
ARIES
PISCES
FABULA SAGITTAE
SAGITTA
AQUILA

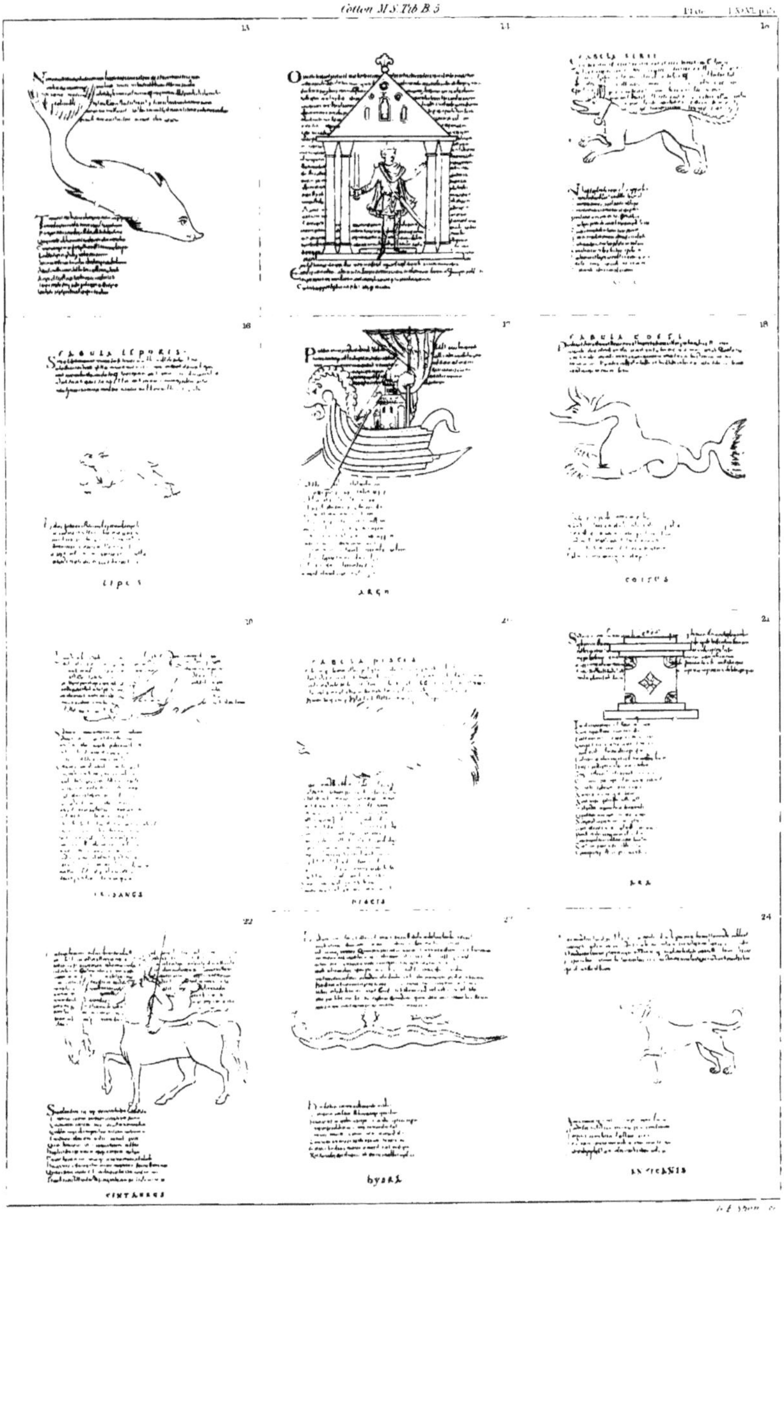
FABULA LEPORIS
LEPUS
ARGO
FABULA CETI
CETUS
ERIDANUS
FABULA PISCIS
PISCIS
ARA
CENTAURUS
HYDRA
ANTICANIS

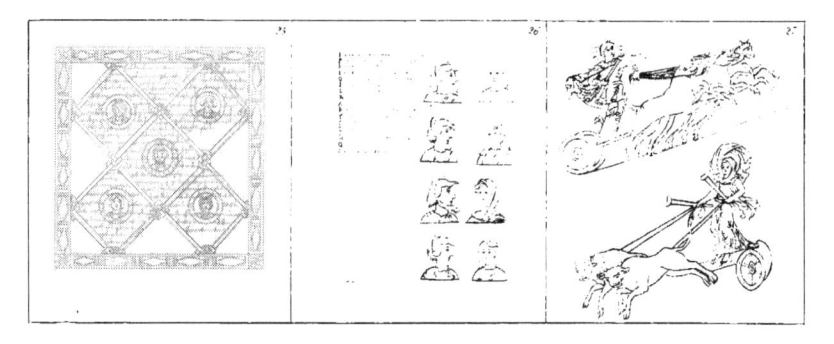

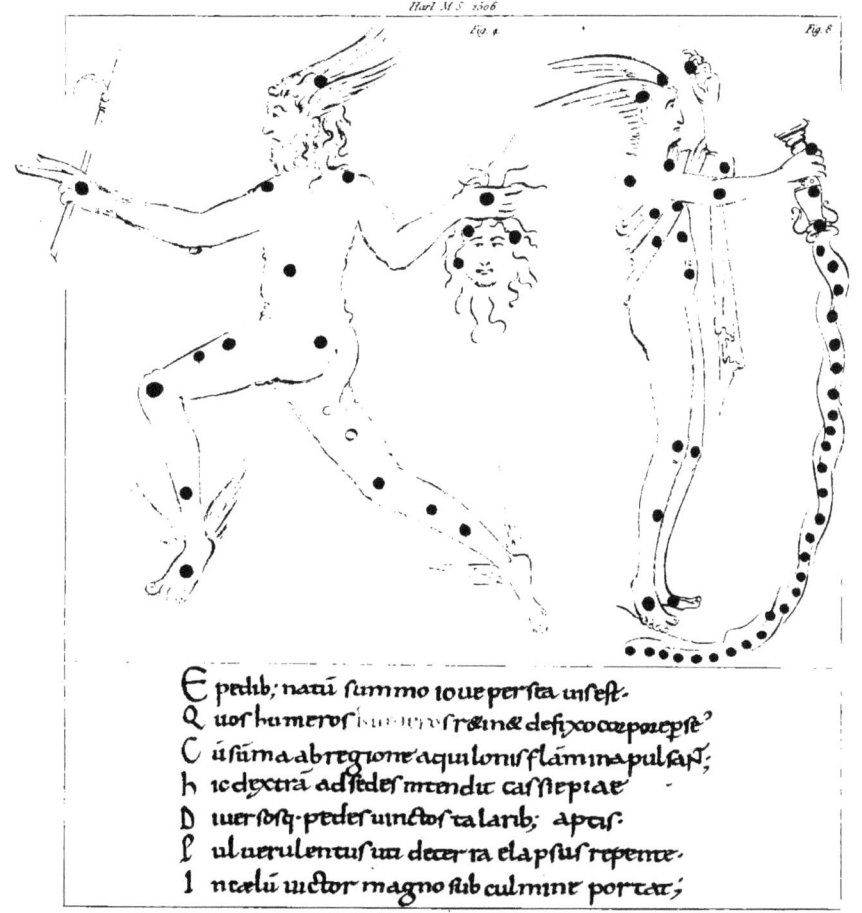

E pedib; natū summo ioue persta infest.
Q uor humeros [...] regine defixo cœpotepse?
C ū sūma a bregione aquilonis flamina pulsans;
h ic dextrā ad sedes intendit cassiepiae
D iuersosq; pedes uinctos talarib; aptas·
P ul uerulentus uia decerpta elapsus repente.
I n cælū uictor magno sub culmine portat;

PERSEUS HIC NOBILITATIS CAUSA
ET QUOD NOVO GENERE CONCUBI
TUS ERAT NATUS AD SIDERA DICITUR
PERUENISSE QUI MISSUS APOLLO DECIT ALIA
SENTISSI POTERAT UIDERI QUAM IS
GRAECIA IDOS DIXERUNT
NON UT QUIDAM INSCI
ENTISSIME INTERPRE
TANTUR EUMORCIGA
LE EUSUM QUAE RES
NEMINI DOCTO PRO
BARI POTEST FERTUR
ETIAM AQUI CANO FAL
CEM ACCEPISSE EX ADA
MANTE FACTAM EX QUA
MEDUSAM GORGONAM
INTER FECIT QUOD FACTUM
NEMO NON SCIT IN PALUDEM
RUPSIT SED UT RIT O NIDAM
AIT AESCHYLUS PROIECIT ITA
IN PHORCI SU QUE CUSTODI
QUAE UTRAE BUS EXCECA
UI UNO OCU IS FACILE IO
LO USAE ET RGO NIDA
ISTI MAN SOMNO DOM
TU RETITIA AMIN TEE SEA
SUO QUAE CITOCULESO
QUE TEMPO PUL MINER
RE ACCEPTO UAD PECTO
OCULO UICI RE BERECU
LASSE HUN ESSENIS
C PERSEUS UA
ETIAM ER
AEMUL
GELLI
SAEST
UISD
UA

SUNT STELLAE

E pedibus natur summo Ioue peractus est
Quo umeros retinet defixo corpore Perseus:
Cum summa a regione aquilonis flamina pulsat:
Hic dextram ad sedes intendit Cassiepiam
Diuersosque pedes uinctos talaribus aptis:
Puluerulentus uti de terra elapsus repente
In caelum uictor magnum sub culmine portat

·PERSEUS·

FABULA PERSEI

Dextra leuaq: pisces extendit adsocer: abstulit ermineue tradidit:
sedem cephei indelica pa- ansandrome- ed illo insuo pectore. Perseum
de cuius pedibus caput prefati pisces aut- uero intersidera collocasse opinatur.
longe stellarum ordi- ne consurcui Habet autem singulas stellas
et dicitur duce fa- bulose- insingulis humeris. Inmanu
inter astra collocatus e dextera nitida una Inmanu
qd Iuppiter insimilitudine aurei sinistra una incubito
imbris se transformans delusa deang- sinistra- Ingorgonis
eum ienuerit. Quæ missa apolidet io capite in uentre
iussu mercurii accepta a uulca- Indextra parce
no falce adamantina pilea lumboru cada i
iter faciens adgorgonas pro- Index tuo femore cada i
ficitur. Que dum tres sorores Ingenu i Insinistra ubi a duas
fierent uno oculo una uidelicet Ingorgonis omnib. iii. Inubia i
pulchritudine utebantur. Equib In sinistro femore unam insinistro-
unaque medusa dicebatur caput sunt insumma decem et
nonam. caput et falx
absque astris
sunt.

E pedibus natum summo ioue perseauis est.
Quos humeros retinet defixo corpore perseus
um summa dbregione aquilonis flamina pulsant
hic dextram adsedes intendit cassie pig
uersosq: pedes uinctos talaribus aptis.
Puluerulentas uti decerta elapsus repente
ncelum auctor magno subculmine postat.

VII. PLIADES MEROPE vel ATHLANTIDES
ALCYONE CELAENO
ELECTRA
TAYGETE ASTEROPE
MAIA

27 At propter leuum genus, omni parte locatas
    Paruas uergilias tenui cum luce uidebis.
    Haec septem uulgo perhibentur more uetusto.
30 Stellae cernuntur uero, exundique paruae.
31 Ac non interiisse putari conuenit unam.
    Sed frustra temere diuulgaratione singulla
    Septem dicier, ut uetere restatuere poetae.
    Aeterno cunctas sano qui nomine dignant.
35 Alcion e, merope que, celaeno, taygete que
36 Electa asterope qu esimul sanctissima maia.
    Haetenues paruo, labenter lumine lucent.
    At magnum nomen signi, clarum que uocatur.
    Propterea quod et, estatis primordia signat.
40 Et post hiberni praepandens temporis ortus.
41 Admonuit ut mandent mortales semina terris.

Quas greci apluralitate / pliadas latini abeo quod ciere exoriant
et uocant. Sunt septem / stellae quarum septima ut dic dratus
uix intu en pot est. Quam / quidam fabulo sae gentilum
pretio re orionis / fugisse putant. Quidam dicte
perse, cutam / arbitran tur uoca amque
electra quide non sustinens uide re casus pro
nepotis fugientis / Un de et illam
dissolutas crinibus propter luctum ire,
adserunt & pro pter comas cometem appel
lare. Non nulli uero mero pen esse
lutū mane qui nup ta a quodam
uiro nomi nata sit ypodormd
sunt enim hdec septem stellae
duce genua quae occasu
suo hie te mem orta aesta tem prime quide
nauigationis tempus ostendant,

At ppter leuum genu omnis pa te locatas
P aruas uergilias tenui cum luce uidebis
30 H e septem uulgo phibentur more ueusto
S tellae cernuntur uero sex unique paruę
A c non interiisse putari conuenit unam
S ed frustra temere ac uulgo ratione sine ulla
S eptem dici et ut uetores statuere poetae,
A eterno cunctas sane qui nomine signant
35 A lcione meropeque celaeno taigeteque
E lectra asteropeque simul sanctissima maia
h e tenues paruo labentes lumine lucent,
A t magnum nomen signi clarumque uocatur
P ropterea quo detestari primordia signat
40 E t post hiberni prepandens temporis ortus
A dmonet ut mandent mortales semina terris.

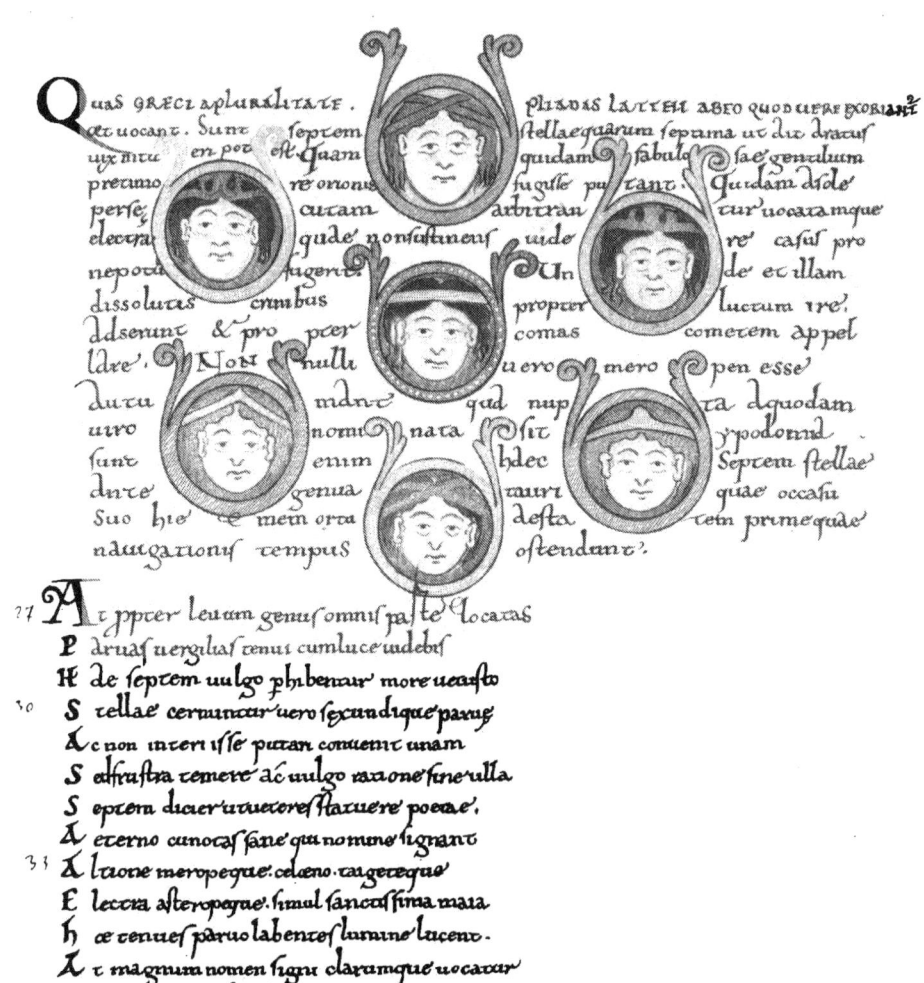

verses in the above brown tint. This figure, with the accompanying writing, is accurately engraved of the full size in Plate XII., and the Saxon copy from it in Plate XIII. In the former we recognise, throughout, the style of Classic times; in the latter, that of a barbarous age. The attitude is the same in both; but, as I before observed, the copyist has indulged his own taste in the details of the draperies, &c.; and has covered the legs of Perseus with garterings, according to the usage of his own time and nation.

There is a painting in the Herculaneum collection, of Perseus delivering Andromeda; in which, as in our ancient MS., he is represented with no other drapery than a light scarf, with the head of Medusa in his left hand, and with the same hooked and pointed weapon in the right. SUNT STELLAE. XVIII.

The figure of Perseus, in the Harl. MS. 2506, is of quite a different design, as may be seen in Plate XI. fig. 4.

5. The PLEIADES. The name over each, is in red, and the verses are in brown, as before. The grandeur of style in these heads is such, that from the first moment I saw them, I became convinced of the antiquity of this MS. I have already (p. 56) contrasted them with the barbarous performance of the Saxon artist; and may confidently appeal to Mr. Storm's Plates XIV. and XV., in which both the drawings are represented of the full size, in justification of my remarks.

Spence observes, that "there is reason to think that the *Pleiades* were represented personally on some of the ancient globes;" though they do not appear on the Farnese Globe.

6. LIRA—truly classical in its shape, and closely resembling that on the Farnese Globe; save that that has only six strings, and that this has eight. We have, however, abundant specimens of the ancient Lyre, both with fewer and more numerous strings. I have already remarked (p. 56) on the strange liberties taken by the Saxon artist in his copy of this drawing; in which, desiring to preserve the general outline of the original, but being at the same time entirely ignorant of the construction of the Lyre, he has presented us with an instrument which neither in ancient nor modern times ever had existence. The reader may compare the two, in our Plates VII. and IX.; besides which, the page representing this constellation in the ancient MS. is engraved of the full size, in Plate XVI. The writing on some parts of the figure in our an-

cient MS. is in red, and in other parts the brown ink is employed ; it having been doubtless the intention of the caligraphist to distinguish, by this means, one member of the instrument from another. The verses below are written with brown.

7. CIGNUS. This constellation, says Spence, is represented on the Farnese Globe, as by the poets, in the attitude of flying ; and so it is in this drawing. Both the verses and the prose text are written in brown. I cannot omit to notice the taste with which the lines of the writing, inside the figure, are accommodated to the forms of the bird by graceful curvatures. HABET (STELLAS). XIIII.

A leaf is here wanting in our ancient MS.; and we therefore recur to the copies of its two pages in the Cottonian MS.

8. AQUARIUS. " According to the old mythology," says Spence, " Aquarius is Ganymedes, the cup-bearer of Jupiter. He holds the cup, or little urn in his hand, inclined downwards ; and is always pouring out of it . . . to form that river which you see running from his feet:" So on the Farnese Globe; and so he is represented here.

The figure of Aquarius, as it appears in the Harl. MS. 2506, is given in our Plate XI.

9. CAPRICORNUS ; wanting, like Aquarius, in our ancient MS.

10. SAGITTARIUS. "*Arcitenens,*" says Spence, " according to Eratosthenes, an ancient Greek writer of very good authority, was represented under the figure of a Satyr ;" and so he appears in the Farnese Globe. But, he adds, that " the artists, in process of time, substituted the form of a Centaur, instead of that of a Satyr,[q] for this sign of the Zodiac; as appears from several gems and medals of good antiquity:[r] and the Roman poets seem to have followed this latter idea, even about the Augustan age." Thus Manilius, i. v. 270:

" In cujus caudam contentum dirigit arcum
Mixtus equo; volucrem missurus jamque sagittam."

[q] It is remarkable that Arcitenens is represented as a Satyr, in the Harl. MS. 2506.

[r] See Polymetis, plate xxv. Nos. 2, 3, in the last of which he exactly resembles in attitude the figure in our MS.

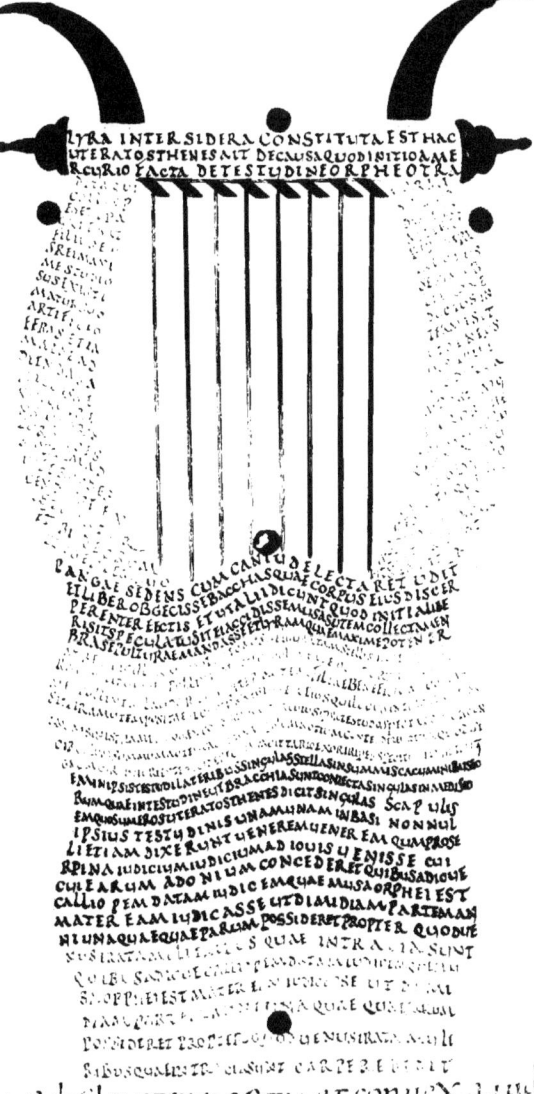

42 Inde fides leuiter posita et conuexa uidetur
Mercurius primum nam bus qua in dicitur olim
Infirmis fabricatus in alta sede locasse
45 Haec genus ad leuum in xide lapsa redit.

FIDES·QUAE LIRA

SAGITTARIUS HUNC CON
PLURES CENTAURUM ESSE DICUNT
RUNT ALII AUTEM NEGANT QUOD CENTAURUS NE
QUE ARCU USUS SIT. QUOD NEMO CENTAURORUM SAGI
TIS SIT USUS HIC AUTEM EQUINA CAUDA NON HABEAT
SAGITTIS SITAM NOMINE EUPHALEMO QUI SIT
QUAERITUR AB EO MUSAE BICIPITEM HABUERINT

SAGITTARIUS.

"The same writer," (iv. v. 561), continues Spence, "speaks as if there was some drapery about this figure:

> 'Nec non Arcitenens primâ cum veste resurgit,
> Pectora clara dabit bello,'......

(exactly agreeing with the drawing in our ancient MS.) "though on the Farnese Globe, Arcitenens and Chiron are both quite naked. Manilius, however," he continues, "marks very strongly that severity of his look, which is distinguishable enough in the figure of *Arcitenens* on the Farnese Globe, and not at all on the face of *Chiron* there; and says, that he looks as scowling and threatening, as Hannibal did in the beginning of the battles of Trebia, Trasimene, and Cannae:" all which corresponds in so remarkable a manner with the figure of Sagittarius, or Arcitenens, in our ancient MS. that one would say the artist must have had the description before him when he painted it. The head, indeed, has prodigious grandeur of character.

The text occupying the human part of this figure is written with minium; and the rest in a greyish-coloured ink, which is also employed in the verses below. SUNT STELLAE XVI. This figure is engraved of the full size of the original in our Plate XVII.

11. SAGITTA. This page is so completely washed out in the ancient MS., that nothing but the faint outlines of a bow are discernible; though I suspect it anciently had also an arrow, placed horizontally over it. The Saxon copy has a bow and arrow. The deficiency of *Sagitta*, in this page of our ancient MS. is supplied, in the next, by the figure of an arrow, having four stars, which is painted over the figure of *Aquila*.

12. AQUILA. Spence tells us that *Aquila*, in the Farnese Globe, makes a very different appearance from what he should have expected. "The poets," he says, "speak of him as flying, and as grasping the fulmen in his talons; whereas here he is without the fulmen, and standing in a quiet posture. No doubt," he continues, "there was some difference, in the different globes used by the ancients, as well as in the modern." In our drawing, the wings of Aquila are fully extended, as in the act of flying, though he holds not the thunder.

The text within this figure is written in brown; except on the tips of the wings and the tail, where, in order to give the bird a more resplendant appearance, minium has been employed. Red has also been used for the commencement of the writing on the neck. The verses below are written with the grey tint above mentioned. SUNT STELL. IIII.

13. DELPHINUS. " Both Manilius and Ovid," says Spence, " speak of the figure of the Dolphin, &c. From an expression used by the former, one may infer that, on the painted globes of the ancients, he was represented of a dark colour." . . . . This is the case with those parts of the figure that are not covered with writing in our ancient MS.; for which, as well as for the prose text itself, a dark blueish tint has been employed. The verses below are written in brown. SUNT STELLAE VIIII.

14. ORION. This figure is represented kneeling on one knee, on the Farnese Globe; though here he is standing: in that, however, as in our MS., he extends both his arms; and so he is described by the poets. This figure, in our ancient MS. has certainly been retouched at a very early period, by an inferior artist: without doubt he originally held a spear in his right hand, which the re-toucher rubbed out in part, and converted into a sword. I have already remarked (p. 56) upon the classical sandals of this figure, which the Saxon copyist changed for the garterings, reaching almost up to the knee, which were worn in his own time.

In all the other drawings of the constellations in this MS. the text of Hyginus, as has been said, is written within the figures. But in this it is otherwise; the account of that author having been here fancifully inscribed, around the figure, partly in red, and partly in a dark greyish ink, in the form of a temple, with a pyramidal top, supported by four columns. This writing is in many parts effaced. Under the figure we read: SUNT STELLAE XVIII. The poem below is written with brown.

In the Harl. MS. 2506, Orion is represented in back view, and in quite a different attitude.

15. SYRIUS. " *Sirius*, or Canicula," says Spence, " (who has so terrible a character in the old poets, and the whole period of whose influence is so particularly dreaded to this day at Rome), was, I doubt not, *represented by the ancient painters with a malign cast of his eyes, and a dark look.* As this could not be expressed on marble, the artist who made the Farnese Globe has given him several odd rays about his head. . . . He is described as running on vehemently after Lepus," &c. It is impossible to describe in a more lively

Plate XVIII Vol. XXVI p.56   Hart M.S. 647.

manner the drawing in our ancient MS.; where Sirius has not only the dark, malign look, above-mentioned, but also the rays surrounding his head. The text within the figure is written with black, and the verses below with light brown. SUNT STELLAE XX.

16. LEPUS. This figure, and the following, occupy the first leaf of a second gathering of eight leaves. A light brown tint is employed for the text within the figure, and a dark blueish ink for the verses below. SUNT STELLAE VII.

17. ARGO. A basso-relievo, representing an ancient ship, with a poop much resembling that of the ship Argo in our ancient MS., may be seen in the first volume, plate xxii. fig. 2, of Mazois's work on Pompeii; and other very near resemblances to it, may be observed on the reverses of medals of Nero, representing the port of Ostia, &c. In the writing within the figure, variety has been studied not a little. Upon the poop of the vessel, the lines are alternately dark red, and light grey. All the upper part of the hulk is written with minium, and the part supposed to be under water with dark brown. The verses below are written with the dark grey ink before-mentioned. SUNT STELLAE XXVI. I have already spoken (p. 56) of the silly extravagances of which the Saxon artist was guilty, in his copy of this drawing in the Cottonian MS. I have caused the original to be engraved of the full size, in Plate XVIII.

18. COETUS. " *Cetus*," says Spence, " or the Sea Monster that was to have destroyed Andromeda, is represented on the Farnese Globe in the attitude of swimming along the water, . . . with great scales on his breast, with his mouth open and threatening, and his tail wreathed; just as he is described by Manilius." The breast and great part of the body of Cetus, are filled with writing in our ancient MS., so that the scales above-mentioned cannot appear; but in all other respects the drawing exactly corresponds with the description. It is the same monster we so often see on ancient bassi-relievi. Both the prose text and the verses are written with dark grey ink. SUNT STELLAE XIII.

19. ERIDANUS. I very much suspect that this drawing was retouched almost all over at an early period. The river god holds an aquatic plant, a sort of reed, in his right hand, as in many other ancient monuments. The text within the figure is done with minium; the verses below with ink of the same hue as the last, but not so dark. SUNT STELLAE XIII.

20. PISCES. Both the prose text and the verses are written with the blueish

tint before-mentioned. š. STELLAE XII. On the left, another star, very large, is represented, under which is inscribed STELLA CANOPUS.

21. ARA. Very classical in its shape, but entirely covered with the writing. Upon it, however, are flames, painted red. Spence observes that, "according to Manilius's account, Ara should be represented in any coloured globe, with lighted coals upon it, and the frankincense flaming up, though there is nothing of this kind appears on the Farnese Globe:

'Ara, ferens thuris stellis imitantibus ignem.' *Manil.* 5. v. 335."

and so we have it in our ancient manuscript.

The prose text, occupying the figure, is written with very dark brown; the verses below, with the same blueish tint as the last. š. STELLAE IIII. In the Cott. MS. the Saxon copyist, though he has maintained the general outline of this figure of Ara, has sought to enrich it with ornaments of his own taste.

22. CENTAURUS. He is represented of a mild, though rustic character, very different from that of Sagittarius; and in conformity with what is said of him by the poets. He has just returned from the chace, and holds in his right hand a leveret, intended by him as an offering to the gods, and in the left a short spear In the Farnese Globe, Centaurus is represented in a back view; here he is seen in front.

The whole of the prose text, within the figure, is written with minium; the verses underneath are in the same blueish tint as those in the two last pages. š. STELLAE XXIIII.

23. HYDRA, with *Crater* and *Corvus*, is so like the figure on the Farnese Globe, that one would almost think that one had been taken from the other.

"Near *Argo*," says Spence, " is *Hydrus*, or the water-serpent; which Manilius says was very well marked out with stars. We cannot verify that here; because the Farnese Globe (which is the only ancient celestial globe I know of) has only the figures of the constellations wrought on it; and not the particular stars which were contained in them." *Crater*, in the Farnese Globe, stands on the back of Hydra, and is a vase with two handles, much like that in our drawing; and *Corvus* also, as in the MS., is perched on the tail of the serpent, and bending down, as if pecking at it. The want of the stars contained in the different constellations, in the Farnese Globe, might, if Spence had known of it, have been supplied to him by our very interesting manuscript.

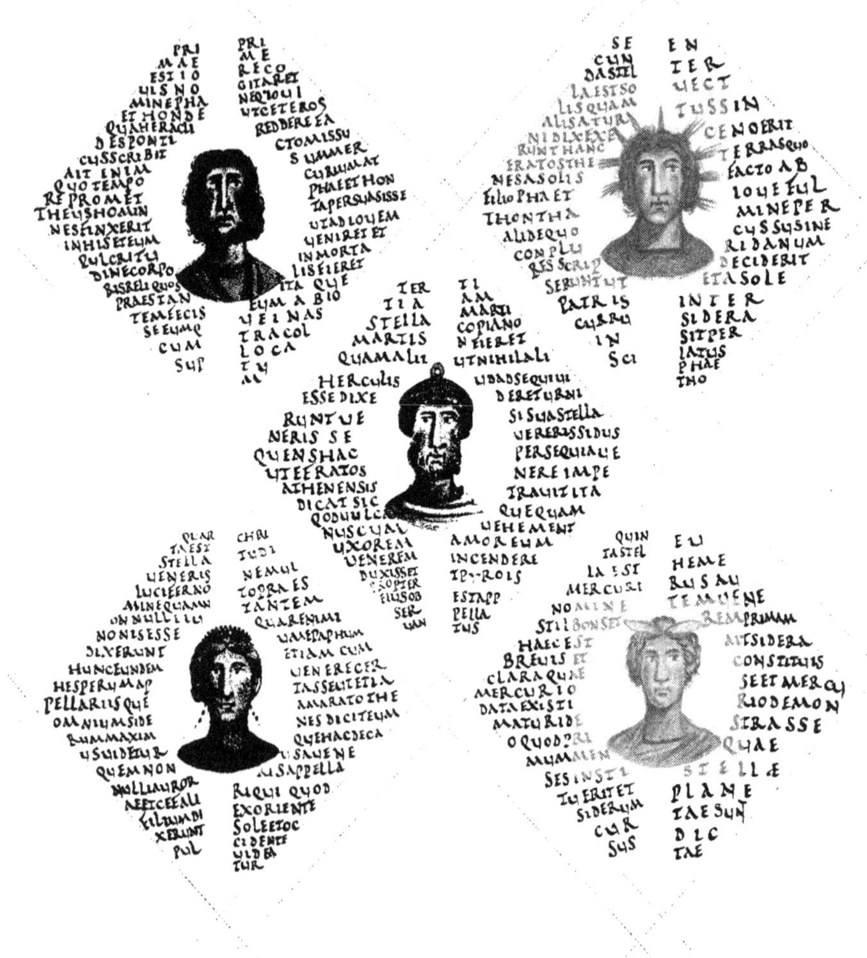
PRI
MAE
ESTIO
ULSNO
MINEPHA
ET HONDE
QUAMHERACLI
DESPONTI
CUSSCRIBIT
AIT ENIM
QUOTEMPO
RE PROMET
NESFINXERIT
INHISETEUM
PULCRITU
DINECORPO
PRAESTAN
TEMEECIS
SEEUMQ
CUM
SUP
PRI
ME
RECO
GITARET
UTCETEROS
REDDERE EA
CTOMISSU
SUMMER
CURUMAT
PHAEETHON
TAPERSUASISSE
UTADIOUEM
UENIRET ET
INMORTA
LISFIERET
ITA QUE
EUM A BIO
UEINAS
TRACOL
LOCA
SE
CUN
DASTEL
LAESTSO
LISQUAM
ALISATURA
NIDIXERE
RUNTHANC
ERATOSTHE
NESASOLIS
FILIO PHAET
THONTHA
ALIIDEQUO
CONPLU
RES SCRIP
SERUNTUT
PATRIS
CURRU
IN
SCI
EN
TER
UECT
TUSSIN
CENDERIT
TERRASQUO
FACTO AB
IOUE FUL
MINEPER
CUSSUSINE
RIDANUM
DECIDERIT
ETASOLE
INTER
SIDERA
SITPER
LATUS
PHAE
THO
TER
TIA
STELLA
MARTIS
QUAMALII
HERCULIS
ESSE DIXE
RUNTUE
NERIS SE
QUENSHAC
UTEFRATOS
ATHENENSIS
DICAT SIC
NUSCUM
UXOREM
UENEREM
SER
UAN
TI
AM
MARTI
COPIANO
UTNIHILALI
UBADSEQUIUI
DERETURNI
SI SUASTELLA
UENERISSIDUS
PERSEQUIAUE
NERE IMPE
TRAUITITA
QUEQUAM
UEHEMENT
AMOREEUM
INCENDERE
ESTAPP
PELLA
TUS
QUAR
TAEST
STELLA
UENERIS
LUCIFERNO
MINEQUAM
NONEISESSE
DIXERUNT
HUNCEUNDEM
HESPERUMAP
PELLARIUSQUE
OMNIUMSIDE
RUMMAXIM
QUEMNON
PUL
CHRI
TUDI
NEMUL
TOPRAES
TANTEM
QUARENIMI
ETIAM CUM
UENERECER
TASSEUITETIA
NES DICITEUM
QUEHACDECA
RIQUI QUOD
EXORIENTE
SOLEETOC
CIDENTE
UIDEA
TUR
QUIN
TASTEL
LA EST
MERCURI
NOMINE
HAECEST
BREUIS ET
CLARAQUAE
MERCURIO
DATAEXISTI
MATURIDE
OQUODPRI
SESINSTI
TUERITET
SIDERUM
CUR
SUS
EU
HEME
RUS AU
TEMUENE
REMPRIMAM
CONSTITUIS
SEET MERCU
RIODEMON
STRASSE
QUAE
STELLAE
PLANE
TAE SUN
DIC
TAE

Cotton. M. S. Tib. B. 5.

Plate XX. Vol. XXVI. p. 157
To face Plate XIV.

Published by the Society of Antiquaries of London, 23rd April 1835.

G. T. Stone sc.

The lines of prose text on the reptile, in this drawing, are made to undulate, according to the bendings of its body. They are written with a dark greyish tint, except the bottom line, which is done with minium. ⁊. OMN̄. STELLAE XXXVI. The verses below are written with a dark ink of a cold hue.

24. ANTICANIS. The text on the figure is written with a warm brown; the verses below, with the same dark tint as those in the last. ⁊. STELLAE III.

25. The *Heads* of *Jupiter, Sol,* (or *Saturn,*[r]) *Mars, Venus,* and *Mercury*.

No person who is conversant with the paintings of the ancients, of which so many have at different times been discovered in the baths of the Emperors at Rome, and in ancient sepulchres, &c.; and recently, in such vast numbers, in the excavations of Herculaneum and Pompeii; no one, I would say, who is well acquainted with these, and will attentively examine the five heads of the planets in this drawing (not to speak of the other drawings already enumerated) will entertain any doubt of the genuine antiquity of this manuscript. They are slightly executed; but with great boldness of hand, and breadth of light and shadow. They are full of vivacity, replete with classic feeling, and, in every detail of the costume, correspond with the productions of classic times. The head of Jupiter, and the small portion of drapery which covers his bust, are decidedly antique; the head-dress of Venus is over and over again to be found in the paintings of Herculaneum, and in other ancient monuments; and even the helmet of Mars, singular as it is for having a sort of ring at the apex, has its counterpart in one of the pictures of that collection, (vol. iii. tav. xxxix.) in which a trophy is represented. But in order to appreciate duly the merits of the original artist, his performances should be confronted with those of the Saxon copyist in the Cottonian manuscript. See Plates XIX. XX. The prose text accompanying these heads is written in minium.

The two leaves which follow (viz. the sixth and seventh of this second gathering) have no drawings; and, as I have said, the text on the verso of the last of them terminates abruptly, half way down the page, with the line:

"Signifero ex orbi sex signorum ordine fultum."

The eighth and last leaf of the gathering is wanting. We find from the Cottonian MS. which was copied from the ancient one before it had suffered mutilation, that the recto of this leaf contained representations of *Sol* and

---

[r] "Secunda Stella est Solis, quam alii Saturni dixerunt," &c.

Luna; the former standing in a car drawn by four horses; the latter standing with a torch in each hand, in a car drawn by two oxen; as Diana occasionally appears, in her character of " *Luna Lucifera,*" upon ancient medals.[s] The loss of this drawing in the ancient MS. is the more to be lamented, as the figures in it do not appear to have been obscured by text written within their outlines, as is the case with the others, and as it must therefore have afforded the artist a fairer opportunity of displaying his talents. In the Saxon copy, which is accurately engraved in our Plate XXI., the legs of Apollo, like those of Perseus and Orion before spoken of, are covered with garterings; but we cannot doubt that in the original manuscript he had sandals.

In the first instance, our ancient MS appears to have ended with this drawing, the back of the leaf containing which was left blank: but the poem was afterwards continued, on the verso of the leaf, by another hand, in a somewhat smaller character; which this second scribe adopted, in order that he might be enabled to introduce certain prose matter in the margin, bearing more or less on the subjects treated of in the poem. [*] These prose passages are all copied, in both the Saxon MSS. after the last line of the poem. The first three have for titles: "De concordia Solaris et Lunaris;" "Item de eadem Ratione;" and "De concordia Maris et Lunae." I give these passages below; as they appear to be curious on account of their Latinity.[t]

[s] I found her thus drawn by two bulls, and holding a torch in each hand, in a medal of Julia Domna, and in another, I think of Lucius Verus: but I have lost or mislaid my references to them. She is represented drawn by two bulls, and holding one torch, in Gessner, plate clxxiii. fig. 23.

[t] " De concordia Solaris et Lunaris.

" Novem horis in luna pro quinque diebus in sole computatis, idem luna novem horis tantum itineris peragitur quantum sol in quinque diebus, et ideo unius signi horis iuxta lunarem velocitatem enumeratis, inveniuntur quinquaginta quatuor quod sunt sexies novem. Duobus enim diebus & sex horis luna per singula pervolat signa. Triginta vero diebus per quodque signum sol spatiatur. Quo partito tricenario in quinque et quinque invenies sexies quinos, quod est sexta pars solaris circuitus in singulis signis, ita ut novem iuxta lunæ cursum sexta pars signi repperiuntur cuiusque, et sic demum possunt novem horæ lunares cum quinque diebus solaribus concordare.

" Item de eadem ratione.

" Luna lucere dodrantis semuncias dicitur. Duodecim unciæ libram faciunt, viginti quatuor horæ diem integrum; totidem enim sunt semunciæ in libra plena; quas si diviseris in quatuor,

Cotton M.S. Tib. B.5. Plate XXI. Vol. XXVI. p. 98

Published by the Society of Antiquaries of London, 23rd April, 1835.

Mr. Prevost thinks them very ancient; and that they may be from some lost work either of Varro or Pliny. The way, used in them, of measuring time by *dodrantes* and *semunciæ*, indicates, he observes, a writer of a very early age. An example of this way of counting hours is in Pliny's Nat. Hist, lib. xviii. cap. lviii.: " *Dodrantes* horarum cum minimum intervalla," &c.

These passages shew also the use of *punctus-i*, for *punctum-i*; not *punctus-punctus*, as inferred by most lexicographers. The existence of this word, as belonging to the second declension, is, my friend observes, very sensibly insisted upon by Facciolati in his Dictionary; though the only proof he had of it was the following passage in Pliny:

" Hæ tot portiones terræ, imo verò, ut plures tradidere, mundi *punctus* ; neque enim est aliud terra in universo."

For *punctus-ûs* cannot mean a point; but a stinging or pricking, or rather the act of so doing; the same as *punctio* and *punctura:* but the only synonyme of *punctum*, is *punctus-i*; of which the second of these passages gives three examples; viz. " *quatuor punctos ;*" " *per punctos cotidianos ;*" and " *quinque puncti* horam faciunt."

The remaining prose extracts, written by the side of the poem in the ancient MS., are from Pliny, Nat. Hist. lib. xviii. cap. lxxviii., the title of the first pas-

quarta pars quadrantis nomen sortita est, reliquæ tres dodrantis ; & ideo dixi dodrantis semuncias horarum, id est, quatuor punctos ; quapropter, si scire velis quot horas luceat una quælibet, ex quatuor punctis cognoscis. Ut puta quinta luna, multiplica quinque per quatuor, hoc est, ætatem lunæ presentis per punctos cotidianos, fiunt viginti ; partire per quinque, quinque puncti horam faciunt, quatuor quinquies, quatuor horas lucet luna quinta.

"DE CONCORDIA MARIS ET LUNAE.

" Unius semper horæ dodrante et semuncia transmissa, idem diviso unius horæ spatio in viginti quatuor semuncias, quia tot sunt semunciæ in libra plena ; iterumque divide viginti quatuor in quatuor, hoc est, quater sex, et ter sex dodrans dicitur ; semel vero quadrans ; et hoc est, quod ait, unius horæ dodrante, idem tribus partibus, decem et octo semunciis. Quod vero ait et semuncia, sex reliquarum semunciarum ad quadrantem pertinentium unam voluit adjungi dodranti, ut essent decem et novem semunciæ, quo æstus oceani cotidie tardius veniret, tardiusque recederet."

Whoever was the author of these passages, they appear to have been well known to Bede, who in his book, " De Temporum Ratione," cap. xxii. (beginning " Tradunt quoque argumentum *veteres*," &c.) and in cap. xxvii. evidently makes use of them; omitting, however, the mode of counting by *dodrantes* and *semunciæ*, but retaining *punctus-i*.

sage being, " DE PRESAGIIS TEMPESTATUM. PRESAGIA SOLIS;" and the text commencing: " Purus oriens atque non fervens serenum diem nunciat," &c. and continuing to the end of the chapter. I suspect that, as far as it goes, this part of our MS. (or rather of our MSS. as the early portion of it is lost in our ancient MS.) might here and there furnish the means of correcting the present received text. For example, in the printed edition that I have turned to, I find: " Quum orientis *atque* occidentis radii rubent, coire pluvias;" whilst in the Cottonian MS. we have: " Cum occidentis *aut* orientis radii videntur, coire pluvias;" which is surely better; as it is not likely Pliny intended to speak of rays, issuing from the east and the west at the same time. I may observe that, throughout these Prognostics, *cum* is used, and not *quum*, in all the three manuscripts.

I have spoken of two gatherings, each composed originally of four sheets of parchment, folded in the usual manner, (that is, the first leaf and the eighth forming one sheet, the second and seventh another, and so on); and containing together, therefore, sixteen leaves. The remaining part of the MS. is comprised in six leaves; but it is remarkable that the parchment composing these has not been folded and gathered with the same regularity. For, of these six leaves, the *first* and *fifth* (and not the first and sixth) form one sheet, and the *third* and *fourth* another; whilst the *second* and *sixth* are single leaves. The continuation of the poem, and the accompanying prose extracts above noticed, fill the first three pages of this gathering; the ten last lines of the poem occupy the upper part of the verso of the second leaf, and immediately underneath these ten lines, the extracts from Macrobius, and Felix or Martianus Capella, before-mentioned, begin; written by a different hand, and with ink of a different hue; as is shewn in Mr. Storm's fac-simile, Plate XXIV. No. 1. Of course the first line of text, on the recto of the third leaf, joins properly with the last line on the verso of the second: but as this second leaf, as I have said, has no corresponding leaf, a deficiency in the text might naturally be expected to occur after the fourth leaf: this however is not the case: as the last words on the verso of the fourth leaf, " *Sed tū maxime plurib: dieb: non*," join perfectly with the first line, " *cerni sidera*," &c. on the recto of the fifth leaf; thereby proving satisfactorily that no intermediate leaf has been lost in this place, since these extracts from Macrobius and Capella were written; but that the leaf, which originally joined and made one sheet of parchment with the second leaf, was cut out before those extracts were written: for that it once had a correspondent leaf appears quite certain, upon a careful examination of its inner edge; where the original needle-holes of the bookbinder may be perceived, and indeed a small remaining edge of the said corresponding leaf itself. But, in order to be more perfectly understood, I subjoin what may be termed a dissection of this gathering:

Leaf 1. The poem continued on both sides.

2. On the *recto*, the poem continued: on the *verso*, the last ten lines of the poem and the beginning of the extracts from Macrobius.

3. *Recto*, and *verso*, Macrobius and Capella, continued.

5. Continuation of Macrobius, &c. on the *recto*: "cerni sidera," &c. joining with "non," which is the last word of the last line on the *verso* of leaf 4. *Verso*, blank.

No corresponding leaf.

4. *Recto*. Planetary system in circles; with text underneath. *Verso*, text continued; ending with " Sed tū maxime plurib: dieb: non," joining with the first line of leaf 5, " cerni sidera," &c.

6. Single leaf: *recto* blank, *verso* the Planisphere by Geruvigus.

After I had discovered so far, it struck me as not impossible that the leaf removed, upon the above occasion, might have been that containing the planisphere of Geruvigus; and upon applying the inner edge of that leaf to the inner edge of the second leaf, I found them to correspond so exactly, as to leave no doubt that such had been the case. This leaf, therefore, was cut out upon the occasion of writing the above extracts, in order that the writer might not be cramped for room; for the entire of leaf five was gained by it. Whether or not the sheet of parchment containing leaves three and four, was then introduced for the first time, I undertake not to determine; for both those leaves bear decided marks of having been washed, before the writing they at present have, was put upon them; and it is very possible that they before contained other writing, perhaps by this very Geruvigus, which some subsequent possessor of the book considered of little import, and therefore washed out, in order to make room for the above passages of Macrobius and Capella, both of whom were writers of reputation on astronomical subjects.

I may here mention, that I have lately had the pleasure of shewing this ancient MS. to one of our oldest and most respected academicians, Mr. Howard, so well known by his beautiful pictures of classic imagery, and whose unremitting study of the works of the ancients, during more than forty years, renders him, without doubt, one of the best judges in a matter of this kind in Europe; and that Mr. Howard not only agrees with the eminent artists before named by me (p. 53), as to the antiquity of the coloured drawings contained in it, but is also of opinion, that the figures in the above planisphere exhibit too much of the remains of classic taste and costume, to justify our ascribing that drawing to a later period than the fourth or fifth century. In fact, the form of the Lyre, as he observed, is such as we often see in antique paintings and bassi-relievi; and it is so well understood in its parts, that one cannot doubt that Geruvigus was familiar with this ancient instrument: the Altar (Ara) also, though not elegant in shape, is still such as we may suppose to have been used by the Pagans in the early part of the middle ages; and similar observations might be applied to many of the other figures.

I have already said, that I think it probable the above Geruvigus was the first Christian possessor of this MS. and the author of the Christian account of the Constellations, the concluding page of which now occupies the recto of the second leaf. And now let me observe of the inscription under the above Planisphere, " EGO INDIGNUS SACERDOS ET MONACHUS NOMINE GERVVIGUS REPPERI AC SCRIPSI, PAX LEGENTIBUS," that the words *repperi ac scripsi* (the former in the sense of *excogitavi*) must be taken to apply to a written treatise, as well as to the invention and design of the planisphere; for it is impossible that the expression, " pax legentibus," can have been intended to refer only to the names of the Constellations, written here and there over the figures, in the drawing. I may further observe, that the judgment of Mr. Howard, as to the antiquity of Geruvigus's planisphere, accords extremely well with the opinion which I before ventured to give, that the above Christian account of the Constellations is, properly speaking, original; in favour of which, I may also mention that the circumstance of the prayer to the Holy Trinity being placed at the end, in our ancient MS., instead of at the beginning, as in the two Saxon copies, (for the prayer is prospective,) is not easily to be ac-

counted for, except upon the supposition that this pious address to the Almighty was an afterthought of the writer; and further, that that prayer terminates with a doxology in the original MS. which is omitted in the said copies.

Besides that this Christian treatise is written, as I have said, in very good Latin, it contains several expressions which seem to indicate that it was composed in an early century. In speaking of the ancient philosophers, Plato and Aristotle, the author uses the past tense: and so when he treats of the origin of the names given to the heavenly bodies; whilst, upon other occasions, he employs the present tense; as if referring to usages of his own time; as " Item hyadas a sucu et pluviis *nominarunt:* Grece enim ΥΕΛΟC pluviæ *dicuntur*, quas Latini suculas *appellant*. Plyades a pluralitate *dixerunt*; quas Greci ΑΠΟ ΤΟΥ ΠΛΙCΤΟΝ *appellant*..... Has Latini vergilias *dicunt* a vere." Again: " Cometes autem Latine crinitæ *appellantur* ... quas philosophi *dixerunt*," &c. An expression in the following passage, (see Plate XXIV. No. 2), seems to indicate a very early period of the Christian era: " His depositione quarundam stellarum, iuxta opinionem antiquorum, &c., et *a filiis Dei*, id est Christianis," &c.; and so the expression, " et, *tempore novissimo*, per eundem incarnatum totum mundum reformasti," in the prayer; which appears indeed, throughout, very much like what we might expect to have been written soon after the famous Nicene Council: for which reason, though it is engraved entire in our plate, I here give it in type, for the convenience of those who are unaccustomed to the abbreviations used in ancient manuscripts:

" Domine Deus omnipotens, Sancta Trinitas, et indivisa unitas, Domine Pater, qui per unigenitum Filium tuum dominum nostrum Jesum Christum, tecum coaeternum et aequalem in substantia divinitatis, in unitate et virtute Spiritus Sancti, omnia condidisti, et tempore novissimo per eundem incarnatum totum mundum reformasti; presta, Domine, ut tua misericordia inspirante per apertionem illam, qua sensus Apostolorum post resurrectionem aperuisti, de volubilitate firmamenti et stellarum astrorumque cursu, secundum modulum nostrae fragilitatis, capere et aliis ministrare valeamus:[u] per eundem dominum nostrum Jesum Christum filium tuum, qui tecum vivit et regnat, Dominus in unitate ejusdem Spiritus Sancti, per omnia secula seculorum. Amen."[x]

Although my opinion of the age of this MS. was at first entirely formed

[u] The Harleian MS. omits the whole of what follows; the Cottonian, Tib. B. v. ends with the words, " per eundem dominum."

[x] It is not impossible that our Geruvigus may have been one of the first professors of Christianity

upon an examination of the drawings it contains, I have since employed some diligence, in order to ascertain whether or no it might not afford other internal evidence of its antiquity: for, if upon a doubtful fact we chance to make a right guess, it will generally be found that whatever evidence is discovered afterwards, will go to prove that that first guess was well founded. With this view (after satisfying myself that the use of minuscule writing in the poem is not against it), I have endeavoured to inform myself concerning those peculiarities, which the best writers on these subjects have noticed in the most ancient MSS. abroad; and which they speak of, as the *criteria* by which such MSS. are generally distinguished from those of later centuries. I shall insist no further on the evidence of the antiquity of our MS. which is drawn from the style and costume of the figures, except by observing that, as far as I can collect, the best judges of early MSS. on the continent, from Mabillon to those of near our own time, would in a similar case, I think, have readily admitted this kind of evidence to be superior to any other.

First, then, these writers agree, that all the most ancient MSS. known, with scarce an exception, are remarkable for *the squareness of their form.* Schawartzius, in his work " De Ornamentis Librorum," already cited in this paper, particularly dwells on this characteristic of the most ancient MSS., enumerating various examples, and among them the celebrated Virgil of Florence. The writers of the " Nouveau Traité," speaking of the famous MS. of the Pandects of Justinian at Florence, inform us that it is in two volumes

in this country, where, at all events, we are assured this MS. existed before the tenth century. It is true, that the writer of the Harleian Catalogue describes this part of it as being written in a *Gallican* hand; but this and other misnomers of the ancient Roman writing, have already been sufficiently remarked upon. This kind of writing was doubtless practised after the decline of the Western Empire, in all countries where the Romans had had dominion; and more especially, we may conclude, by those people among whom they had the longest resided. I find in the " Nouveau Traité de Diplomatique," a notice, stating that, in the eighth century, St. Boniface, having experienced great difficulty in reading the books which he had been enabled to procure in Germany, made application to Daniel Bishop of Winchester, praying that prelate to send him books clearly and distinctly written: *" libros claris, discretis, et absolutis litteris scriptos:"* whence we may conclude with certainty, that at that time we were celebrated for the goodness of our writing, and reasonably conjecture that we had been so long previously.

of *nearly a square form, their height being only two inches more than their breadth.* In another place, speaking of a MS. in the Library of S. Germain des Prés, which contains the Gospel of St. Matthew and part of that of St. Mark, and which they think may be as old as the fourth or fifth century, they tell us that this MS. is *ten inches high* and *eight inches broad.* The MS. No. 3225, in the Vatican, containing the fragments of Virgil, with the drawings which Bartoli engraved, measures, according to D'Agincourt, *eight inches one line in height,* by *seven inches two lines in width*; this MS., which is probably the most ancient Latin MS. existing, appearing to be broader in proportion to its height than any other.

So far, therefore, we find nothing to render the antiquity of our MS. questionable; since it measures twelve inches seven-eighths in height, by eleven inches one-eighth in width, and therefore appears to be of a squarer proportion than any of those mentioned above, except the last.

In the next place, I find it observed, as a general rule, that the *rarity of abbreviations in manuscripts is generally in proportion to their antiquity.* In the Vatican fragments of Virgil, I have found, occasionally, a dot after *q.* to denote *que,* but no other abbreviation whatever; in the Virgil of Medicis this abbreviation is constant, and we have also very commonly a dot after the letter *b.* at the end of a word, to signify *bus,* and occasionally, also, at the end of a line, a straight or curved stroke, to mark an *m,* or an *n.* Nor are they much less rare in the Pandects of Florence: Brinckman, say the writers of the "Nouveau Traité," found only in that MS. the stroke at the end of a line, to denote *m,* and *n*; *id.* for *idem*; *n.* for *non*; *edm* (with a stroke at top) for *edictum*; and the letter I, for *primum.* Now it happens that in our MS. throughout the whole of the poem of Cicero's Aratea, I *have not found even one abbreviation*; and that in the text of Hyginus, written in the figures, Mr. Storm tells me, he only in one instance found *b,* followed by two dots, standing for *bus.* Not that an abbreviation, here and there, can at all make against the antiquity of any MS.; as we find them in abundance in ancient Latin inscriptions, and, among others, in those of Pompeii. Had the leaves of our MS. been of less ample dimensions, the above common abbreviations would, I doubt not, have been sometimes resorted to in the poem, in order to gain space; and indeed, we find this to have been done in the prose extracts from Pliny, which were written at the time, in narrow columns, by the side of the latter verses of the poem.

The omission of stops, marking periods, and distinguishing the members of sentences, is, according to the last mentioned writers, another sign of high antiquity in MSS. *Scarcely one* is to be found in a page of the most ancient part of our MS., either in the poem, or in the prose text above; unless, indeed, such as were added, probably some centuries afterwards, by the person who undertook the task of correcting, in the former, the blunders of the original transcriber; a duty which it does not appear he was very well qualified to perform.

Speaking of *Ornamented Capitals, (lettres grises,)* the same writers say: "In general *their rarity* in MSS. where in other respects elegance has not been neglected, *is in proportion to the antiquity of the MS.* If their omission is not to be accounted for upon this or some other good ground, the MS. may be esteemed of the fifth century, or of the sixth at least, if no one of these ornamental letters occurs in it." It has been sufficiently shewn, that elegance has been in a more than ordinary degree sought for in the execution of this MS. I need only add, that *not one ornamented initial letter* is to be found in the whole; that in the prose text, written in capitals within the figures, the initial letters of the sentences are not larger than the other letters; and that the initial letters of the verses below are of the size proper to range with the minuscule characters used for the poem, and no larger.

"*The less frequently the letter Y is found, surmounted by a point, the more ancient ought we to esteem the MS. in which such letters occur.*" So say the writers of the "Nouveau Traité;" and they add in a note, that "*those MSS. in which the letter Y is always, or almost always, without this point, bear the marks of the highest antiquity; of the fifth century at least,*" &c. They have, I take it, used the expression *always, or almost always,* guardedly; because the Y, with a point over it, is sometimes, though rarely, found in ancient monuments. Indeed Mabillon, in the first plate of his large work, gives a specimen from an ancient engraved brass tablet, *Fragmentum legis Romanae,* which appears from the orthography to be of high antiquity, and in which the V with a square point over it is used for Y.

Now it happens that the letter *y* is only once admitted in the first part of the poem, in our ancient MS.; although we have it in some of the titles of the Constellations, at the bottoms of the pages, and occasionally in the text of Hyginus above. I find it in the name *Phryxum*, in the prose account of Aries; in the name *Alcyone*, written over one of the Pleiades; in the word *Lyra*, in the prose account written within that figure; in that of *Cignus*, where the word is twice spelt with this letter; in the title *Syrius*, at the bottom of the page containing that constellation; in the word *Cyclopas*, in the prose account of Ara; in the title *Hydra*, at the bottom of the page exhibiting the figure of that constellation; and in the same word, at the beginning of the 292d line of the poem; and *in all these instances it is without the point*. In the latter part of the poem, written, as has been said, by a different hand from the former, I, for the first time, find the point over the *y* in the word *Hydra*, in line 376, and the letter again so occurs, in the same word, in verse 449. Neither the remainder of the poem, nor the prose extracts from Pliny, furnish any other example of the letter *y* at all; nor have I observed it in the extracts which follow from Macrobius and Capella: but we have it twice, with the point over it, in the Planisphere of Geruvigus, on the last leaf of the MS.; besides which, I find it once with the point, in the worn *Moysen*, at the end of the Christian account of the Constellations, prefixed, as has been shewn, to the most ancient part of the volume. If, therefore, the authors of the " Nouveau Traité," are to be depended upon, the chief part of this MS. bears *the most decided marks of high antiquity:* not that I am disposed to admit the antiquity of the latter part of the poem to be rendered questionable, from the circumstance of its twice having the letter *y* surmounted by a point; since, as has been shewn, sufficient evidence appears to exist that this mode of marking this letter was not an invention of the low ages, but was known and occasionally practised in very ancient times.

It is a common notion that, in the most ancient MSS., the words are not separated from each other, by intervening spaces; and as they often are so in this MS., more especially in the poem, it has been suggested to me, that I ought, if I can, to answer this supposed objection to its antiquity. It might be going too far, were I to say that this opinion is absolutely without foundation; but I think it will be easy to shew, that the exceptions furnished by ancient MSS. to such a supposed rule, are so numerous, as to prove that it ought not to be considered as a general one.

In many inscriptions of high antiquity, we find the words divided by points; in others, spaces are left between them, with more or less regularity; and in a smaller number, I should say, the words appear to run one into another; neither spaces nor points having been used to separate them. A fourth kind, again, unite both these modes of separating one word from another: and, in short, any person who will be at the pains to turn over any work of Roman antiquities, will immediately perceive, that the circumstance of an ancient Latin inscription having the words thus divided, or not, can make nothing for or against its genuineness. But, without going further, sufficient proof of all this will be found in Plates IV. and V. accompanying this Dissertation; and containing, as before said, ancient inscriptions written on the walls of Pompeii, and others taken from the works of Buonarruoti and Koppius. In the former plate, it will be observed, that all the inscriptions, excepting only the small specimen from an ancient Greek MS., have the words divided by points, or by spaces, or by both. Most of the inscriptions on the other, we may conclude to be of a somewhat later date: that in cursive characters, of *Mercurius*, we know, indeed, to be of the first half of the fourth century, and it is scribbled with little or no attempt at separation between the words: but not so that of the sculptor *Atticianes*, which is doubtless much earlier, wherein they are very distinctly divided by spaces; as is the case also in the first line of that of *Vero*, and throughout that of *Rincentius*; whilst in those of Q. *Terentius*, *Priscianus*, *Evagrenus*, and *Auxentius*, the words are separated from one another by points.

Now, it is not reasonable to suppose, that a practice, so necessary to facilitate the reading of what was written, and which we are certain prevailed in the first century, and I think we may conclude long before, should at any time afterwards have been generally abandoned, as unimportant or useless; or that it should have been continued in inscriptions, but, by common consent, disused in writing books; and if, therefore, we sometimes find very early MSS. in which the words are neither separated by points or spaces, we must, in great part at least, account for it in some other way.

In the Latin MS. poem, the fragments of which are published in the second volume of the Herculaneum Collection, and of which a specimen is given in our Plate IV. the words throughout are distinctly divided from each other by points; besides which, a little more distance is commonly allowed, between the last letter of one word and the first of the word following it, than between the characters composing the words themselves; so that, before that MS. had suffered mutilation, it must have been as easy to read as possible; and would indeed have been so, even without the points. I understand that no erasures, no errors, have been detected in this MS.; whence we may conclude that it was transcribed by some lover of literature for his own use; and not by one of that ignorant class of persons, who in the most ancient times were commonly employed by the Roman booksellers, to multiply copies of the works of eminent authors for sale. If we could now see the MS. in which, according to Plutarch, the elder Cato wrote his "Origines," in large characters, for the use of his son, we should probably find the words regularly divided, as they are in the above papyrus.

Angelo Mai, in the preface to his edition of the Palimpsest discovered by him of Cicero "de Re Publica," observes, that the more finely-formed and larger the characters in ancient MSS., the grosser the errors he has commonly found them to contain. It is well known, he says, that the persons employed in ancient times to copy MSS. were often of the lowest order of servants; nay, he seems to think the opinion of Poggius, that women also were employed in this kind of labour, may not be ill-founded. This class of unlearned persons copied what was put before them, often without understanding it.[y] Hence the fine large letters they used were termed by Seneca *litteras serviles*; and hence the frequent blunders which they fell into; which occasioned Cicero to complain, "that, as for Latin MSS. he did not know which way to turn himself, they were written and sold so full of errors."

After the copyist had done his part, a critic or grammarian, real or pretended, was sometimes employed to correct his errors, and perhaps to separate the words by points placed between them: but this, it is probable, was not

[y] Hence it is, perhaps, that in ancient MSS., written in capitals, it often happens, where a word begins with the same letter with which the preceding word terminates, that one of the two letters is omitted. There are many instances of this in the Medicean Virgil, where the corrector of the MS. has afterwards inserted the letter which was wanting at top.

often done immediately, by direction of the bookseller; but was commonly left to the care of the purchaser of the MS.; who in a great majority of cases, I am disposed to believe, placed the volume on his shelf without having it done at all. In a MS. Virgil, written in very large capitals, No. 3867 of the Vatican Collection, before-mentioned, the words are separated from each other by points, added by a more recent hand, who however omitted them in some pages. According to the writers of the "Nouveau Traité," this person must have had but an imperfect knowledge of Latin, or else have been very negligent. In fact, say they, "in inserting these points, he has not unfrequently cut words in two, and made nonsense of them; as in the second book of the Æneid, v. 30, where, instead of *certare solebant*, we read *certa. res. olebant*." What I have said may suffice to account for the want of divisions between the words, which no doubt is observed in several very ancient MSS. This I may add, that in these very MSS., in their titles and at the beginnings and endings of their books or chapters, those *formulæ*, which, from the frequency of their occurrence, the copyists employed could not but well understand, are generally written in words distinctly separated from each other; as in the title, "Saeculi novi interpraetatio," engraved in plate xxxv. of the third volume of the "Nouveau Traité de Diplomatique" from the above MS. of Virgil, where the words have considerable spaces between them; and in the *formulæ* at the ends of the different books, in the Medicean Virgil; as " P. Vergili Maronis Georgicon Lib. iiii. Expl. Incipit Aeneidos Lib. i." &c. &c.

But all that has been hitherto said relates to MSS. written in *capital letters*, and especially to MSS. of the ancient classics; and if this want of a due separation between the words be an evidence of high antiquity in a MS. (which I do not entirely deny), the MS., which is the subject of this paper, surely possesses it in a very ample degree, in the text of Hyginus written within the figures; where, at first sight, the words bear the appearance of not being at all distinguished from each other; though, upon a more close examination, small spaces between them will be perceived, here and there, enough to shew that the writer was not one of the very low class of copyists above spoken of; but that, besides being familiar with Latin, he had some knowledge of the fables which he was employed to transcribe; such as might enable him, perhaps, in this or that passage, to alter or abridge the text of the original author, whenever the limits of the figure made such change necessary. This I conjecture he may have occasionally done; as, although these prose accounts agree for the most part with the printed copies of Hyginus, they do not do so always.

But, admitting that the want of spaces or points, separating the words, is really a characteristic of several of the most ancient MSS. written in capitals, it is not the case with all of them: for in the fine MS. of Germanicus Cæsar's translation of Aratus, enriched with coloured figures of the Constellations, which was celebrated by Grotius in his Syntagma, and which, as I before observed, I lately saw at Leyden, the words, (although the whole is written in capitals) are quite as well divided as they are in the verses of Cicero in our MS.; and yet there is, I think, every reason to believe the Leyden MS. to have been written and decorated in ancient Roman times.

The want of a proper division between the words is, without doubt, found also in some very early MSS. written in those separate round characters, (some capital letters and others minuscules,) which the authors of the "Nouveau Traité" term *uncials*.[z] Thus, in the specimen, "*dixit autem*," &c. given in our Plate VI. and which is taken from a MS. of the Gospels, said to have been written in the fourth century by St. Eusebius, Bishop of Vercelli, (for I do not vouch for the truth of this, since the writing seems to be that of a calligraphist), the words in the different lines are neither divided from each other by points nor distinguishing spaces; though, as here the lines are so short as to contain only, upon an average, two words apiece, little inconvenience could be occasioned by the circumstance to the reader; especially as when a sentence, or a member of a sentence, terminates in the middle of a line, the remainder of that line is left blank, and the line that follows commences with a character larger than the others. An entire page of this MS., beginning "Mulier abscondit in farina," &c. is given in fac-simile by Blanchinius, in the last volume of his "Evangeliarium Quadruplex;" where, on the same plate,

---

[z] In speaking of a Psalter, supposed of the beginning of the fifth century, in the collection of the Queen of Sweden, the writers of the "Nouveau Traité" say (tom. iii. p. 91): "On y voit par tout *ae*; & *plusieurs mots distingués les uns des autres*;" which proves, as they observe, that this distinction of words is not always a good reason for dating a MS. so low as the seventh century.

is the fac-simile of part of another MS. of the sixth century, beginning : " Notum ergo," &c. written in characters a good deal similar in shape, but a little smaller. Here the columns are wider; and therefore, although individual words are not separated from each other by points or spaces, a point, followed by a considerable space, is used to separate the members of sentences. In the plate immediately preceding, we have part of a page, in much larger characters, from a MS. supposed of the sixth century, beginning: " Et a foro cum venerit," &c., where, though we have no points, not only the smaller members of sentences, but even occasionally individual words, are separated by spaces; and in one of the plates following, we have three lines : " Omnia haec temptavi," &c. written in smaller separate characters, and with less neatness and regularity than all the above, taken from a MS. of Ecclesiasticus at Fulda, which is said to have belonged to St. Boniface, who suffered martyrdom in the eighth century, and in which most of the words are decidedly separated from each other by spaces. It is no uncommon thing to find two, and perhaps sometimes three words, joined together in very early MSS.; I speak of such as were written by persons who may be supposed to have fully understood the meaning of what they wrote : but when we find a MS. written in finely formed characters, and in which the letters of a dozen consecutive words follow each other at equal distances, we may generally, I think, conclude, that it is the work of a calligraphist; who, if not utterly unqualified to understand the subject matter of what he was copying, was in no degree interested by it, and thought only of the mechanism of his art and the beauty of his penmanship.

But the poem in our MS. is not written in what are termed *uncials*, but in *minuscules*. It will be found, by turning to plates xlvii.—xlix. in the third volume of the " Nouveau Traité," that a considerable proportion of the earliest MSS., written in this kind of character, have the words divided by spaces, with greater or less regularity, in proportion, we may conclude, to the intelligence and care of the individuals who wrote them; and it is therefore unnecessary that I should offer any thing further in answer to the above supposed objection. It will be seen, in our third Plate, that they are so in the MS. of *Sulpicius Severus*, which was written at Verona in the year 517 ; and also in the Vatican *Terence*, from which we have given specimens, and which, as has been said, there is reason to believe to be much earlier. When we get to the latter part of the eighth century, we often find MSS. written in beautiful small minuscules, with the words more often separated than not, so as to be very easy to read: and such is the famous Bible, formerly preserved in the Convent of St. Paul outside the walls of Rome, which was probably written for Charlemagne before he was Emperor, and of which a page is given in fac-simile in the last volume of the "Evangeliarium Quadruplex" of Blanchinius, already mentioned.

But although, in the poem in our ancient MS. the words in the different lines bear, at first sight, the appearance of being properly separated from each other, they are often not so in reality. On the contrary, they are sometimes strangely divided in the middle, and the latter part of a word is joined to the beginning of that which follows; which again, perhaps, is treated in the same manner: thus, in the first line, under the figure of Perseus, instead of,

"*E pedibus natum summo Jove persea vis est,*"

the last part of the line in the ancient MS. reads, "*summo io ueperse auis est,*" as may be seen in the engraving; and so, in the fourth line under the Pleiades, we have, "*ueros exundique parvae,*" instead of, "*uero sex undique paruae.*" In fact this part of our MS. is full of similar evidences of the carelessness, or ignorance, or both, of the person who wrote it: and the circumstance is worthy of consideration, since Mai and other authors on these subjects speak of these kind of errors, as of frequent occurrence in the most ancient MSS. Under the supposition that the same person who wrote the text of Hyginus within the figures, wrote also the poem underneath them, (and I think this more likely than not, as the ink, when its colour has not been purposely changed for the sake of the variety before-mentioned, appears to be the same), I should account for the grosser errors, observable in the latter, by the circumstance of poetry being in its nature more difficult to understand than prose; besides which, we may reasonably suppose that greater errors had previously crept into the text of Cicero's juvenile performance, than into the prose of Hyginus, which was written long afterwards; and, moreover, that the remains, here and there in the poem, of the very ancient mode of spelling certain words, quite unlike that commonly used in the time of the copyist, could not but render him more liable to make mistakes in this part of his work.

The peculiarities in the orthography of this MS. (I speak more especially of the poem) furnish such evidence of its antiquity as is not I think to be withstood. It is true that the two Saxon MSS. copy several of these; and, I admit that, did they copy the whole, nothing would be proved by them; except that when Cicero was a youth (for it was then that he wrote this translation) this orthography prevailed; and that the different scribes, who in various after ages copied the poem, had, from a particular feeling of respect, been careful to preserve throughout the original spelling. But this, as has been shewn, was never customary with the copyists of MSS., and the two Saxon MSS. though they follow this ancient orthography in some cases, correct it, according to modern usage, in others; and, therefore, a very sound argument in favour of the antiquity of the MS. in which *all* these peculiarities, all these *archaisms*, are found, is to be drawn from them.

Between the probable date of this poem by Cicero, and the time when Virgil wrote his Æneid, we may count an interval of perhaps seventy years. There seems no doubt that during this period considerable changes were gradually introduced in Latin orthography, especially in the writing of compound words commencing with a preposition. The most ancient usage of all was to maintain the preposition in its original form, and to write *adpello, conlucens, inmortale, inlustrem,* &c. But Cicero, at a later period of his life, if we can judge from the Palimpsest "de Re Publica," published by Mai, sometimes wrote *appellabit, collocabit,* &c.; and Virgil, it appears from the most ancient MSS. of his poems (and, for the reasons already given, I am very much disposed to think that the Vatican MS., containing the fragments so often mentioned, was written not very long after his death), wrote sometimes one way, and sometimes the other; nay, it would seem from these fragments, that, more frequently than not, he changed the last letter of the preposition into the letter with which the word joined to it commenced; preferring *immemor, immota, immanis, immeritam, aggredior,* &c. to *inmemor, inmota, inmanis, inmeritam, adgredior,* &c. though I have little doubt he occasionally wrote these and other similar words both ways; as, indeed, writers in general did for many centuries afterwards.

In the poem in our ancient MS., on the contrary, I have not observed an instance in which the last letter of the preposition in a compound word is so changed; but we have always *adpositum, admonet, conmiserans, conlucens, inlustrem, inlustria, inponit,* &c. which orthography is commonly, though not always, copied in the Cottonian MS., but not unfrequently altered in the Harleian copy; where I find *ammonet* instead of *admonet, illustrem* for *inlustrem,* and *imponit* in place of *inponit.*

Not unfrequently we have *p*, instead of *b*, in our ancient MS.; as in *opscura, opservans,* &c. which are written in the usual manner, *obscura, observans,* &c. in the two Saxon copies; also *supter* for *subter*; and sometimes also, *t* for *d, at* for *ad.*

Instead of *arcitenens,* we have always *arquitenens,* which is the most ancient orthography: again, we have *oblicus,* and *longincum,* for *obliquus,* and *longinquum*; in which latter mode those words are spelt in the Harleian copy. The interchange, which was often made by the ancients, in the letters *c* and *q*, is well known. We shall notice another instance of it in this MS. presently.

The *h* is very seldom used in our ancient MS.; which, in almost every instance, has *umero, umeris, umeros,* as is commonly the case in the oldest MSS. of Virgil; instead of *humero, humeris, humeros:* it has also *aud* for *haud,* and in one instance *Idra* for *Hydra.* This initial *h*, is commonly supplied in the two copies.

We have always the ancient orthography in *pinnis, pinnati, pinnas,* as in all the earliest MSS. of Virgil; which words are constantly written with an *e*, *pennis, pennati, pennas,* in the two Saxon MSS.

In the 53d line, we have the contraction *vemens,* for *vehemens,* necessary because of the verse. Neither of the Saxon copyists appear to have understood the propriety of this, having both written *vehemens.*

We have also, over and over again, the termination *is* for *es*; as *partis tris,* for *partes tres*; *expertis omnis,* for *expertes omnes*; *quadruplicis* for *quadruplices*; *stirpis* for *stirpes*; *consimilis* for *consimiles*; *horribilis* for *horribiles*; which orthography is sometimes altered by the Saxon copyists, though oftener not.

In this MS. we have often the dipththong, in words where we are not accustomed to use it, whilst, *vice versa*, it is omitted in others where, according to our received orthography, it ought to be found; in which respect, also, it agrees with the most ancient Latin MSS. known. It is remarkable that *equus* is sometimes written *aequus,* and so in the Cottonian copy; and that in one instance (in verse 385) it has originally been written *aecus.* I may observe that I have occasionally found the word written with this dipththong, in the Medicean Virgil; as at pages 61, v. 6, 215—27, and 373—15, where we have *aequarum, aequum,* and *aequorum,* in each of which cases the corrector of the MS. has struck his pen across the first letter; that at page 2, v. 24, of the Medicean MS. I find *eequae* for *eque,* the first letter and the last but one being struck out in the same way; and that at pp.15—13, 120—14, 123 —24, 246—21, and 402—13, we have *ecus,* and *ecum;* besides which that MS. has sometimes *equs* written with one *u,* and sometimes in the ordinary manner with two. Our MS. of Cicero has also *querellis,* with the double *l,* which is written, according to the common orthography, *querelis,* in the Harleian copy, and *sollertem,* also with the double *l;* both of them according to the most ancient way of spelling those words. But all this will more fully appear in the text of the poem, in printing which care will be taken to preserve, as much as possible, the ancient orthography.

I must not omit to mention, that upon the margins of many of the pages of this MS., especially those with the figures, we have *the monogram of Christ* (☧) as it is termed, slightly drawn in with a pen, and generally with ink different from that with which the pages themselves are written. Upon first noticing the circumstance, I was of opinion that this had been done by the first Christian possessor of the MS., in order, as it were, to sanctify these Pagan performances: but I now find (Nouveau Traité, vol. iv. p. 598, n. 1.) that this monogram does not always denote Christianity; but that in early times it was often used by the Greeks in the margins of their MSS. (as in later centuries a hand pointing has been employed) in order to draw the attention of the reader to any thing that particularly deserved notice.

I must add, that the MS. bears decisive evidence of having been from the first, and perhaps during many centuries, folded in the middle; in consequence of which the parchment, strong as it is, has been worn through in three or four of the leaves. This I conceive to have been done by the original possessor of the MS. because of the great breadth of the leaves, and in order that it might the more conveniently go into one of those *oval* or *circular* boxes, in which the ancients were accustomed to keep their rolled MSS.: for though we have sufficient evidence that square MSS. began to come into use at a very early period, (probably in some parts long before the commencement of the Christian era), still there appears little doubt that, for a long time afterwards, rolled MSS. also continued to be used; and as this kind of MS. was the most ancient, it probably continued to be the most commonly adopted for a considerable time.

I have taken great pains, in the course of this inquiry, in order to come at truth; and may now fairly say, that whatever evidence I have chanced to find, bearing on the subject, appears to me to be confirmatory of the opinion which I originally expressed upon the age of this MS. on first seeing the drawings it contains; namely, that the most ancient part of it is anterior to the time of Constantine.

A very curious fact remains to be stated; namely, that the whole of the parchment of which this MS. is formed, (except the leaf with Saxon writing at the beginning), has formerly had other writing upon it, which was anciently washed and rubbed out, in order to make it available for the writing which it now has; in short that, ancient as it is, it is a Palimpsest.[a] The marks of this

[a] *Angelo Mai*, in his preface to the Palimpsest, discovered and published by him, of Cicero "De Re Publica," pag. xxx. produces the following passage in a letter of Cicero to Trebatius, in proof of the antiquity of the custom of making palimpsests; that is of rubbing out old writing from paper or parchment, and dressing the parchment a second time, in order to fit it for the reception of new: "Ut ad epistulas tuas redeam, cetera belle; &c. nam quod in *palimpsesto*, laudo equidem parsimoniam: sed miror quid in illa chartula fuerit, quod delere malueris quam haec non scribere; nisi forte tuas formulas. Non enim puto te meas epistulas delere, ut reponas tuas. An hoc significas, nihil fieri? frigere te? ne chartam quidem tibi suppeditare?" Mai observes, that Cicero here points out the three great causes of the practice; viz. a contempt for the matter contained in the old writing, economy in study, and the scarcity of parchment. He adds, that though parchment, from its strength, would seem alone qualified to undergo the above operation, and afterwards to receive new writing, yet he had seen an instance of a diploma of the ninth century, written upon papyrus, from which former writing had been washed out, the remains of which were apparent; and he therefore recommends the learned to be diligent in their examination of ancient papyri, as well as of MSS. on parchment: and indeed the fact of paper having been used in this way in ancient times, as well as parchment, may be inferred from the words of Catullus, (Carmen xxii.):

" Puto esse ego illi millia aut decem, aut plura,
Perscripta: nec sic, ut fit, in palimpsesto
Relata; chartae regiae, novi libri," &c.

When

washing, rubbing, and scraping, are every where to be seen in the MS., unless here and there in the margins of the pages, where we may suppose there was little or nothing to erase; and some of my friends think that they see in several places the stains occasioned by the former writing, although the letters cannot be distinguished.[b] Four or five words of the original MS., and I am sorry to say no more, have escaped the above process; which, as I have said, was less rigorously performed on the margins of the first MS. than on the pages themselves. I was long without noticing them: but happening one day to turn the book the bottom upwards, I observed, to my great surprise, on the page with the figure of *Lepus* (on what now became the upper margin,) the words s̃eq. deapostolis,[c] *(Sequitur de Apostolis)*, written in minium, grown black, in

---

When it was determined to make an old book serve for new writing, the whole was removed from the cover, the gatherings were unstitched, and the sheets, after being separated, were washed, scraped, and scowered, one by one, by the workman employed; after which they were dried and polished, in order to fit them to receive the new matter intended. In making the parchment, thus re-dressed, into new books, the sheets would of course seldom or never occupy the same situations as they did before; and that which in the former book had been the top of a page would as often as not become the bottom: but besides this, a book which had originally the form of a quarto was sometimes folded into an octavo; and sometimes a new volume would chance to be made of parts of several old ones; and this, although it consists of so few leaves, may possibly have been the case with our MS. of Cicero's Aratæa.

[b] It is possible that, by the application of the infusion of galls, some parts of the original writing might be made to re-appear: but the operation is a nice one; and if it be ever attempted in this MS. the greatest care ought to be taken not to injure either the writing or the drawings which it now has.

[c] " Seq'. de Apostolis," not " de SS. Apostolis," as it would most probably have been written, after the middle of the fifth century. *Buonarruoti*, (pp. 83-84, of the work already so often mentioned), describing certain fragments of drinking-glasses, whereon are the figures of St. Peter and St. Paul, speaks as follows, of the period at which the usage commenced, of prefixing the title of *Sanctus* to the names of the Apostles and other Saints and Martyrs:

" Around the portraits of these holy Apostles, we read their names, without the title *Sanctus*, or the letter *S*. which is so often used to signify it: it could not be otherwise with these very ancient monuments; as the custom of using the term in this way, was not introduced for a century or two after their date. In the Old and New Testament, this term, which properly means any thing separated from common use, is applied to whatever was in an especial manner consecrated to God, and appertained to his religion. Hence it is, that, in the infancy of the Christian Church, all Christians were called *Saints*, as being the children of God, and his favourite

capital letters of nearly the same size as those used in the text of Hyginus, but sensibly differing from them in shape; the E, especially, being quite unlike any I have observed in the book. (See Plate XXIII. No. 3.)

These words, I cannot doubt, were the title of some account of the preaching of the Apostles, with which that page, and probably some others following, were originally filled; other pages preceding it having been, I conclude, devoted to an account of the life and doctrine of Christ himself; whether a copy of one of the Gospels in Latin, or one of those shorter accounts which many learned men suppose to have been current in the Christian world before some of the Gospels themselves were written, I pretend not to say. In the middle of the upper margin of the page having the figure of *Coetus*, also, (near the edge of the leaf), we have the two words " *in nomine*," written with black ink in beautifully formed minuscule, which chanced to escape the above process: (Plate XXIII. No. 2.) besides which, in the inner margin of the recto of the second leaf of the third gathering, we have a capital C, and a small cross, done with the same black ink, and both turned upside down. (Plate XXIII. No. 1.) It is possible, that the two words, " *in nomine*," may originally have formed the first line of a page, or column of text, (for some very ancient

people. This title, in the course of time, was no longer applied to the Christians generally; but was given only to such as were eminent for virtue and piety; and so we find it used in the time of St. Jerome: not that the application of it was then so limited as it became afterwards; as it was commonly given to Bishops, Priests, Deacons, Monks, and Nuns. As, therefore, the title was not understood to distinguish, in an especial manner, men of very extraordinary sanctity from all others, so, in those times, it was by no means considered necessary to prefix it always, as we do now, to the names of Saints. In the Roman Calendar, supposed to be of the middle of the fourth century, and of the time of Liberius, which was published by Bucherius, and by Ruinart, we never find the word *Sanctus* prefixed to the names of the Pontiffs or Martyrs; whilst, on the contrary, it is seldom omitted in the Carthaginian Calendar, which was published for the first time by Mabillon, and afterwards by Ruinart, and which is believed to be of the fifth century. In this calendar, however, it is omitted before the names of some of the Saints; and we may therefore conjecture that the custom of using it began then to be introduced, and that this calendar was in part copied from a more ancient one, which in no instance had this title of *Sanctus*: in the Calendar of Polemius, of the year 449, (Act. SS. tom. i. Jan. p. 43), it is never wanting. And, with little variation of date, we find the same usage to have been by degrees introduced, in our paintings in Mosaic: as, in those in the church of S. Giovanni in Fonte at Ravenna, executed about 451, (Ciampini, tom. i. tab. 70), the Apostles are without

MSS. appear to have been written in three columns,[d] all the rest of which has been washed and rubbed out. I say this, because the word " *est*," alone, forms the first line of a column of the text in the Palimpsest of Cicero " de Re Publica," published by Angelo Mai,[e] as may be seen in the fac-simile given by him of that very ancient MS.

this title; but had it in the mosaic formerly in the church of St. Agatha, in the suburbs of Rome, which was executed about 472 (ibid. tom. i. tab. 77); as have also the figures of St. Cosmus and St. Damianus, in their church at Rome (ibid. tom. ii. tab. 17), which was decorated by Felix III. about the year 530."

[d] In the Edinburgh Review, Dec. 1828, there is an interesting paper on *Palimpsests*, in which those discovered by Mai are described. Speaking of one of those containing Orations of Cicero, the writer says: " He (Mai) read the titles '*pro Scauro*,' '*pro Tullio*,' and '*pro Flacco*,' and was able, with some trouble, to decipher the whole of the fragments of these three lost orations. They are written in large and very beautiful letters, each page being divided into *three columns*," &c. Speaking of another, he says: " The more ancient writing was in large and handsome characters, larger, but less beautiful, than that which contained the fragments of the three orations already named; and these were *two columns only in each page*, which circumstance testifies that the writing is somewhat more modern, than where there are *three*." I know not the grounds of this observation; but one of the pages of our MS. has three columns of writing; though the page preceding it has only two. See Plate XXIII Nos. 5, 6.

[e] Since the preceding pages were printed, I have turned over the Fragments of a *Palimpsest MS. of Plautus*, I did not know of before, which was published by Mai in 1815. Mai thinks this MS. was written in the time of the Antonines, and I suspect from the orthography that it is still older. The greater part is written in capitals, very like those of the Vatican fragments of Virgil; but part is in a mixed character, in which *minuscules* greatly preponderate.

I may add, that my attention has also lately been called to a very long *Inscription*, existing at *Eski-hissar*, supposed to be *the ancient Stratonicea*; whereof we have a *fac-simile* upon a reduced scale, (apparently done with great accuracy,) which was made by direction of Mr. William Bankes, who, in the year 1817, caused the whole to be carefully copied from the original. This inscription contains *an edict of Diocletian, A. D. 303*, with a *tariff* of the prices to be paid, for all sorts of commodities and labour, throughout the Roman Empire. Many of the letters are *minuscules*: the *b*, the *d*, the f (s), and the *u*, are always, or almost always, so; the *g* is oftener so than not; and we have several times the round ϵ, the minuscule *m*, the *q*, &c. See an interesting Article, upon the subject of this Inscription, by W. M. Leake, Esq. in the ' Transactions of the Royal Society of Literature.'

336 Sex omnes semper cedunt labentia nocte
Tot cælum rursus fugientia signa revisunt
Hoc spatium transeunt cæcis nox conficit umbris
Quod superud terras prima denocte relictum est

MARCI TULLII CICERONIS ARATÆA.*

(Figure of Aries.)   ANC. MS.

E quibus hinc subter possis cognoscere fultum.
I*am* [1] caeli mediam partem terit, ut prius illae   [1] Ima
Chel*ae*,[2] tum pectus quod cernitur Orionis.   [2] Chele
Et pro*p*e [3] conspicies paruum, sub pectore clarae   [3] prole conspiciens

(Deltoton.)

5 Andromedae signum, Deltoton dicere Grai*i* [4]   [4] Grai
   Quod solit*i*,[5] simili quia forma littera claret :   [5] solita
   Huic spatio ductum simili latus extat utrumque ;
   At non tertia pars lateris, nam non minor illis,
   Sed stellis longe densis praeclara relucet.
10 Inferior paulo est Aries, et flamen ad austri
   Inclinatior, atque etiam uehementius illi

---

* The Poem, in our ancient MS. has been corrected throughout by some old grammarian, who in some cases has marked misplaced letters, or such as he thought erroneous, by points placed over or underneath them ; but oftener has rubbed out, more or less effectually, the letters he disapproved of, substituting others in their place. The two Saxon copyists have generally adopted these corrections. I give the orthography, as far as possible, as it was originally. Where a letter is necessarily changed or added, it is printed in italic ; besides which, the word, as it stands in the MS. is repeated in the margin.

(verse 1) " *E quibus,*" &c. The two Saxon MSS. have " *A quibus.*"

(2) The ancient MS. and the Cottonian Saxon MS. have " *Ima caeli mediam,*" &c. ; the other Saxon copy has " *Ima poli,*" &c.

(3) The ancient MS. has " *Cheletum pectus,*" &c. the two first words being written as if one

(4) Anc. MS. " *Et prole conspiciens,*" &c.; the Cott. MS. has " *Et prole conspicies ;,*" the other Saxon MS. has " *Et prope conspicies.*"

(6) The ancient MS. and the Cottonian have " *solita ;*" the latter has also " *littore,*" instead of " *littera.*"

(8) " *At non,*" &c. ; the Cott. MS. has " *Et non,*" &c. " *nam non minor illis ;*" the other Saxon MS. has " *neq. est minor illis.*

(10) " *et flamen ;*" the Cott. MS. has " *ad flamen ;*" the other Saxon MS. has " *et flumen.*"

(Pisces.)

                                                            ANC. MS.

Pisces, quorum alter paulo praelabitur ante
Et magis horrissonis Aquilonis tangitur alis:
Atque horum e caudis duplices uelut esse catenae
15 Dices, quae diu diuersae per lumina serpunt,
Atque una tamen in stella communiter haerent,[1]   [1] haeret
Quem ueteres soliti caelestem dicere nodum.
Andromedae leuo ex umero, si quérere perges,
Adpositum poteris supra cognoscere piscem.

(Perseus.)

20 E pedibus natum summo Joue Persea vises,[2]   [2] vis est
Quos umeros retinet defixo corpore [3] Perseus,   [3] corrore
Cum summa ab regione Aquilonis flamina pulsant.

(v. 12.) Here we have "*praelabitur,*" instead of "*prolabitur,*" which was the reading of the older editors. Grotius first restored "*praelabitur,*" probably upon the authority of Cicero, quoting himself, in his "*De natura Deorum,*" ii. 43.

(13) "*Horrissonis:*" thus, with the double *ss*. Here the reading "*horrisonis,*" given by Grotius and Morel, is confirmed, against the "*horriferis*" of the older editors. At the end of this line, the Cott. MS. has "*alas,*" instead of "*alis.*"

(14) Both the Saxon MSS. have "*aere catenae.*"

(15) In the ancient MS. the "*a*" in "*quae,*" and "*di*" in "*diversae,*" appear to have been erased. The two Saxon MSS. have, "*Dicessuque diu verse,*" &c.

(16) The ancient MS. has "*haeret.*" Both the Saxon MSS. have the verb plural.

(18) All the three MSS. have "*levo*" and "*querere,*" without the diphthong, and so we sometimes find them in the palimpsest of Cicero de Re Pub. and in the Medicean Virgil. Indeed the diphthong is often omitted in this MS. in words in which we are accustomed to use it. In the same line, the two Saxon MS. have "*humero.*" We shall have future occasion to notice the frequent omission of the *h* in our ancient MS.

(19) "*Adpositum,*" for "*appositum,*" according to the ancient orthography; and so it is in the two Saxon copies, the writers of which sometimes copied what they saw, and at others altered the spelling according to the usage of their own times.

(20) Orig. "*perseauis est,*" and so in the two Saxon copies.

(21) "*Quos umeros,*" &c. The two Saxon MSS., as before, have the *h*. "*Humeros*" was the reading of Aldus in this line; but other editors give "*humeris.*" "*Humeros,*" however, may be maintained by supposing "*secundum:*" this accusative, instead of the ablative, is common in poetry,

supposed to be of the 2d or 3d century.

ANC. MS.

  Hic dextram ad sedes intendit Cassiepiae,[1]   [1] Cassiepiam
  Diuersosque pedes, uinctos talaribus aptis,
25 Puluerulentus uti de terra elapsus repente
  In caelum uictor magno[2] sub culmine portat.   [2] magnum

(Pleiades.)

  At propter leuum genus omnis parte locatas
  Paruas uergilias tenui cum luce uidebis.
  Hae Septem uulgo perhibentur more uetusto
30 Stellae, cernuntur uero sex undique paruae.
  Ac non interiisse putari conuenit unam,
  Sed frustra temere a uulgo ratione sine ulla
  Septem dicier, ut ueteres statuere poetae,
  Aeterno cunctas sane[3] qui nomine dignant: [3] sano
35 Altione Meropeque, Celaeno Taugeteque
  Electra[4] Asteropeque, simul sanctissima Maia.   [4] Electa
  Hae tenues paruo labentes lumine lucent;
  At magnum nomen signi, clarumque vocatur,

as every one knows; and seems very justifiable in this verse, in order to avoid a redundancy of ablatives. Virgil has, "Os humerosque deo similis," &c. In the same verse, the ancient MS. and the Cott. MS. have "*corrore*," instead of "*corpore*;" the other Saxon copy has rectified the error.

(23) The ancient MS. has "*cassi epiam*," the Saxon copies read as above.

(26) The ancient MS. has "*magnum*;" but both the Saxon MSS. have "magno."

(32) "*Ac vulgo*," was the reading of a MS. at Leyden, which Grotius used; notwithstanding which he preferred "*a vulgo*." It is gratifying to observe that the emendations suggested by this great scholar almost always agree with the readings of our ancient MS. We have another instance in the next line but one.

(34) The ancient MS. has "*sano*," which in both the Saxon MSS. is corrected "*sane*." But they also give "*signant*," instead of "*dignant*." Grotius maintains "*dignant*," probably against the authority of his own MS. "*Dignare*," actively used, is to be found in Accius, Cicero himself, and Virgil: the latter has,

" Conjugio Anchisae Veneris dignate superbo,"

where "*dignatus*," passive, warrants the above use of the active verb; which we also find in Accius (apud Nonnium): "*Exuvias dignavi Atalantae dare*."

(35) All the three MSS. have "*Altione*," instead of "*Alcione*."

(36) The *r* omitted in "*Electra*."

Propterea quod et estatis primordia *clar*at,
40 Et post hiberni praepandens temporis ortus
Admonet, ut mandent mortales semina terris.

(Fides quae Lira.)

Inde Fides leuiter posita et conuexa uidetur,
Mercurius paruus manibus, quam dicitur olim
Infirmis fabricatus, in alta sede locasse.
45 Haec genus ad leuum Nixi delapsa resedit.

(Cignus.)

Atque inter flexum genus, et caput alitis hesit :
Namque est ales auis, lato sub tegmine caeli

(39) In our ancient MS. the first four letters of the last word of this line have been erased. The word was probably the best reading of Grotius, "*clarat.*" The common reading has been "*claret.*" The Cottonian Sax. MS. has "*signat*," and the other has "*signant.*"

(41) The Harl. Saxon MS. has "*Ammonet;*" but the Cottonian has "*Admonet*," as in our ancient MS. "*Ammoneo*," in MSS. vett." says Ainsworth, " pro *Admoneo.*" By " MSS. veteres," he means those of the early centuries of the Christian era, till perhaps the eighth or ninth ; for *admoneo*, in which the preposition is preserved in its original state, (as in our ancient MS.) is the oldest orthography of all. In the time of Priscianus, it was customary to change the last letter of the preposition to the first letter of the word joined to it, in many cases where we do not do it now.

(43-4) Aldus and Morel have also "*parvus*," which is said to have been the reading of other old editions ; and the passage, as we here have it, renders very well the sense, if not the letter, of the Greek original ; παρὰ λίκνῳ Ἑρμείας—Mercury in his cradle. Grotius, Gruterus, and others, without the authority it appears of any MS. have somewhat too boldly altered these two lines as follows,

" Mercurius parvis manibus quam dicitur olim
In cunis fabricatus in alta sede locasse."

As if the Greek, παρὰ λίκνῳ, were not sufficiently implied by "*parvus*," and "*infirmis manibus.*"

(45) The line appears divided thus, in our ancient MS. ; whence we may conjecture that the writer of it did not very fully understand the meaning of his author :

" Haec genus adle uum nixide lapsare sedit."

One of the most ancient Latin MSS. existing, is supposed to be the Virgil in large capitals, No. 3867, in the Vatican library. In it the authors of the " Nouveau Traité de Diplomatique," (tom. iii. p. 61), notice the words, "*certare solebant,*" cut in pieces, by points, in the same strange manner ; "*certa. res. olebant.*"

(46) "*hesit*," without the diphthong ; and yet, at v. 16, we have "*haeret.*"

(47) The Harl. Saxon MS. has "*Jamque*," instead of "*Namque;*" and so has the MS. at Leyden. But "*Namque*" is better. Aratus says, ἤτοι γὰρ.

supposed to be of the 2d or 3d century.

ANC. MS.

Quae uolat, et serpens geminis secat aera[1] pinnis   [1] era
Altera pars huic opscura est et luminis expers:
50 Altera nec paruis, nec claris lucibus ardet,
Sed mediocre iacit quatiens e corpore lumen.
Haec dextram[2] Cephei dextro pede pellere palmam   [2] dextrim
Gestit; iam uero clinata est ungula uemens
Fortis Equi,[3] propter pinnati corporis alam.   [3] Foris eque

(Aquarius.)   COTT. MS.

a 55 Ipse autem labens multis Equus[4] ille tenetur   [4] aequus
Piscibus: huic ceruix dextra mulcetur Aquari.
Serius haec obitus terrai[5] uisit Equi uis,   [5] terrae
Quam gelidum ualido de corpore frigus anhelans

(48) The latter part of the line appears thus in our ancient MS. *geminisse catera pinnis,"* the words not being properly divided. Both the Saxon MSS. have "pennis," according to present usage. But "*pinnis*" is the most ancient orthography; and the word so spelt recurring several times in our MS. is among the proofs of its antiquity. This word, and its derivatives, are also written in this ancient manner with an *i*, in the celebrated Medicean MS. of Virgil, before-mentioned.

(49) "*Opscura*," for "*obscura.*" The ancients often substituted the *p* for the *b*, especially before a hard *s*, as in "*obscura*," "*observari*," &c. or before *t*; and the change has been consecrated by grammar, as in *scribo, scripsi, scriptum; nubo, nupsi, nuptum*, &c. Both the Saxon MSS. have "*obscura.*"

(52) Our ancient MS. has "*dextrim.*"

(53) Both the old Saxon copyists, ignorant of the justifiable contraction used in the last word, have written "*vehemens.*" There can be no doubt that Horace, like Cicero, wrote:

"Vemens et liquidus puroque simillimus amnis,"

and not "*vehemens et liquidus;*" a spondee, and not an anapest, being here required.

(54) "*Foris eque,*" in our ancient MS.: the *t*, omitted by mistake, was added at top by the person who in early times corrected it. Here, again, we have "*pinnati*," which in both the Saxon copies is altered to "*pennati.*"

a A leaf being here wanting in the ancient MS. we must supply the deficiency in the best way we can, by reference to the two Saxon copies, more especially the Cottonian.

(57) In this verse, Aldus has "*equinis.*" Grotius, however, ingeniously hit upon the true reading, "*equi vis*," notwithstanding the Leyden MS., which he used, had "*terrae pervisit equinis.*" The Harl. Saxon MS. has "*pervisit.*"

(Capricornus.)   COTT. MS.

Corpore semifero magno Capricornus in orbe :
60 Quem cum perpetuo uestiuit lumine Titan,
     Brumali flectens contorquet tempore currum.
     Hoc caue te in pontum studeas committere mense;
     Nam non longincum spatium labere[1] diurnum,   [1] habere
     Non hiberna cito uoluetur curriculo nox :
65 Humida non sese uestris aurora querellis
     Otius ostendit clari prenuntia solis ;
     At ualidis aequor pulsabit uiribus Auster :
     Tum fissum tremulo quatietur frigore corpus.
     Sed tamen anni iam labuntur tempore toto,
70 Ne cui signorum cedunt, neque flamina uitant,
     Nec metuunt canos minitanti murmure fluctus.[b]

(Sagittarius.)   ANC. MS.

Atque etiam super hoc,[2] naui pelagoque uagator[3]   [2] superos [3] vagato

(61) Turnebus and Grotius restored this line. The former, in company with Morel, gave "*contorquet*," instead of "*cum torquet;*" and Grotius changed "*cursum*" into "*currum*," in perfect agreement with our Cottonian MS. The other Saxon copy has "*Brufnali*," and "*cum torquet.*"

(62) We doubt not that our ancient MS. read "*conmittere.*"

(63) The Cottonian MS. has "*habere*," instead of "*labere*," which may be considered as a slip of the pen. The Harl. Saxon copy has "*longinquum :*" but the Cottonian has the archaism "*longincum*," which was doubtless the reading of our ancient MS. Most or all of the MSS. hitherto known appear to have had "*longe cum*," which editors have changed into "*longinquum.*"

(65) "*Querellis*," instead of "*querelis.*" Gruterus, Fabrettus, and Aldus Manutius have many proofs of the antiquity of this orthography ; as appears from Facciolati's Lexicon. It is indeed of constant occurrence in the most ancient MSS. The Harl. Saxon MS. has "*querelis.*"

(66) Buhle has "*Ocyus ostendet*," &c. Both our Saxon MSS. have "*ostendit ;*" and "*prenuntia*" without the diphthong.

[b] Although the leaf immediately following, containing the constellations *Sagittarius* and *Sagitta*, is not wanting in our ancient MS. ; the writing under those figures is so obliterated as to be illegible ; the same is the case with that under *Aquila*, which succeeds them ; and we must therefore still have recourse to the two Saxon copies.

(72) Although this page of our ancient MS. is almost entirely effaced, the word "*superos*," instead of "*super hoc*," is discernible. The Cottonian MS. has "*aetiam ;*" and both it and the

supposed to be of the 2d or 3d century. 187

  Mense, Sagittipotens solis cum sustinet orbem :   COTT. MS.
  Nam iam cum minus exiguo lux tempore presto est,
75 Hoc signum ueniens poterunt praenoscere nautae ;
  Iam prope praecipitante licebit uisere nocti,
  Ut sese ostendens ostendat Scorpius alte,
  Posteriore trahens flexum ui corporis arcum.
  Iam super hunc cernes Arc*ti*[1] caput esse minoris, [1] Arci
80 Et magis erectum ad summum uersarier orbem.
  Tum sese Orion toto iam corpore condet
  Extrema prope nocte, et Cepheus condit*ur* alte[2] [2] Cæpheus conditor
  Lumborum tenus a prima depulsus ad umbras.   [altæ

(Sagitta.)

  Hic m*iss*ore[3] uacans fulgens iacet una Sagitta, [3] messore
85 Quam propter nitens pinna[4] conuoluitur ales :   [4] penna
  Haec clinata magis paulo est aquilonis ad auras.

other Saxon MS. have "*vagatur,*" instead of "*vagator.*" The ancient MS. appears to have had "*vagato,*" which the original corrector of it changed to "*vagatur.*"

(76) Both the Saxon MSS. have "*Jam,*" and the ancient MS. appears to have had the same. The common reading of this line formerly was :

   " Jam prope praecipiti ante licebit visere nocti."

Grotius suggested the correcting of it as above ; save that he changed "*nocti*" into "*nocte.*" Nevertheless, the supposition that "*nocti*" may have been anciently used as an ablative, seems probable from the "*orbi*" for "*orbe,*" elsewhere to be found in this MS. Grotius styles such ablatives as "*orbi,*" "scriptura antiqua." The Cottonian MS. retains "*nocti:*" the Harl. Saxon MS. has "*nocte.*"

(77) Mr. Prevost, following Buhle, suggests "*emergens,*" instead of "*ostendens ;*" but both the Saxon copies have "*ostendens.*"

(79) Both the Saxon MSS. have "*Jam,*" and the ancient MS. appears to have had the same. The Saxon MSS. have both "*arci,*" instead of "*arcti.*"

(82) The Cottonian MS. has "*conditor.*" "*Alte*" was suggested by Grotius ; the common reading having been "*conditur ante.*"

(84) This reading confirms the correction of Morel. Before his time the adopted line was : "*Hic misso revocans,*" &c. Grotius himself gave it so in his Syntagma ; although, approving of Morel's correction, he says in his notes : "Non dubium est legendum : *missore vacans.*" The Cottonian MS. gives erroneously "*messore,*" but the other Saxon copy has "*missore,*" which word is also discernible in our ancient MS.

(85) Both the Saxon MSS. have "*penna.*" The word was certainly "*pinna*" in our ancient MS.

(Aquila.)

  At propter se Aquila ardenti cum corpore portat,
  Igniferum mulcens [1] tremebundis aethera pinnis,
  Non nimis ingenti cum corpore, sed graue mestis
90 Ostendit nautis, perturbans aequora, signum.

COTT. MS.

[1] mulcis

(Delphinus.)

  Tum magni curuus Capricorni corpora propter
  Delphinus iacet, haud nimio lustratus nitore,
  Praeter quadruplicis stellas in fronte locatas,
  Quas interuallum binas disterminat unum :
95 Cetera pars late tenui [2] cum lumine serpit.
  Illae quae fulgent luces ex ore corusco,
  Sunt inter partes gelidas Aquilonis locatae,[3]
  Atque inter spatium et laeti uestigia solis.
  At pars inferior Delfini fusa uidetur

ANC. MS.

[2] tenul

[3] locatas

(88) Before the time of Grotius "*mulgens*," instead of "*mulcens*," was the received reading; which, as he observed, was indefensible. The archaism, "*pinnis*," is not entirely obliterated in our original MS. The Saxon copies have "*pennis*."

(89) This reading, adopted by Morel and Grotius, is said to be found only in two MSS. on the continent: all the others have "*non minus*," &c.

(92) The Cottonian MS. has "*haut*," instead of "*haud*."

(93) One of the Saxon MSS. has "*Propter*," instead of "*Praeter*." "*Quadruplicis*," for "*quadruplices*," in this verse, is according to the most ancient orthography. The two Saxon MSS. have also "*quadruplicis*."

(95) This reading of our ancient MS. save that by a slip of the pen we have "*tenul*," instead of "*tenui*," confirms the "legendum" of the learned Grotius. Both the Saxon copyists altered the line thus: "Caetera pars latet et nullo cum lumine serpit."
Some of the printed editions, with still less regard to sense, and heedless of grammar and prosody, read: "Cætera pars lata nullum cum lumine serpit."

(97) All the three MSS. have "*locatas*."

(99) Our ancient MS. has "*Delfini:*" and yet in verse 92 we read "*Delphinus*." Similar variations of orthography, in writing the same word, are frequent in the most ancient MSS. of Virgil. Both the Saxon copies have "*Delphini*." In the word "*fusa*," in the ancient MS. the traces of two obliterated letters, apparently an *l* and an *o*, are to be perceived, between the *u* and the *s*. It is to be regretted, that the ancient corrector of this MS. did not throughout content himself with marking erroneous or superfluous letters by points placed over or underneath, instead of rubbing them out.

supposed to be of the 2d or 3d century.

100 Inter Solis iter, simul inter flamina uenti,
    Uiribus erumpit qua summi spiritus Austri.[1]

ANC. MS.
[1] Astri

(Orion.)

    Exinde Orion obliquo corpore nitens,
    Inferiora tenet truculenti corpora Tauri:
    Quem qui suspitiens in caelum nocte serena
105 Late dispersum non uiderit, aud ita uero
    Cetera[2] se speret cognoscere signa potesse.

[2] Ceteras speret

(Syrius.)

    Namque pedes subter rutilo cum lumine clare*t* [3]
    Feruidus ille canis stellarum luce refulgens.
    Hunc tegit obscurus subter praecordia uesper;
110 Et uero toto spirans de corpore flammam
    Aestiferos ualidis erumpit flatibus ignes.
    Totus ab ore micans iacitur mortalibus ardor.
    Hic ubi se pariter cum sole in lumina caeli
    Extulit, haud patitur foliorum tegmine frustra
115 Suspensos animos arbusta ornata tenere:
    Nam quorum stirpis tellus amplexa prehendit,

[3] clare

(101) The ancient MS. has "*astri*," which is corrected, "*austri*," in both the Saxon copies.

(104) In our ancient MS. "*suspiciens*" is written with a *t*; indeed, the *t* is often used in our MS. instead of the *c*, in words of similar termination.

(105) Instead of "*aud ita*," (the first word being written without the *h* in our ancient MS.) all the MSS. known to previous editors are said to have "*abdita*," a reading out of which it is not easy to make sense. Both the Saxon MSS. have "*haud ita.*"

(106) The ancient MS. reads, *ceteras speret*," &c. the *e* in *se* having been left out, or perhaps obliterated: both the Saxon copies have "*cetera se speret*," &c.

(107) The ancient MS. has "*clare*," and so has the Cottonian MS. The other Saxon copy has "*claræ.*"

(108) The two last words in this line read, "*lucere fulgens*," in our ancient MS.

(114) The Harl. Saxon MS. has "*filiorum*," instead of "*foliorum.*"

(116) "*Stirpis*," for "*stirpes*," another instance of *is* long, for *es*. Both the Saxon MSS. also have "*stirpis.*" The word "*tellus*" appears originally to have been written "*stellus*" in our ancient MS. and the *s* to have been afterwards rubbed out.

		ANC. MS.
	Haec augens anima uitali flamine[1] mulcet:	[1] flamina
	Ad quorum nequeunt radices findere terras,	
	Denuda*t*[2] foliis ramos, et cortice truncos.	[2] Denuda

(Lepus.)

120 Hunc propter subterque pedes, quos diximus, ante
Orionis iacet leuipes Lepus: hic *fugit*,[3] ictus   [3] leuipedes . . eugit
Horrificos metuens rostri tremebundus acuti,
Nam Canis infesto sequitur uestigia cursu,
Praecipitantem agitans: oriens iam denique paulo,
125 Curriculum numquam defesso corpore sedans.

(Argo.)

At Canis ad caudam Serpens prolabitur Argo
Conuexam prae se portans cum lumine puppim:
Non aliae naues ut in alto ponere[4] proras   [4] pondere
Ante solent, rostro Neptunia prata secantes;
130 Sed conuexa retro caeli se per loca portat
Sicuti cum coeptant tutos contingere portos,
Obuertunt nauem magno cum pondere nautae
Aduersam que trahunt obtata ad littora puppim:
Sic conuersa uetus super aethera uertitur Argo,
135 Atque usque *a* prora ad *celsum*[5] sine lumine malum,   [5] caeli sum

(117) All the three MSS. have "*flamina*."
(119) The ancient MS. has "*Denuda*."
(120) Both the Saxon copies have, "*Hanc propter*," &c.
(121) The ancient MS. has "*leuipedes lepus*," and "*eugit*," instead of "*fugit*." The two Saxon MSS. instead of "*fugit*," have "*quoq*." The "*eugit*," in the ancient MS. may, I think, reasonably be accounted for, by supposing this MS. to have been copied, by a person not very well versed in Latin poetry, from one written entirely in capitals; where an ғ might readily have been mistaken for an ᴇ.
(125) The ancient MS, has "*numquam*," instead of "*nunquam*."
(128) All the three MSS. have "*pondere*."
(135) The *a* before *prora* is wanting in all the three MSS. Instead of "*ad celsum sine*," &c. the ancient MS. has "*ad caeli sum sine*, &c. The two Saxon copies have the line thus:
     "Atque usque proram ac caeli summum sine lumine malum."

supposed to be of the 2d or 3d century. 191

  A malo ad puppim clara cum luce uidetur.   ANC. MS.
  Inde gubernaclum disperso lumine fulgens,
  Clari posteriora canis uestigia tangit.[1]   [1] candit

(Coetus.)

  Exin semotam procul in tutoque locatam
140 Andromedam tamen explorans fera querere Pistrix
  Pergit et usque sitam ualidas Aquilonis ad auras[2]   [2] aures
  Caerula uestigat, finita in partibus austri
  Hanc Aries[3] tegit, et squamoso corpore Pisces   [3] aues
  Fluminis in*lustri tangentem corpore ripas.

(Eridanus.)

145 Namque etiam Eridanum cernes in parte locatum
  Caeli, funestum magnis cum uiribus amnem,
  Quem lacrimis mestae Phaethontis sepe sorores
  Sparserunt, letum merenti uoce canentes.
  Hunc Orionis sub leua cernere planta
150 Serpentem poteris : proceraque uincla uidebis

(138) The ancient MS. has "*candit*," instead of "*tangit*;" the Cottonian MS. has "*candet*," and the other Saxon copy has "*clarent*."

(141) The ancient MS. has "*ad aures;*" both the Saxon copies have "*ad auras.*"

(143) The ancient MS. has "*Hanc aves tegit*," &c. the Cottonian has "*avis*," and the other Saxon copy "*navis.*" Buhle gives the line as above.

(144) "*Fluminis* inlustri." The "*in*" is omitted in the ancient MS. Both the Saxon copies have "*illustri.*"

In another place (verse 254), the writers of these two MSS. both wrote *inlustria*, copying what was before them: and at verse 213. where the ancient MS. has "*inlustrem*," the Harl. Saxon MS. has "*illustrem*," and the Cottonian "*inlustrem*."

(147) In this line we have "*lacrimis*," without the *y*. Facciolati, in his Lexicon, says: "veteres.... inscriptiones plurimae pro hac scriptione (*lacrima*, pro *lacryma*) stant."

(148) "*Letum*," for "*lethum*." Facciolati observes: .... "in antiquis libris et lapideis monumentis nulla est aspiratio; testibus Manutio et Cellario in orthographia." It is worth observing, that the word is so spelt in the fifth column of the ancient Latin Papyrus, published in vol. ii. of the "Herculanensium Voluminum quae supersunt," (Neapoli 1809), where we read : "*Omne vagabatur leti genus.*" The two Saxon MSS. have "*loetum.*" All three have "*merenti.*"

Quae retinen*t* Pisces caudarum parte locata, ANC. MS.
Flumine mixta retro ad Pistricis terga reuerti.
Hac una stella nectuntur, quam iacit ex se
Pistricis spina [1] ualida cum luce refulgens.   [1] spinae
155 Exinde exiguae tenui cum lumine multae
Inter Pistricem fusae sparsaeque [2] uidentur,   [2] quae
Atque gubernaclum stellae, quas contigit omnis
Formidans acrem [3] morsu Lepus : His neque nomen, [3] acram
Nec formam ueteres certam statuisse uidentur.
160 Nam qua*e* sideribus claris natura poliuit,
Et uario pinxit distinguens lumine formas,
Ha*ec* ill*a* astrorum custos ratione notauit,
Signaque *d*ignauit caelestia nomine uero :
Has autem quae sunt paruo cum lumine u*er*s*ae*
165 Consimilis spetie stellas, parilique nitore,
Non potuit nobis nota clarare figura.

(151) The last letter in "*retinent*," has been erased and changed to a *t* in the ancient MS. I suspect it to have been originally an *s*.

(153) The first word of the line in the ancient MS. has perhaps originally been "*hanc ;*," but the third letter has been erased, and an *e* inserted in its place. Both the Saxon copies have "*Haec*."

(154) The ancient MS. has "*spinae*," the Cottonian MS. has "*spine*, and the other has "*spinæ*."

(156) The ancient MS. has "*quae ;*" the two Saxon copies have "*que*."

(158) The ancient MS. has "*acram*," the two Saxon MSS. have "*acrem*."

(160) The ancient MS. has "*Nam qua*," the letter following (probably *e*) having been erased, and an *s* inserted in its place. Both the Saxon copies have "*quas*."

(162) The ends of the two first words are erased in the ancient MS. Both the Saxon copies have "*Has ille*." The ancient MS. instead of *o* in "*notavit*," has originally had some other letter, perhaps an *a*, which has been rubbed out, and the *o* substituted ; the Saxon MSS. have "*notavit*."

(163) The *d* in "*dignavit*," (if indeed we are correct in our suspicions that that was the original word) has been erased in the ancient MS. and an *s* substituted. Both the Saxon MSS. have "*signavit*," which is also the reading of Buhle.

(164) The end of the last word has been erased in the ancient MS. and the whole changed to "*uelquae ;*" which is also the reading of both the Saxon copies.

(165) "*Consimilis speti..*," in the ancient MS. the end of the latter word being erased. *Consimilis*, for *consimiles*, is according to the ancient orthography. Both the Saxon copies have, "*Consimiles specie*."

(*Piscis.*) ANC. MS.

Exinde australem soliti quem dicere Piscem
Uoluitur inferior Capricorno uersus ad austrum,
Pistricem opseruans, procul illis piscibus herens.
170 Et prope conspicies expertis nominis omnis
Inter Pistricem, et Piscem quem diximus austri,
Stellas sub pedibus stratas radiantis Aquari.
Propter Aquarius obscurum dextra rigat amne*m*;
Exiguo qui stellarum candore nitescit.
175 E multis tamen his duo late lumina fulgent;
Unum sub magnis pedibus cernetur Aquari,
Quod superest gelido delapsum flumine fontis,
Spinigeram supter caudam Pistricis adhesit:
Hae tenues stellae perhibentur nomine Aquari.
180 Hic aliae uolitant paruo cum lumine clare,
Atque prior*a* pedum subeunt[1] uestigia magni [1] subsunt
Arquitenentis et opscurae sine nomine cedunt.

(169) "*Opseruans,*" for "*observans,*" *p* for *b*, as in a word noticed in the 49th line. In this and other similar instances where the *p* is used for *b* before a hard consonant in our ancient MS. the Saxon copyists have altered the word according to modern usage. All the three MSS. have "*herens,*" without the *a*.

(170) "*Expertis....omnis,*" for "*expertes....omnes,*" *is* for *es*, as before. Both the Saxon MSS. have the same.

(178) "*Supter,*" for "*subter.*" Both the Saxon MSS. have "*subter.*"

(179) This line confirms the correction of Morel and Grotius. In some MSS. the readings were: "*Et tenues stellae,*" and "*Etenus stellae.*"

(181) The *a* in "*priora*" is added, in the ancient MS., by the person who in early times corrected it. All the three MSS. have "*subsunt,*" instead of "*subeunt.*"

(182) Our ancient MS. gives constantly "*Arquitenens,*" which was the orthography of the oldest poets, as Nævius, quoted by Macrobius, Lucretius, &c. There can be no doubt that Cicero, who was so well read in the old poets of his country, wrote the word as we have it in our ancient MS. and, indeed, as this translation was a work of his early youth, (for in his "De Natura Deorum" he speaks of himself as then "admodum adolescentulus") we may conclude that the old orthography was at that time in vogue. In this line we have also "*opscurae,*" for "*obscurae,*" (it is written with the *b* in both the Saxon copies); also "*cedunt,*" the very reading of Grotius, instead of the "*condunt*" of previous editions.

194   *On a MS. of Cicero's translation of Aratus,*

(*Ara.*)   ANC. MS.

    Inde Nep*a*e [1] cernes propter fulgentis acumen   [1] nepe
    Aram, quam flatu permulcet spiritus austri,
185 Exiguo superum quae lumin*a* tempor*e* [2] tranat: [2] lumine tempora
    Nam procul Arcturo est aduersa parte [3] locata.   [3] de parte
    Arcturo magnum spatium supero dedit, orbem
    Juppiter hic [4] paruum inferiori in parte locauit.   [4] huic
    H*a*ec [5] tamen aeterno inuisens loc*a* curriculo nox,   [5] Hic
190 Signa dedit nautis, cuncti qu*a*e [6] noscere possent,   [6] que
    Conmiserans hominum metuendos undique casus.
    Nam cum fulgentem cernes sine nubibus atris
    Aram sub media caeli regione locatam,
    A summa parte opscura caligine tectam,
195 Tum ualidis fugito deuitans uiribus austrum ;
    Quem si prospiciens uitaueris, omnia caute
    Armamenta locans tuto labere per undas.
    Sin grauis inciderit uehementi flamine uentus
    Perfringet celsos defixo robore malos,
200 Ut res nulla feras possit mulcere procellas,

(185) Here, in all the three MSS., we have erroneously "*lumine*" for "*lumina*," and "*tempora*," instead of "*tempore*." In other respects the line confirms the correction of Turnebus, adopted by the modern editors. "*Limina*" was the previous reading.

(186) All the three MSS. have "*aduersa de parte*."

(187–8) Again, the very reading suggested by the sagacious and learned Grotius ; if we except "*supero*," for "*supera ;*" though, according to his usual practice, when the MSS. he knew of were not in favour of his corrections, he preserved the old reading "*hunc paruum*," in his text. All the three MSS. have "*huic paruum.*" We should observe, that the *m*, in "*orbem*," has been inconsiderately erased in the ancient MS. and that the two Saxon copies, have "*orbe.*"

(189) All the three MSS. have "*Hic tamen.*"

(190) The ancient MS. has "*que*" without the *a*: the two Saxon MSS. have a mark under the *e*, denoting the diphthong.

(191) "*Conmiserans*," for "*commiserans.*"

(194) "*Opscura*," again, for "*obscura* ." The two Saxon MSS. have "*obscura.*"

supposed to be of the 2d or 3d century. 195

Ni parte ex Aquilonis opacam pellere nubem
Coeperit et subitis¹ auris diduxerit Ara.

ANC. MS.
¹ subditis

(*Centaurus.*)

Sin umeros medio in caelo Centaurus habebit,
Ipseque caerulea contectus nube feretur,
205 Atque Ar*am* tenui caligans uestiet² umbra,
At signorum obitum³ uis est metuenda fauoni.
Ille autem Centaurus in alta sede locatus,
Qua⁴ sese clare conlucens Scorpios infert,
Haec subter partem perportans⁵ ipse uirilem
210 Cedit, equi partis properans⁶ coniungere Chelis.
Hic dextram porgens, quadripes qua uasta tenetur,

²arma .. uestigiet
³obitu

⁴Quae
⁵perpotans
⁶properat

(202) The ancient MS. has had "*subditis*," instead of "*subitis*;" but the *d* is erased. Both the Saxon MSS. have "*subitis*."

(203) Again, "*umeros*," without the *h* in our early MS., for the two Saxon copies have "*humeros*." It was very much the practice of the ancients to drop the *h*. H. Stephanus says, in his Lexicon, that on the tombs of the early Christians they wrote "*abet sedem*," for "*habet sedem*;" and we have an instance of it, in Arringhi's "Roma Subterranea."

Quinctilian also, (lib. i. cap. 5), bears testimony to the frequent omission of this letter by the ancients; "Parcissimè eâ (littera *h*) veteris usi, etiam in vocalibus, cum ædos, ircos, dicebant." Again, Cassiodorus says, in his valuable treatise "de Orthographia:" "Omnis vocalis м sequente leniter enunciatur, ut. ... umor, umeros, umus, et quicquid ab his fit." The dropping of the *h* in "*humeros*," is peculiarly justified by etymology; the Greek ὦμος having the soft aspiration. Hence it is, perhaps, that the *h* is omitted in this word, with scarce any exception, throughout the MS.

(205) Here we have two gross errors in our ancient MS., "*arma*" for "*aram*, and "*vestigiet*" for "*vestiet*," only to be accounted for by the ignorance or carelessness of the copyist. These and similar blunders, however, are evidence of the genuineness of the good readings, when we find them; as it is impossible to attribute these latter to the ingenuity of the scribe. Both the Saxon MSS. have "*aram*;" but one of them, the Cottonian, has retained "*vestigiet*."

(206) "*At*," for "*ad*;" in the same line, the ancient MS. and the Harleian Saxon MS. have "*obitu*;" the Cottonian has "*obitus*."

(208) "*Conlucens*," for "*collucens*."

(210) "*Partis*," for "*partes*." The Harl. Saxon MS. has the same; but the Cottonian has "*partes*." In the same line, all the three MSS. have "*properat*."

(211) The ancient MS. has "*quadripes*," and so has the Cottonian MS. The other Saxon copy has "*quadrupes*."

Quam nemo certo donauit nomine Graium,   ANC. MS.
Tendit et inlustrem truculentus cedit ad Ar*am*.

(Hydra.)

Hic sese infernis e partibus erigit Idra
215 Praecipiti lapsu, flexo cum [1] corpore Serpens.   [1] qum
Haec caput atque oculos torquens a*d* [2] terga Nepai,   [2] a
Conuexoque sinu subiens inferna Leonis,
Centaurum leui contingit lubrica cauda,

(213) "*Inlustrem*," for *illustrem*. The Harl. MS. has "*illustrem*;" but the Cottonian copies the old orthography: as it does, indeed, in most of these compound words, throughout the poem.

(214) The *s*, in "*infernis*," is wanting in the ancient MS.; but both the Saxon copies have it. This line certainly runs smoother with the preposition *è*, than with the *de* of some of the editions. Some MSS. appear to have had *a*, which is less proper. The Leyden MS., not disapproved, though not followed by Grotius, had *è*.

In this line we also read "*Idra*," for "*Hydra*." The frequent omission of the *h* has already been sufficiently noticed, as an evidence of the antiquity of this MS. As for the *i*, instead of the *y*, we read in the Lexicon of Stephanus: "Latini veteres ab hâc Græcorum vocali abstinebant: dixerunt enim vel cum *i*, silva, silvanus; vel cum *u*, ut *Burrhum, Bruges*, i. e. *Pyrrhum, Phryges*." The Harl. Saxon MS. has "*Hydra*;" the Cottonian "*Idra*," like the ancient MS. The *y* came much into fashion afterwards. In the latter part of the fifth century the celebrated Medicean MS. of Virgil was corrected, as has been said, by Turcius Rufius Apronianus: and in doing this, it is remarkable that in numerous cases he converted the I into Y. See the notes at the end of Foggini's edition of this manuscript, printed at Florence in 1741.

(215) In this verse, the ancient MS. has "*qum*," for "*cum*;" which the two Saxon MSS. have altered to "*cum*." We have several instances of the *q*, used instead of *c*, in Gruterus's Inscriptions; as in tom. i. p. 202, where we read "*pequdes*," for "*pecudes*," and several times "*pequnia*," for "*pecunia*;" and at p. 205, where we find, "*pequsque*," instead of "*pecusque*."

(216) The ancient MS. has "*a terga*;" both the Saxon copies have "*ad terga*."

(218) All the editions, and the MSS. hitherto known, the Leyden MS. excepted, read "*leni*," instead of "*levi*;" which last epithet is certainly more applicable, than the other, to a hard and scaly substance like that of the tail of the Hydra. Thus, Virgil has:

      ...... "*Levi* de marmore tota
      Saxa ciet."......

And   "*Levibus* huic hamis consertam."......
And Horace: "Galeæ que *leves*."
And in Valerius Flaccus we find:

    ...."*levique* manus labuntur ab auro."—Argonaut, lib. i. v. 290.

Lenis

supposed to be of the 2d or 3d century. 197

    In medioque sinu fulgens Cretera relucet   ANC. MS.
220 Extrema[1] nitens plumato corpore Coruus   [1] extrema
    Rostro tondit, et hic geminis est ille sub ipsis,

(Anticanis.)

    Antecanem, Graio Procyon qui nomine fertur.
    Haec sunt quae uises[2] nocturno tempore signa,   [2] uisens
    Legitimo cernens caeli lustrantia cursu,
225 Aeternumque uolens[3] mundi pernoscere motum.   [3] uoles

Lenis is applied to very different substances: such as the water: also to the wind, sound, &c. Therefore Virgil says: ...." *leni* fluit agmine Tybris."
...."*sic leni* crepitabat bractea vento."
" *Lenibus* horrescunt flabris "....
.... " *lenis* crepitans vocat Auster in altum."
And Horace: ...." *leni* fuit Austro
    Captus "....
And Valerius Flaccus, in one of his best lines:
    "Nox erat et *leni* crepitabant aequora sulco."
And in another: .... " *leni* modulatur carmen avena."
where *leni* is applied to the sound, not to the hard substance of the reed. And again:
    " *Lenibus* alludit flabris levis Auster."
From these quotations the excellence of *levi cauda* (hydrae) is evident. Unfortunately, however, it has not been adopted in any edition we know of; not even in that of Grotius, who nevertheless had the use of the Leyden MS. The German editor, Buhle, contents himself with saying: "Melius forsitan *levi*," but did not admit it in his text; perhaps because there was only known one MS. in favour of the reading: now, happily, we have three others.

(219) The ancient MS. has " *cretera,*" and so the word is spelt in verse 387. Both the Saxon copies have " *cratera.*"

(220) All the three MSS. have " *Extrema.*"

(223, 4, 5) These three lines stand thus in our ancient MS. and in the Saxon copy in the Harleian collection. All the three MSS. have " *visens,*" and " *cernens,*" and the Cottonian MS. has also " *volens.*"

    " Haec sunt quae uisens nocturno tempore signa.
    Legitimo cernens caeli lustrantia cursu,
    Aeternumque uoles mundi pernoscere motum."

The last verse is given by Aldus, as it is here placed; but is omitted by Morell and some other editors; either perhaps in consequence of the difficulty they found in making sense of it, or because, in the opinion of the censors of the press, it might be supposed to imply the motion of our globe, as

	ANC. MS.
Nam quae per bis *sex*[1] signorum labier orbe*m*	[1] bis ex
Quinque solent stellae, simili ratione notari	
Non possum ; qu*ia* quae faciunt uestigia cursu	
Non eodem[2] semper spatio protrita teruntur :	[2] eadem
230 Sic malunt errare uagae per nubila caeli,	
Atque suos[3] uario motu metirier orbes.	[3] suo
Hae faciunt magnos longinqui temporis annos,	
Cum redeunt ad idem caeli sub tegmine signum :	

well as of the heavenly bodies which surround it ; a doctrine then considered at variance with the true Catholic faith.

Mr. Prevost, upon the passage being first shewn to him, immediately suggested the following transposition and alteration of the last line; which he afterwards found had been also thought of by Grotius ; and, indeed, the lines are placed in this order, in the edition of Buhle.

"Haec sunt quae visens nocturno tempore signa,
Aeternum que volens mundi pernoscere motum,
Legitimo cernes caeli lustrantia cursu."

But had Grotius known of three MSS. all having the rare verse, "*Aeternumque*," &c. in the same place it occupies in the Aldine edition, he would perhaps have sought out some other means of rectifying the passage ; and it occurred to me that, without any transposition, it might stand as follows ; and as it is given above :

"Haec sunt quae vises nocturno tempore signa,
Legitimo cernens caeli lustrantia cursu
Aeternumque volens mundi pernoscere motum."

Thus, the sense is rendered perspicuous, by merely taking the *n* from *visens*, and giving it to *voles*, at the same time that the solecism, "*voles pernoscere*," is got rid of. The superiority of *pernoscere*, as in our MS. over *cognoscere*, which has been the more common reading, is evident. Mr. Prevost thinks I have chanced to hit upon the right correction of this passage. In support of *vises*, he observes, that we have in the 342d line :

"Ortus signorum nocturno tempore vises,"

and in this other line :

"Ac si nocturno convises tempore caelum ;"

in which two passages, Cicero himself appears to point out the correction : the text of Aratus he also finds implies the same order in the lines :

Ταῦτά κε θηήσαιο, παρερχομένων ἐνιαυτῶν,
Ἐξείης παλίνωρα· τὰ γὰρ καὶ πάντα μάλ' αὔτως
Οὐρανῷ εὖ ἐνάρηρεν ἀγάλματα νυκτὸς ἰούσης.

(229) The ancient MS. has "*eadem*." See Buhle's note upon "*teruntur*;" for which he substitutes "*feruntur*."

supposed to be of the 2d or 3d century. 199

  Quare ego nunc nequeo tortos euoluere cursus.
235 Uerum haec quae semper certo euoluuntur in orbe
  Fixa simul, magnos edemus gentibus orbes.
  Quattuor aeterno lustrantes lumine mundum,
  Orbes stelligeri portantes signa feruntur,
  Amplexi terras caeli sub tegmine fulti.
240 E quibus annorum uolitantia lumina nosces,
  Quae densis distincta licebit cernere signis.
  Tum magnos orbes magno cum lumine latos,
  Uinctos inter se, et nodis caelestibus aptos,
  Atque pari spatio duo cernes esse duobus.
245 Ac si nocturno conuises tempore caelum,

(234) Here the reading of Aldus "*quare,*" is confirmed; whose MS. had "*Quar.*" Grotius approves of this reading, instead of the common one "*quarum ;*" and in his note on this line mentions his father's conjecture that, in place of "*totos,*" we should read "*tortos.*" We see from this MS. that the idea was a happy one. The common reading of the line had been:

  "Quarum (or quorum) ego nequeo totos evolvere casus."

and was adopted by Grotius, in his text; according to his usual custom, when he had not what he thought sufficient authority in favour of his conjectural amendments.

(239) Grotius gives "*Amplexi terra,*" &c. according to the MSS. known to him; but he says in his notes: "Lege *terram*, vel *terras.*".... Modern editors have adopted "*terram ;*" but "*terras,*" as in our MS. is better.

(242) So is the Aldine reading, and it is better than the "*Tum multos,*" of the subsequent editions. Grotius, though he adopted "*tum multos,*" evidently approved the Aldine "*magnos,*" quoting in support of it this other line of the poem:.... "magnos edemus gentibus orbeis." Besides, the repetition "*magnos....magno,*" in the same line is more forcible; and, indeed, the German editor, Buhle, taking the hint of Grotius, adopted "*magnos.*"

(245) The word "*conuises*" has been erroneously changed to "*invises*" in our ancient MS. by the individual who, in early times, undertook to correct the errors of the text, a task for which he appears to have been not very competent. "*Invises*" is also the reading of the two Saxon MSS. and is one among other proofs of the same kind, that they were copied from this, subsequently to its being so altered. "*Conuises*" was thought of by Grotius, who besides suggested "*Et si,*" or "*En si,*" equivalent to our "*Ac si,*" instead of "*Nec si.*" The common reading was "Nec si nocturno cognoscens tempore caelum," and so the verse is given by Grotius; though in his notes he says: "Pro '*cognoscens*' omnino '*conuisens*' legendum; nam visere et conuisere sunt verba poetica Ciceroniana." Indeed, we have elsewhere:

  "Et loca conuisit cauda tenus infera Piscis."

Besides, it corresponds exactly to the σκεψαμένῳ of Aratus.

	Cum neque caligans detergit sidera nubes	ANC. MS.
	Nec pleno stellas superarit¹ lumine Luna,	¹ superaret
	Uidisti magnum candentem serpere circum :	
	Lacteus hic nimio fulgens candore notatur.	
250	Is non perpetuum detexens conficit orbem ;	
	Sed spatio multum super*est* :² praestare duobus	² superes
	Dicitur et late caeli lustrare cauernas	
	Quorum alter *tangens* Aquilonis uer*t*itur auras,	
	Ora petens geminorum inlustria : tum genus ardens	
255	In sese retinens aurigae³ portat utrumque.	³ auriga
	Hunc supera leua Perseus humeroque sinistro	
	Tangit, ad Andromedam⁴ hic dextra de pa...e tenetur ;	⁴Andromedan
	Inponitque pedes duplices Equus *et* simul Ales	
	Ponit auis caput et clinato corpore tergum :	
260	Anguitenens humeris conititur ille recedens :	
	Austrum consequitur deuitans corpore Uirgo.	
	Ut uero totum spatium conuestit et orbis	
	Magnus Leo, et claro conlucens lumine Cancer,	
	In quo consistens conuertit curriculum sol	
265	Aestiuus, medio distinguens corpore cursus :	
	Hic totus medius circo disjungitur ipse	

(247) The ancient MS. has "*superaret.*"

(250) This verse, in all the editions, except the Aldine, which has "*his*," begins: "*Hic non perpetuum,*" &c. Grotius sagaciously conjectured "*Is*" to be the proper reading : as we have it in this MS.

(253) The word "*tangens*" is wanting in the ancient MS. Perhaps the omission ought to be considered as a mere oversight.

(254) Grotius, in his notes, suggests this reading ; though, being unsupported by MSS. he, in his text, gave the line as he found it, thus :

"Ora petens geminorum illustratum genus ardens."

We need not again remark upon the *inlustria,* for *illustria.*

(257) The ancient MS. has "*Andromedan,*" the Greek accusative, but probably by a mistake of the copyist, as, in order to retain it, it would be necessary to expunge the "*de.*"

(258) The "*et*" is wanting in our ancient MS. The archaism "*Inponit*" in this line, is copied in the Cottonian MS. but the word is written "*imponit*" in the other Saxon MS.

(266) The old reading was "*disjungitur ipso,*" &c. from which no plausible sense could be made. Grotius suggested "*iste,*" instead of "*ipso.*"

supposed to be of the 2d or 3d century.

      Pectoribus ualidis, atque aluo possidet orbem.   ANC. MS
      Hunc octo in partes diuisum [1] noscere circum   [1] diuersum
      Si potes, inuenies supero conuertier orbe
270 Quinque pari spatio partis tris esse relictas,
      Tempore nocturno quas uis inferna frequentat.
      Alter ab infernis austri conuertitur auris,
*   Arquitenens humeris connittitur ille recedens,
      Distribuens medium subter secat hic Capricornum,
      Atque pedes gelidum riuum fundentis Aquarii,
275 Caeruleaeque feram caudam Pistricis, et illum
      Fulgentem Leporem; inde pedes Canis, et simul amplam
      Argolicam retinet claro cum lumine nauem;
      Tergaque Centauri, atque Nepai portat acumen;
      Inde Sagittarii deflexum possidet [2] arcum.   [2] posidet
280 Hunc a clarisonis auris Aquilonis ad austrum
      Cedens postremum tangit rota feruida Solis.
      Exinde in superas brumali tempore flexu
      Se recipit sedes; huic orbi quinque tributae
      Nocturnae partes, supera tres luce dicantur.
285 Hosce inter mediam partem retinere uidetur
      Tantus quantus erat conlucens lacteus orbis,
      In quo autumnali, atque iterum Sol lumine uerno [3]   [3] uero

(268) Our ancient MS. has "*diuersum*," and so have the two copies. Grotius and Buhle have *diuisum*.

(270) "*Partis tris*," for "*partes tres*," according to the most ancient orthography.

(272*) This line, "*Arquitenens humeris*," &c. is not to be found in any of the printed editions, and is wanting, we may conclude, in all the MSS. hitherto known. And although, if we except the first word, it be a repetition of ver. 260, it ought to be maintained, as very appropriate. It is remarkable that Buhle, the German editor, observes, that a gap has been suspected in this place by some editors. *Connititur* is here spelt with a double *t*; but in v. 260 it has only one.

(281) Before Grotius, "*condens*," instead of "*cedens*," was the received reading. Grotius restored "*cedens*," as he had before given "*cedit*" for "*condit*," as already mentioned, guided by the παρερχόμενος of Aratus.

(282) The "*in*," perhaps by an oversight, is omitted in our ancient MS.

(286) "*Conlucens*," for "*collucens*."

(287) Our ancient MS. has "*lumine uero*," and so has the Cottonian MS.

		ANC. MS.
	Exaequat spatium lucis cum tempore noctis.	
	Hunc retinens [1] Aries sublucet corpore toto,	[1] retinet is
290	Atque genuflexo Taurus connititur ingens :	
	Orion claro contingens corpore fertur :	
	Hydra tenet flexu Crateram, Coruus adhaeret ;	
	Et paucae Chelis stellae : simul Anguitenentis	
	Sunt genua, et summi Jouis ales nuntius instat :	
295	Propter equus [2] capite et ceru*icum* lumine tangit.	[2] aequus
	Hosce aequo spatio deuinctos sustinet axis,	
	Per medios summo caeli de uertice tranans.	
	Ille autem claro quartus cum lumine circus	
	Partibus extremis extremis continet orb*is*,[3]	[3] orbes
300	Et simul a medio media de parte secatur,[4]	[4] sequatur
	Atque oblicus in his nitens cum lumine fertur :	
	Ut nemo cui sancta manu doctissima Pallas	
	Sollertem ipsa dedit fabricae rationibus artem,	
	Tam tornare cate contortos possiet [5] orbes,	[5] posceret

(295) In the ancient MS., instead of "*Equus*" we have "*aequus*," and the last syllable of the last word but two, in this line, has been erased and altered to "*cis*."

(300) The *c* in "*secatur*," has been inserted in our ancient MS. by the early critic, who throughout attempted to correct its errors. It was, I think, originally written "*sequatur*."

(301) "*Oblicus*," for "*obliquus*." This substitution of the *c* for the *q*, is very ancient. Stephanus says: "Literam *q* veteres ignorabant ;" (he must mean to speak of a period very remote indeed) " unde *locuntur* scribebant, non *loquuntur*, ut testantur vetustissimi codices. Item, *oblicum* pro *obliquum*," &c. One of the Saxon copies, the Harleian, has " *obliquus*," according to the modern orthography ; the other retains " *oblicus*." We have in the sixty-third line, " *longincum*," for " *longinquum*," and, elsewhere, other specimens of the same kind.

(303) " *Sollertem*," for " *solertem ;*" also an archaism in orthography , and copied in both the Saxon MSS. Pompeius Festus, an ancient grammarian, doubles the *l* in this word : he wrote a treatise "De verbis priscis," and may therefore be supposed to have had a predilection for the ancient way of spelling it. We learn in Facciolati's Dictionary, that Aldus Manutius and Cellarius also prefer " *sollertem*."

Aldus, in his treatise on Orthography, refers to a MS. Virgil in the Vatican (No. 3867) written in very large capitals, and believed by some to be of higher antiquity than any other, in proof that the ancients wrote "*sollers*," instead of "*solers*." (Nouv. Trait. de Diplom. vol. iii. p. 61.)

(304) Our ancient MS. has " *posceret*."

305 Quam sunt in caelo diuino lumine flexi, ANC. MS.
Terram cingentes, ornantes lumine mundum,
Culmine transuerso retinentes sidera fulta,
Quattuor hi motu¹ cuncti uoluuntur eodem : ¹ motus
Sed tantum supera terras semper tenet ille
310 Curriculum oblique inflexus tribus orbibus unus,
Quantum est diuisus Cancer spatio a Capricorno ;
At supter terras spatium par esse necesse est.
Et quantos radios iacimus de lumine nostro,
Quis hunc connixum caeli contingimus orbem,
315 Sex tantae poterunt sub eum succedere partes,
Bina pari spatio caelestia signa tenentes.
Zodiacum hunc Graeci ² uocitant, nostrique Latini ² greci
Orbem signiferum perhibebunt nomine uero ;
Nam gerit hic uoluens bis sex ardentia signa.
320 Aestifer est pandens feruentia sidera Cancer :
Hunc subter fulgens caedit uis torua Leonis,
Quem rutilo sequitur conlucens corpore Uirgo ;
Exin prosectae claro cum lumine Chelae ;

(308) Our ancient MS. has " *hi motus.*"

(309) The MS. reads, "*Sed tantum superat erras ;*" the first letter of "*terras,*" having been erroneously supposed by the copyist to belong to the preceding word.

(312) "*Supter,*" again, for "*subter,*" as at ver. 178.

(314) "*Quis* pro *queis* (vel quibus) apud veteres," says a critic, and indeed it appears to claim the same antiquity as the "*ques*" of Ennius for "*qui.*" The elder Pliny, alone, we believe, retained that old form, in this passage : " Mille sunt arborum usus, sine quis vita degi non possit."

In this line Grotius restored "*hunc,*" for " *lunae,*" of the preceding editions, among which was the Aldine ; but "*connixum*" appears to be peculiar to our ancient MS. ; all the editions having "*convexum :*" "*connixum*" seems more proper in this place, and more poetical : as the portion of the sky, which is seen above the horizon, has the appearance of resting on the earth, and as fabled Atlas bore the heavens on his shoulders. Besides, Cicero, in other parts of the work, occasionally uses the same word, and on the whole it sounds more genuine.

(322) "*Conlucens,*" for "*collucens,*" as before.

(323) "*Prosectae,*" in this line, is badly changed to "*prolectae,*" in the two Saxon copies : "*prosectae*" is, we think, the true reading, and, as far as we know, it is peculiar to our ancient MS. After the constellation of the Virgin, the fore-claws of the Scorpion rise on the horizon, and are

Ipsaque consequitur lucens uis magna Nepai : ANC. MS.
325 Inde Sagittipotens dextra flexum tenet arcum :
Post hunc ore fero Capricornus uadere pergit :
Humidus inde loci conlucet Aquarius orbem.
Exin squamiferi serpentes ludere Pisces,
Quis comes est [1] Aries, obscuro lumine labens [1] et
330 Inflexoque genu prosecto corpore Taurus,
Et Gemini clarum iactantes lucibus ignem.
Haec Sol aeterno conuestit lumine lustrans,
Annua conficiens uertentia corpora cursu.
Hic quantus terris consectus pellitur orbis,
335 Tantumdem pandens supera mortalibus edit.
Sex omnes semper cedunt labentia nocte,
Tot caelum rursus fugientia signa reuisunt.
Hoc spatium tranans caecis nox conficit umbris,
Quod supera terras prima de nocte relictum est,
340 Signifero ex orbi sex signorum ordine fultum.

then apparently "*prosectae,*" or cut: the modern correction, "*projectae,*" is therefore not so happy an expression We shall presently find the same word applied to Taurus (v. 330), and again erroneously altered by the Saxon critics.

(329) "*Quis,*" for "*queis,*" as in line 314.

(330) The constellation Taurus here presenting only the fore-part of the body, "*prosecto*" is evidently the genuine reading; though hitherto it has not been suggested by any editor of this poem. See our note on v. 323.

(337) Here we have the suspected "*rursus,*" of Grotius. The old insignificant reading was "*jussus,*" changed by some into "*jussu.*" Turnebus substituted "*juxta,*" which is little better. "*Rursus*" corresponds to the Greek αἶει of Aratus, meaning continued succession.

(340) In consequence of the imperfect and erroneous separation of the words (of which instances have been before given), the line appears thus in our ancient MS.:
" Signifero exorbis exsignorum ordine fultum."
Grotius has :   " Signifero ex orbi 'st et signorum ordine fultum,"
which is not so good : for, as at all times six of the constellations of the Zodiac are above the horizon, "*sex*" ought to be maintained. This reading appears to be peculiar to our MS.; for "*sex*" is not to be found in any of the editions. Here we must also observe, "*orbi,*" as an ablative, which Grotius, in another place, terms "scriptura antiqua." The two Saxon copies have also, "*ex orbi.*"

With this line, the larger minuscule writing in our ancient MS. terminates; and as the half page

supposed to be of the 2d or 3d century.

(COTT. MS.)

    Quod si Solis habes tetros cognoscere cursus,
    Ortus signorum nocturno tempore uises ;
    Nam semper signum exoriens Titan trahit unum.
    Sin autem officiens signis mons obstruet altus,
345 Aut adimet lucem caeca caligine nubes,
    Certas ipse notas calido de tegmine sumes,
    Ortus atque obitus omnes cognoscere possis.[1]   [1] poscis
    Quae simul existant[2] cernes, quae tempore eodem   [2] existunt
    Praecipitent obitum nocturno tempore nosces.
350 Iam simul ac primo *ad* superos se *lumine*[3] Cancer   [3] flamine
    Extulit, extemplo caedit delapsa Corona,
    Et loca conuisit cauda tenus infera Piscis :
    Dimidiam retinet stellis distincta Corona
    Partem etiam supera atque alia de parte re*f*usa ;[4]   [4] reuisa
355 Quam tamen insequitur Piscis, nec totus ad umbras

below it is left blank, a careless observer might be naturally led to suppose, that the sense and the poem were completed ; which is not the case.

The leaf that should immediately follow, containing thirty-one lines, is here wanting in the ancient MS., and we must therefore once more have recourse to the two Saxon copies, which happily were made before it had suffered mutilation. I think there is no doubt, that the *recto* of the leaf, wanting in the ancient MS., exhibited the representations of *Sol* and *Luna Lucifera* in their chariots, from which the drawing in the Cottonian MS. was copied ; and that the thirty-one lines wanting, with the first part of the prose extracts in the margin, occupied the *verso* of it.

(341) The common reading has been :
        " Quod si solis aves certos cognoscere cursus."
Both the Saxon MSS. have " *habes tetros ;*" which reading seems better than " *aves certos ;*" as Aratus is here giving instructions how, in case of need, a person may discover the true situation of the Sun, at a time when it is hid by lofty mountains, or dark clouds.

(346) Here we have " *calido de tegmine,*" instead of " *caeli de tegmine.*" This reading has not been hinted at by any editor : the idea conveyed by it of the heated vault (of heaven) is highly poetical.

(347) The Saxon MSS. have "*poscis.*"

(348) The MSS. have " *existunt.*"

(350) Our Saxon MSS. omit the " *ad,*" and have "*flamine,*" instead of " *lumine.*"

(354) The MSS. have " *reuisa,*" instead of " *refusa.*" Grotius and Buhle have " *repulsa est.*"

Jactus, sed supero contectus corpore caedit   COTT. MS.
Atque humeros usque a genibus, clarumque recondit
Anguitenens[1] ualidis magnum *a* ceruicibus Anguem :   [1] Inguitenens
Nam uero Arctophylax non aequa parte secatur,
360 Nam breuior clara caeli de parte uidetur,
Amplior infernas depulsus possidet umbras.
Quattuor hic obiens secum deducere signa
Signifero solet ex orbi, tum [2] serius ipse,   [2] cum
Cum supera sese satiauit[3] luce, recedit,   [3] sociavit
365 Post mediam labens claro cum corpore noctem.
Haec obscura tenens conuestit[4] sidera tellus :   [4] conuertit
* Dimidiam retinet stellis distincta Corona ;
At parte ex alia claris cum lucibus enat
Orion humeris et lato pectore fulgens,
Et dextra retinens non cassum luminis ensem.
370 Sed cum de terris uis est patefacta Leonis,
Omnia quae [5] Cancer praeclaro detulit ortu,   [5] que
Cedunt obscurata simul uis magna Aquilai

(356) "*Jactus (Piscis) sed supero*, &c. This also, we can affirm, is peculiar to our MSS., both the copies have it so. "*Tractus*," instead of "*Jactus*," is the common reading. The last word in the line is spelt in our MSS. with the diphthong, "*caedit* ;" of which kind of orthography the whole work abounds with examples.

(358) Our MSS. have "*Inguitenens*," instead of "*Anguitenens*," and omit the "*a*" before *cervicibus*.

(363) Our MSS. have "*cum*," instead of "*tum*."

(364) The MSS. have "*sociavit*."

(366) The MSS. have "*convertit* ;" which is also the reading of Buhle.

(366*) An exact repetition of ver. 353.

(367) This is the reading of both the Saxon MSS. and we may safely assert it to be better than that of the editions which have "*lucibus errat*." The propriety of "*enat*," as applied to the emerging of a constellation from the bosom of the ocean, is obvious. In another line of this poem, Cicero has used "*tranans*," a word of the same family, in reference to another constellation.

(372) Our ancient MS. beginning from this verse, inclusive, being no longer deficient, we gladly return to it.

And here it is proper to observe, that after the 340th line, ending with "*fultum*," the poem appears to have been continued by a different copyist, and in a somewhat smaller character

supposed to be of the 2d or 3d century. 207

ANC. MS.

Pellitur de*f*lexo ¹ confidens pectore Nixus: ¹ delexo
Jam supero ferme depulsus lumine cedit;
375 Sed laeuum genus, atque inlustrem linquit in alto
Planta*m*: ² tum contra exoritur clarum caput Hydrae,   ² Plantan
Et Lepus et Procion qui sese feruidus infert
Ante Canem; inde Canis uestigia prima uidentur.

than had been before used. One leaf, containing from verse 341 to 371, inclusive, is, as we have said, wanting in our MS. Beginning from the present line, " *Cedunt obscurata,*" &c. (which last word the reader will perceive to be written with a *b*, and not with the *p*, so commonly employed in the early part of the MS.) the writing is not only smaller but different in the forms of some of the characters, (the minuscule *a* for example, which is often quite unlike what it ever appears in those verses which are introduced under the drawings), so as to leave, I think, no doubt that it was written by a different person from the one employed before. The poem, also, in this latter part, occupies only half the breadth of the page; the remainder being devoted to what at first sight might be taken for a prose commentary on the verses; but which, as has been said, proves to be a part of one of the books of Pliny.

The old reading of this verse (372) was:

" Cedunt obscurata simul vis magna Aquari."

But as this *Aquari* did not correspond to the Greek, καὶ ἀἐρος, some attempted to correct the error, by substituting " *aeti:*" but then, again, " *vis major,*" had there no sense. Turnebus happily conjectured that the three last words should be " *vis magna Aquilai,*" as they are in our MS. and his emendation was approved by Grotius.

(373) The ancient MS. has, by error, " *delexo,*" and so has the Harleian Saxon MS. but the Cottonian has corrected it, " *deflexo.*" The printed editions generally have " *Pellitur ac flexo* "

(375) Here, again, we have the archaism, " *inlustrem,*" for " *illustrem.*" The above reading of this line is more strictly grammatical than the " *linquit in altum* " of the printed editions; as no change of place is here intended in the object " *plantam,*" in the following verse, to which " *in alto* " refers; though we are aware that very ancient authors, in imitation of the Greek, have sometimes used the accusative upon similar occasions. Virgil has (Æn. v. 517):

" Decidit exanimis, vitamque reliquit in astris,"

which warrants our " *linquit in alto plantam* ;" and although the same author uses the accusative, " *in altum,*" (iv Georg. 528), " Se jactu dedit aequor in altum ;" the passage implies change of place.

(376) Our ancient MS. has " *Plantan.*" The *y*, in *Hydrae*, in this line, is for the *first time* surmounted by a *point*. But we have observed, that beginning from line 372, the poem is written by a different hand from that which wrote the preceding part.

(377) " *Et Lepus et Procion,*" *i* for *y* ; not unusual with ancient Latin writers; as we have observed in speaking of " *Idra,*" for " *Hydra,*" in the 214th verse. Both the Saxon copies, also, have " *Procion.*"

Non pauca e caelo depellens signa repente,   ANC. MS.
380 Exoritur pandens inlustria lumina Uirgo.
    Cedit clara Fides Cyllenia, mergitur unda
    Delphinus, simul obtegitur depulsa Sagitta,
    Atque Auis at summam caudam, primasque recedit
    Pinnas, et magnus pariter delabitur amnis.
385 Hic E*quus* [1] a capite et longa ceruice latescit :   [1] aecus
    Longius exoritur iam claro corpore Serpens,
    Creteraque tenus lucet mortalibus Hidra.
    Inde pedes Canis ostendit jam posteriores,
    Et post ipse trahit claro cum lumine puppim,
390 Insequitur labens per caeli lumina Nauis ;
    Et cum iam toto processit corpore Uirgo,
    Haec medium ostendit radiato stipite malum.
    At cum procedunt obscuro corpore Chelae,
    Existet pariter larga cum luce Bootes,
395 Cujus in aduerso est Arcturus corpore fixus,
    Totuque jam supera fulgens prolabitur Argo,

(380) "*Exoritur pandens,*" &c. All the printed editions have "*candens.*" Had Grotius fallen upon this MS. he would, no doubt, have joyfully adopted its reading, which, on all accounts, is far superior. Cicero has used "*pandens,*" on a similar occasion, in the 320th verse :

"Aestifer est pandens ferventia sidera cancer."

After "*Exoritur pandens,*" we have again the archaism of "*inlustria,*" for "*illustria.*"

(383) "*Atque avis at summam,*" &c. "*at,*" for "*ad.*" The ancients also sometimes wrote "*ad,*" for "*at,*" "*aput,*" for "*apud.*" See Stephanus. The Harl. Saxon MS. has "*ad,*" and so has the Cottonian.

(384) "*Pinnas,*" again, for "*pennas,*" see our note on v. 48.

(385) In our ancient MS. the word "*Equus*" has been originally written "*aecus,*" and the *a* afterwards erased, leaving "*ecus,*" which has been since altered to "*equs,*" and a second *u* added at top. I have already noticed the various ways in which this word is spelt, in the celebrated Medicean Virgil, and have spoken of the interchange between *c* and *q*, which is of such frequent occurrence in the most ancient MSS.

(387) Our MS. has "*creteraque,*" instead of "*crateraque,*" as at ver. 219.—Ibid. "*Hidra,*" for "*Hydra.*" See our remarks on ver. 214.

(392) The three last words of this line are thus strangely divided in our ancient MS. "*radiat os tipite malum.*"

  Hidraque quod late caelo dispersa[1] tenetur,   [1] disparsa
  Nondum tota latet nam caudam contegit umbra.
  Iam dextrum genus, et decoratam lumine suram
400 Erigit ille uagans uulgato nomine Nixus,
  Quem nocte extinctum atque exortum uidimus una
  Persaepe, ut paruum tranans geminauerit orbem.
  Hic genus et suram cum Chelis erigit alte ;
  Ipse autem praeceps obscura nocte tenetur,
405 Dum Nepa et Arquitenens inuisant lumina caeli.
  Nam secum medium pandet Nepa, tollere uero
  In caelum totum exoriens conabitur Arcus.
  Hic tribus elatus cum signis corpore toto
  Lucet ; at exoritur media de parte Corona,
410 Caudaque Centauri extremo candore refulget.
  Hic se iam totum caecas Equus abdit in umbras,
  Quem rutila fulgens pluma praeteruolat ales.
  Occidit Andromedae clarum *caput*, et fera Pistrix
  Labitur horribilis epulas funesta requirens :
415 Hanc contra Cepheus non cessat tendere palmas :
  Illa usque ad spinam mergens se caerula condit ;
  At Cepheus caput atque umeros palmasque reclinat.

(397) Here we have "*Hidra*," for "*Hydra ;*" and not "*Idra*," as at line 214. But, as has been observed in our note on the 372d line, this part of the poem is not written by the same person that wrote the beginning. The Cottonian MS. also reads "*Hidra ;*" the Harleian Saxon MS. has "*Hydra*." Our ancient MS. also has "*disparsa*," instead of "*dispersa*."

(405) "*Arquitenens*," for "*Arcitenens*." See our remarks on verse 182. The first four words of this line are thus strangely divided in our ancient MS. : "*Dum nepae tar quitenens*," &c.

(411) The fifth and sixth words of this line appear thus in our ancient MS. "*caecase quus*."

(413) The word "*caput*" is omitted in the MS.

(414) "*Labitur horribilis*," &c.—"*horribilis*," for "*horribiles ;*" an archaism in orthography before noticed.

(417) Again "*humeros*" without the *h*. See our note on v. 203. To which I may add, that there is a passage in Aulus Gellius (lib. ii. c. 3) respecting this letter or aspirate, which I cannot help thinking has been misunderstood by some late grammarians. He says : "In his enim verbis omnibus litterae seu spiritus istius nulla ratio visa est, nisi ut firmitas et vigor vocis, quasi quibusdam nervis additis, intenderetur. Sed quoniam *aheni* quoque exemplo usi sumus, venit nobis in memo-

Cum uero uis est uehemens exorta Nepai
Late fusa uolat ; per terras fama uagatur,
420 Ut quondam Orion manibus uiolasse Dianam
Dicitur, excelsis errans in collibus amens,
Quos tenet Aegeo defixa *in* gurgite Chius,
Brachia quae uiridi conuestit tegmine uitis.
Ille feras uaecors amenti corde necabat,
425 Oenopionis auens epulas ornare nitentis.
At uero pedibus subito percu*l*sa Dianae

riam Fidum Optatum multi nominis Romæ grammaticum ostendisse mihi librum Æneidos secundum, mirandæ vetustatis, emptum in Sigillariis xx aureis, quem ipsius Virgilii fuisse credebat : in quo duo isti versus quum ita scripti forent,

'Vestibulum ante ipsum primoque in limine Pyrrhus
Exsultat telis et luce coruscus *aena,*

Additam supra vidimus *h* litteram, et *ahena* factum. Sic in illo quoque Virgilii versu in optimis libris scriptum invenimus :

'Aut foliis undam tepidi dispumat *aheni*.''

It has been supposed from this, that the ancient Romans were accustomed to place an *h* over a vowel intended to be strongly pronounced, instead of inserting it in the word. Facciolati says : " Aspiratio autem (ut idem *Gellius, ibid.* auctor est) non solebat litteris interseri, quemadmodum nos hodie facere consuevimus, sed more Græcorum supra litteras annotari, quod et ipsum se vidisse affirmat in quondam vetustissimo codice, quem Virgilii autographon fuisse putat," &c. But Gellius, I believe, meant to say, that Virgil had written *aena,* without the *h* (and so we find it in the Medicean Virgil and in the Vatican fragments) and that some grammarian, who thought the word ought to be written with the *h* (as became the custom) had afterwards placed that letter over the space separating the two first letters, to shew that it ought to be there ; in the way constantly used by the ancient correctors of MSS. ; and indeed the corrector of the ancient MS. before us, has done this in every page.

(422) Our MS. has " *aegeo,* instead of " *egeo,*" and omits the " *in,*" after " *defixa.*" Instead of " *chius,*" in this line, Aldus read " *echinus ;*" whence the " *echinei*" of the subsequent editors. But as the *Echinades*' islands are not in the Egean sea, but in the Achelous, that reading did not answer. At length Grotius thought of " *Chius,* as we have it in this ancient MS.

(424) " *Vaecors,*" for " *vecors.*" Aulus Gellius tells us that the word was so spelt of old. See our note on v. 356. Both the Saxon MSS. have " *vecors.*"

(425) The constant reading, before Grotius, was " *cænare nitentis.*" Grotius proposed " *ornare ;*" though having only one old MS. in his favour, he did not introduce it in his text. In his notes he says : " Imo *epulas ornare,* ut habet vetus codex...... feris enim quas venatus erat Orion Oenopionis *epulas* condecorabat. Nil clarius."

supposed to be of the 2d or 3d century. 211

	ANC. MS.
Insula discessit, disiectaque saxa reuellens [1]	[1] reuellins
Perculit, et caecas lustrauit luce lacunas;	
E quibus ingenti existit *cum* corpore prae se	
430 Scorpios infest*us* [2] praeportans flebile acumen.	[2] infesta
Hic ualido cupide uenantem perculit ictu,	
Mortiferum in uenas fu*nd*ens per uulnera uiros;	
Ille graui moriens constrauit corpore terram.	
Quare cum magnis sese Nepa lucibus effert,	
435 Orion fugiens commendat corpora terris.	
Tum uero fugit [3] Andromeda, et Neptunia Pistrix	[3] fuit
Tota latet: cedit conuerso corpore Cepheus,	
Extremas medio contingens corpore terras.	
Hic caput et superas potis est demergere partes,	
440 Infera lumborum nunquam conuestiet umbra; [4]	[4] umbras
Nam retinent Arctoi [5] lustrantes lumine summo.	[5] arctoe
Labitur illa simul gnatam lacrimosa requirens	
Cassiepia, neque ex caelo depulsa decore	
Fertur; nam uero contingens uertice primum	
445 Terras, post umeris euersa sede refertur.	
Hanc illi tribuunt poenam Nereides almae,	
Cum [6] quibus, ut perhibent, ausa *est* contendere forma.	[6] Quam

(427) MS. "*reuellins.*"

(429) In our MS. "*cum*" is omitted.

(430) Instead of "*infestus,*" we have "*infesta,*" in our ancient MS.

(432) The letters "*nd,*" in "*fundens,*" are wanting in our ancient MS. In this line we have "*viros*" for "*virus:*" this change of *us* into *os* is, as every one knows, very frequent in the old poets. The Harleian Saxon MS. has "*virus:*" the word is accidentally omitted in the Cott. MS.

(436) Our ancient MS. has "*fuit,*" instead of "*fugit.*"

(441) Our MS. has "*Arctoe.*" Grotius in his notes recommends "*Arctoe;*" though, having no MS. of this poem in his favour, he preserves the common reading, "*Arcti,*" in his text. His reason for preferring *Arctoe* is, that he always found the word so written in a very early MS. before mentioned, of Germanicus Cæsar: "Libro antiquissima manu exarato."

(445) Again, "*humeris,*" without the *h*. The most common reading has been "*post humeros;*" and Grotius retained it in his text; though in his notes he says: "melius alii *humeris.*"

(447) The ancient MS. appears originally to have had "*Quam,*" from which the *a* was afterwards erased, leaving "*Qum,*" which the ancient corrector of the MS. altered to "*Cum.*" Both the Saxon MSS. have "*cum.*" The "*est*" is wanting in the ancient MS.

212   *On a MS. of Cicero's translation of Aratus,*

ANC. MS.

Haec[1] obit inclinata ; at pars exorta Coronae est   [1] Hae .. corona
Altera, cum caudaque omnis iam panditur Hydra.
450 At caput et totum sese Centaurus opacis
Eripit et tenebris, linquens uestigia parua
Ante pedum contecta ; simul cum lumine pandit,
Ipse feram dextra retinet. Prolabitur inde
Anguitenens capite et manibus ; profert simul Anguis
455 Iam cap*ut*[2] et summum flexo de corpore lumen.   [2] capit
Hic ille exoritur conuerso corpore Nixus,
Aluum, crura, umeros, simul et praecordia lustrans,
Et dextrae radios laeto cum lumine iactans.
Inde Sagittipotens superas conuisere luces
460 Institit, et mergit Nixi caput, et simul effert
Sese clara Fides, et promit pectore Cepheus.
Feruidus ille Canis toto cum corpore cedit,
Abditur Orion, obiit simul abditus umbra est.
Inferiora cadunt Aurigae[3] lumina lapsu.   [3] aurige ... lapsum
465 Crus dextrumque pedem li*n*quens[4] obit infera Perseus   [4] liquens
In loca ; tum cedens a puppi linquitur Argo.
Inde obiens Capricornus ab alto, lumine pellit
Aurigam, instantemque Capram, paruos simul Haedos,
Et magnam antiquo depellit nomine Nauem,
470 Obruiter Procion ; emergunt alite lapsu[5]   [5] lapsum
E[6] terris uolucris ; existit clara Sagitta.   [6] Et
SED CUM SE MEDIUM CAELI IN REGIONE LOCAUIT
MAGNUS AQUARIUS, ET UESTIUIT LUMINE TERRAS,
TUM PEDIBUS SIMUL ET SUPERA CERUICE IUBATA

(449) Here, again, the *y*, in *Hydra*, is surmounted with a point, as in line 376. See our note on that verse.
(455) Our ancient MS. has " *capit,*" instead of " *caput.*"
(458) All the printed editions have " *dextra,*" instead of " *dextrae.*"
(470) Our ancient MS. has " *lapsum.*"
(471) The ancient MS. has " *Et terris volucris ;*" " *volucris,*" for " *volucres.*"
(472–480) What has been hitherto known of Cicero's Aratæa, ends with the last verse (471 ;) and we now come to *nine lines*, the existence of which is not even hinted at in any printed edition

supposed to be of the 2d or 3d century. 213

475 CEDIT EQUUS FUGIENS; AT CONTRA SIGNIPOTENS NOX
  CAUDA CENTAURUM RETINENS, AD SE RAPIT IPSA;
  NEC POTIS EST CAPUT ATQUE UMEROS OBDUCERE LATOS;
  AT UERO SERPENTIS HIDRAE CALIGINE CAECA
  CERUICEM ATQUE OCULORUM ARDENTIA LUMINA UESTIT:
480 HANC AUTEM TOTAM PROPERANT DEPELLERE PISCES.

whence we may conclude that, except in our ancient MS. and the two Saxon copies from it, they are no where to be found.

These nine lines form, happily, one of the best preserved passages of the poem, which, as all are aware, has so much suffered by the injuries of time; and they exactly correspond to these nine original verses:

"Ἵππος δ' Ὑδροχόοιο νέον περιτελλομένοιο,
Ποσσί τε καὶ κεφαλῇ ἀνελίσσεται· ἀντία δ' Ἵππου
Ἐξ οὐρῆς κέντρυρον ἐφέλκεται ἀστερίη νύξ.
Ἀλλ' ὂν οἱ δύναται κεφαλὴν, οὐδ' εὐρέας ὤμους
Αὐτῷ σὺν θώρηκι χαδεῖν, ἀλλ' αἴθοπος Ὕδρης
Αὐχενίην κατάγει σπείρην, καὶ πάντα μέτωπα.
Ἡ δὲ καὶ ἐξόπιθεν πολλὴ μένει· ἀλλ' ἄρα καὶ τὴν
Αὐτῷ Κενταύρῳ, ὁπότ' Ἰχθύες ἀντέλλωσιν
Ἀθρόον ἐμφέρεται.

Grotius, who has so religiously preserved all the lines of Cicero's version that he could find, has thus endeavoured to supply its deficiency in this place:

" At postquam superum convisit Aquarius orbem,
. . . .
Seque humero et pedibus primis Equus exerit altè:
Centauri oppositam devolvit ad infera caudam
Nox, caput, et latos humeros, et pectora magna
Non potis obscurare, et Hydræ quæ proxima collo est
Subducit Spiram, rutilantiaque ora recondit:
Cætera sed longum radianti lumine perstant,
Nec prius à superis cedunt, cum semifero oris
Omnia, quam surgant geminato corpore Pisces."

The genuineness of the above nine lines in our MS. will be acknowledged, we are satisfied, by any scholar who, confronting Cicero with himself, will be at the pains to compare the style and phraseology of them, with those of the rest of the poem. If Cicero ever finished this translation, about 30 verses only appear to be now wanting The first of these nine lines (verse 472):

" Sed cum se mediam caeli in regione locavit,"

immediately calls to our remembrance several lines in other parts of the poem, as (v. 27) " At propter leuum genus omnis parte locatas." (v. 93) . . . . " in fronte locatas." (v. 139) " Exin semotam procul in tuto que locatam." (v. 145) . . . . " in parte locatum." (v. 151) . . . . " caudarum parte locata." (v. 186) .... "adversa de parte locata." (v. 188) .... "in parte locavit." And again, (v. 193) "Aram sub media caeli regione locatam:" where the similarity is very striking.

The tendency that Cicero has here shewn to end his verses by "*locatus*," "*locata*," "*locatam*," "*locavit*," with an ablative, reminds us of his numerous prose sentences ending with his favourite "*esse videatur*." The one and the other are characteristic.

Let us pass to the second line (v 473):

"Magnus Aquarius, et vestivit lumine terras,"

This line is analogous to (v. 60) .... "perpetuo vestivit lumine Titan;" and (v. 332) "Haec Sol aeterno convestit lumine lustrans."

The fourth (v. 475):

"Cedit Equus fugiens, at contra signipotens nox;"

We have two other verses ending with the same monosyllable: (v. 64) "Non hiberna cito volvetur curriculo nox;" and (v. 189) "Haec tamen aeterno invisens loca curriculo nox."

One of the most striking features of our newly-discovered passage, is the compound adjective "*signipotens*;" a most excellent epithet for Night, whose whole power lies in her constellations. We might look in vain in the best poets for so happy an expression as "*signipotens nox*." The Ἀστερίη νύξ of Aratus, and the "*Stelliger*," "*Stellata*," of other poets, bear no comparison to it. In Ennius, as quoted by Varro, we find "*Signi'enens*;" in the third book of Lucan, "*Signifer polus*;" in Valerius Flaccus, "*Signifer crater*." But all fall short of "*Signipotens nox*."

At verses 73, and 459, of this poem, we find "*Sagittipotens*," which is also peculiar to Cicero; a happy circumstance for proving the genuineness of "*signipotens*," which is not to be found in any Dictionary, not even in the Lexicon of Henricus Stephanus, to whom the nine verses must have been of course unknown. Cicero alone has used "*Sagittipotens*," and we may safely conclude that he only was the inventor of the splendid epithet, "*signipotens*," happily preserved in our ancient MS.

The seventh line (v. 478):

"At vero serpentis Hidrae caligine caeca,"

recalls (v. 345) "Aut adiment lucem caeca caligine nubes"—and another, in the fragments of the Prognostics : "Stinguuntur radii caeca caligine tecti." The expression, "*caligine caeca*," in these three lines, evidently proceeded from the same writer.

And, lastly, the ninth line (v. 480):

"Hanc autem totam properant depellere Pisces."

Is analogous to (v. 210) "Cedit equi partes properans subjungere Chelis."

Since the first part of this poem was printed, it has occurred to me that the erroneous reading, "*Ima*," instead of "*Iam*," in the second line, may easily be accounted for, upon the supposition (as is most probable) that the MS. from which our MS. was anciently copied, was written in capitals; as the ancients, in writing, seldom put a cross stroke to the A, and as therefore an Λ followed by an M, and an M followed by an Λ, would look the same: so that IAM and IMA might easily be mistaken for each other.

CPSIA information can be obtained
at www.ICGtesting.com
Printed in the USA
BVHW04s1610030418
512350BV00010B/224/P